S0-BEC-777

Citizen Jane

Citizen Jane

The True Story of One Woman's
Mission to Put a Killer Behind Bars

A True Crime

James Dalessandro

with David Mehnert

New York

CITIZEN JANE

The True Story of One Woman's Mission to Put a Killer Behind Bars

Copyright © 2010 Jane Alexander and James Dalessandro. All rights reserved.

No part of this publication may be reproduced or transmitted in any form or by any means, mechanical or electronic, including photocopying and recording, or by any information storage and retrieval system, without permission in writing from the author or publisher (except by a reviewer, who may quote brief passages and/or short brief video clips in a review.)

Disclaimer: The Publisher and the Author make no representations or warranties with respect to the accuracy or completeness of the contents of this work and specifically disclaim all warranties, including without limitation warranties of fitness for a particular purpose. No warranty may be created or extended by sales or promotional materials. The advice and strategies contained herein may not be suitable for every situation. This work is sold with the understanding that the Publisher is not engaged in rendering legal, accounting, or other professional services. If professional assistance is required, the services of a competent professional person should be sought. Neither the Publisher nor the Author shall be liable for damages arising herefrom. The fact that an organization or website is referred to in this work as a citation and/or a potential source of further information does not mean that the Author or the Publisher endorses the information the organization or website may provide or recommendations it may make. Further, readers should be aware that internet websites listed in this work may have changed or disappeared between when this work was written and when it is read.

Cover Designer: Rachel Lopez Rachel@r2cdesign.com

ISBN 978-1-60037-596-5

Library of Congress Control Number: 2009929147

MORGAN · JAMES
THE ENTREPRENEURIAL PUBLISHER

Morgan James Publishing, LLC
1225 Franklin Ave., STE 325
Garden City, NY 11530-1693
Toll Free 800-485-4943
www.MorganJamesPublishing.com

In an effort to support local communities, raise awareness and funds, Morgan James Publishing donates one percent of all book sales for the life of each book to Habitat for Humanity. Get involved today, visit www.HelpHabitatForHumanity.org.

Dedication

To the memory of Jane Alexander, who inspired us all.

Acknowledgments

Many people contributed to this book. Jan Miller—who co-founded Citizens Against Homicide (CAH) with Jane Alexander—was unfailingly generous with her time and insight. Help also came from many CAH members: Nadine Calvert, Terri de la Cuesta, Nancy Guggeos, Jacque MacDonald, Bill Miller, Jack Miller, Chuck Mitchell, Alice Ostergren, Anne Poverello, Carol Silveira, and Ed Sullivan.

Jane Alexander's personal saviors, Erin and Jim Rohde, Sandy and Ed Sullivan, and Vaux and Bob Toneff, contributed greatly to our efforts. Carnell Rogers and the Honorable Dorothy Von Beroldingen gave helpful accounts, as did Jane's son, Scott Alexander. Polygraph expert George Johnson recounted his experience with Jane many years after the fact.

Investigator Grant Cunningham detailed the workings of the Santa Clara County District Attorney's office. The Honorable Joyce Allegro spoke of her role as prosecutor, taking time from a successful run for Superior Court Judge. The notes of juror Cathy Gyselbrecht provided invaluable insight.

Without the valiant efforts of two great detectives, Sergeants John Kracht and Jeff Ouimet, there would be no story and no book.

Lee Sansum spared no detail in recounting the murder of his sister, Abby Niebauer, and his fourteen-year search for justice. Palo Alto detective Mike Yore, who worked the Niebauer case, graciously spent hours offering his perspective on Jane's work.

I must thank the executives, Rick Frishman, David L. Hancock and Margo Toulouse of Morgan James Publishing for their incredible support and enthusiasm for this book. Peter Miller, our manager, was relentless in seeing the Jane Alexander story come to light, both as a book and now as a Hallmark Channel Movie. In the latter effort, I must thank Hallmark Channel executives, David Kenin and Elizabeth Yost, and my friend, television producer and legendary New York City Police Detective Sonny Grosso and his producing partner, Larry Jacobson and Tara Long. Finally, Kathleen Dallessandro worked long hours helping edit the preliminary manuscript. Our editor at Nal/Signet, Carolyn Nichols, won our hearts for her support and coaching.

Jane Alexander is our heroine. For her devotion to justice, her courage in telling the most intimate details of her life and struggle, we are all forever in her debt. After helping to solve more than 20 homicides, and offering comfort and hope to hundreds of victims' families. Jane Alexander departed this earth in December 2008. We thank her family for allowing us into her life.

James Dalessandro

Introduction

In 1995, I left Los Angeles after a sixteen-year sojourn, and returned to my beloved San Franciso Bay Area. The warm reception for my first novel, *Bohemian Heart*, a noir thriller in the City by the Bay, had led me to decide that I would concentrate my writing efforts on great San Francisco stories.

About a month after returning, I read an article in the Marin County *Pacific Sun* on a remarkable woman named Jane Alexander. Jane had just scored a stunning legal victory by seeing the conviction of a man who had murdered her beloved aunt, Gertrude McCabe. The twisted path to justice had taken thirteen years. Jane had been, at the time of the murder, a widow living on a picturesque, three-acre estate in the hills of Marin County. In the aftermath of the premature death of her husband, a long-time family friend, a dapper, charismatic Irishman named Tom O'Donnell, had rescued Jane from loneliness and depression.

Just as heartbreak turned to happiness for Jane, heartbreak reared its ugly head again. The eighty-eight year old Gertrude, who had raised Jane as a surrogate mother, was brutally murdered in her home in San Jose, California. Beaten, stabbed twenty-seven times, strangled with a bicycle chain. She weighed 90 pounds at the time of her death; one of the most sensational, and repellent crimes that the great Santa Clara Valley had witnessed in decades.

That sent Jane on a most remarkable odyssey; a thirteen-year crusade to identify, track down, and convict the murderer. During that journey, Jane came to grip with an awful truth; the problem was not the criminal, but often the criminal justice system. One jurisdiction would not extradite the suspect because of the cost and volume of paper work, several assistant district attorneys refused to prosecute for an endless stream of reasons, all while the killer walked free to try again.

Jane Alexander did not merely earn justice for her aunt. Jane and another woman, Jan Miller, who had lost a nineteen-year daughter to an assailant as brutal as the one who took Jane's aunt, decided they had to carry the fight even further. They founded Citizens Against Homicide and fought back against criminals, often confronting the criminal justice system itself. They found other frustrated family members who had lost a loved one to violence. They held meetings, they held people's hands, they lobbied lawmakers and cops and proseutors. They convinced politicians to offer reward money, and helped families to contest hundreds of potential paroles for convicted murderers. They have won awards from London to Sacramento. CAH members are now in all fifty states.

People Magazine did three pages on Jane. Then Maury Povich called. And Larry King. Dan Rather and his "48 Hours" asked to do a ten-minute segent on Jane as part of a 'people who found justice' segment, then scrapped the other stories and did a full hour on Jane. The response was overwhelming: "Citizen Jane" continues to be re-run on CBS and other networks.

As of the summer of 2008, Jane Alexander and Jan Miller have worked with families and detectives in scores of homicide cases. Their efforts have been crucial in aiding the resolution of more than twenty murders, some of which were cold cases that had been abandoned by the system. Their filing cabinets now bulge with more than 500 homicide investigations.

This is the story of how it began.

James Dalessandro

Chapter One

"Jane, will you give me a hand with the roast?"

October 23, 1983 seemed like a typical fall Sunday in Marin County. Jane Alexander was attending a 49ers football party, a weekly ritual in thousands of homes throughout Northern California. Nancy Martell, the party's hostess that week, needed Jane's respected advice in the kitchen. It was the custom to eat just after the game, and the hostess had to estimate just when the game would finish so that dinner could be served at the right time.

"Haven't you put the roast in yet?" asked Jane, mother of six grown children.

"No. Should I have?"

"We're at the end of the second quarter. You should have had it in twenty minutes ago. Nancy, if you only knew more about football," Jane said with a laugh, "you'd be a better cook!"

Jane Alexander was in good spirits that day. An athletic, articulate woman of sixty-one, known for her fiery conservative opinions and dedication to family and friends, Jane seemed happier than she had been in years. This was largely thanks to the company of Tom O'Donnell, a tall and charismatic family friend who had become her romantic partner three years after her husband's tragic death. He was fifty-seven, a ballroom dancer, a world traveler, and world-class raconteur. Tom was a welcome addition to the comfortable upper-middle-class social set that Jane had enjoyed for decades.

Thanks to her late husband's foresight and financial planning, Jane owned a large and beautiful home in Sleepy Hollow, a two-and-a-half-acre slice of paradise just fifteen miles north of the Golden Gate Bridge. Her mortgage was a mere forty thousand dollars, less than a tenth of the property's value. Although Jane had not gone to work after her husband's premature death, she was meeting the payments and living securely on Al's modest pension and Social Security benefits.

If Al's early death had caused any financial worry, her fortunes had improved when she and O'Donnell fell in love, since he had amassed a sizable

1

Swiss trust fund that was just months from maturity. Between the two of them, there was more than enough to live comfortably on for the rest of their lives.

The phone rang, and the hostess answered it.

"It's for you, Jane," Nancy said.

"Who would be calling me here?"

She recognized the voice of Hugh Fine, a friend who was spending the weekend with Jane and Tom while studying for his final college examinations. The sixty-two-year-old father of nine was pursuing a lifelong dream of becoming a chiropractor, and Jane and Tom were happy to supply him with a place to stay in her roomy five-bedroom house.

Hugh sounded worried. "Cousin Irma called," he said. "She's very upset. She says she called your Aunt Gert's house about eight thirty last night with no answer. She thinks something awful has happened."

Jane was immediately concerned. Gertrude McCabe was a surrogate mother to Jane, helping to raise her when her parents divorced. Aunt Gert lived alone in San Jose, seventy miles south of Jane's Marin County home. At age eighty-eight, Gert was active, healthy, and predictable as a Swiss watch. At eight thirty, she should have been home watching television or reading.

Jane immediately called her cousin Irma Clark in San Francisco.

Irma was nearly hysterical. "I called just now and a stranger answered, so I hung up, thinking it was a wrong number. When I called back, he told me he was a police officer!"

Irma said the officer refused to answer any questions concerning Aunt Gert. Jane told Irma to stay by the phone and try not to worry.

Among the company was Jim Rohde, Jane's attorney and longtime friend, who advised her to call the San Jose Police Department. All the police dispatcher would offer was a curious statement, "An entry has been made for 165 Arroyo Way in San Jose."

Next, when she telephoned Gertrude's house, the man who answered identified himself as a San Jose police officer.

"This is Jane Alexander. I'm the niece of Gertrude McCabe."

"Where are you calling from? What is your phone number?"

Jane gave him the information he requested then asked, "Why are the police at the house? Is Gertrude sick? Is she in the hospital?"

"I really can't say, Miss Alexander. I'm not in a position to reveal any information at this time." He concluded by telling Jane that someone would call her back in a few minutes.

Jim Rohde waited with Jane until the phone rang a few minutes later, and then listened in on the extension. It was the San Jose coroner, Nat Gossett.

"Mrs. Alexander, are you the niece of Gertrude McCabe?"

"Yes."

"I'm sorry to tell you that your aunt Gertrude has been the victim of a homicide."

"What?"

"Your aunt has been the victim of a homicide."

"Homicide? Was she shot?"

"No."

Jane pressed for more information, but the coroner was no more forthcoming than the police officers had been. Finally, Jane told him she was coming to San Jose.

"I'm sorry, the officers have not yet finished at the crime scene. There's nothing you can do. Please don't come down at this time."

The news quickly dampened the spirit of the football party, and everyone fell silent. What was there to say? A few made a halfhearted effort to watch the game again. Tom came into the kitchen with Jane.

"Should I phone Cousin Irma?" she asked.

"Better if we tell her the news in person," said Tom. "I'll get our jackets. We'll drive to San Francisco."

Tom drove them across the Golden Gate Bridge to Irma's high-rise apartment on Lombard Street, atop picturesque Russian Hill. Jane talked the entire way, wondering aloud how someone could kill an old woman. Why they would choose Gertrude's house, one of the more modest on a street of expensive dwellings? Gertrude McCabe was eighty-eight years old, weighed barely over a hundred pounds, and would have surrendered anything to anyone who confronted her.

Tom and Jane arrived at the building. When they exited the elevator on the fourth floor, Irma's apartment door was open. They could hear her sobbing, "Why? Why? Why would someone do this? Who would do such a horrible thing to an old woman?"

Irma, eighty-four, had been on the phone with Gert's next-door neighbor, Juanita Lennon, who had recounted the little she knew. That morning she had noticed two day's worth of newspapers in front of Gert's door. Normally, Gert read her newspaper early every morning then passed it over the back fence for Juanita.

Chapter One

Juanita had nervously rung Gert's doorbell but had gotten no response. Too frightened to investigate on her own, she summoned a neighbor, who noticed a sliding door on the side of the house was wide open. Through a living room window the neighbor also noticed drawers open and their contents scattered about the room. The police were quickly called and arrived just before ten o'clock. "They carried her body out on a gurney," cried Irma.

Irma spurned Jane and Tom's offers to accompany them back to their house in Marin. Before they left, Jane and Irma made several more calls to the San Jose police and to Gertrude's home. Each was met with a refusal to reveal any further information.

When Jane and Tom arrived back home in Sleepy Hollow, houseguest Hugh Fine was on the phone with a reporter from the *San Jose Mercury News*. He handed the receiver to Jane.

"Mrs. Alexander, was your aunt one of *the* San Jose McCabes?"

Jane replied that she was. The McCabes were one of the original pioneering families in San Jose. At the turn of the century, Jane's grandfather had opened a First Street haberdashery in what later became the city's downtown. The McCabes had a long and distinguished history in Northern California. Gertrude McCabe was part of the second generation of McCabes to live in the Santa Clara Valley.

"When was your aunt born?"

"January 1, 1895."

"Any relation to Jay McCabe?"

"She was his sister," Jane said, "and the last of that generation."

James (Jay) Aloysius McCabe had been a towering figure in San Jose politics. He was a quintessential Irishman who led the St. Patrick's Day parade every year. An inveterate prankster, he was famous for playing elaborate practical jokes on visiting dignitaries—jokes that sometimes involved buckets of green paint. He had a fifty-year career promoting conventions and tourism in San Jose, and helped put the city on the map. Jay was personally credited with attracting more than fifty million dollars in convention revenues to the San Jose area. So important were his promotional contributions to the burgeoning city that the new convention center in downtown San Jose was named Jay McCabe Convention Hall upon his retirement in 1963. When he died in 1971, he left an estate worth more than a quarter million dollars at a time when that figure was still a significant sum. Gertrude McCabe, his younger sister, was the heir to his estate.

The reporter told Jane that her aunt "was bludgeoned several times on the head with a blunt instrument then stabbed in the chest and neck a dozen times. Then she was suffocated."

After the reporter hung up, Jane dropped the phone to her chest.

"Tom, I'll *kill* the animal that did this."

No one who had witnessed the bizarre turn of events that balmy day could ever have predicted the odyssey that the death of Gertrude McCabe would trigger.

Chapter Two

Arroyo Way is seven blocks east of the sprawling San Jose State University campus. A quiet, tree-lined street laid out in the 1930s, the former fruit orchard is now a solidly middle-class neighborhood populated by longtime residents. In the 1960s, Jay McCabe helped Gertrude buy one of the most modest single-story houses on the block. By 1983, the neighborhood real estate prices were booming, and today many of the gracious old homes are worth a million dollars or more.

Although violent crime in adjacent San Jose neighborhoods was rising due to the proliferation of street gangs and drugs, murder was still an unthinkable event on Arroyo Way. That changed on October 23, 1983.

Responding to a 911 call phoned in by Gertrude McCabe's neighbors, Juanita Lennon and Dominic Kovacevic, San Jose patrol officers Santiago Asencio and Ernest Carter arrived at the McCabe home at 9:57 AM, just two minutes after the call was received by the dispatcher.

While police are always reluctant to enter a home without a warrant, Officer Asencio felt the neighbors' concerns were genuine. He and Officer Carter rang the bell and called out to McCabe several times. Since the front door was locked, they circled around the house, continuing to call out Gertrude's name.

The two officers tried the rear door adjacent to Gertrude's laundry room. It was unlocked. Officers Ascenio and Carter made their way through a narrow hallway and kitchen. When they reached the den, Asencio found the body of an elderly woman, prostrate on the floor.

It was a horrible sight.

Gertrude McCabe was lying on her left side, wearing a gray knit skirt with a patterned sweater. Her skirt was hiked up to reveal nylon stockings and black shoes. The left side of her face appeared to be pressed down on a blue and brown oriental rug. Her hair was thickly matted and her face caked with dried blood. It appeared she had crawled or been dragged a short distance. The carpet behind her was soaked with a trail of blood.

Officers Ascenio and Carter knew they had a homicide, but before they could call forensic experts and detectives, they had a more pressing concern. Where there is one victim, there is often another. And a perpetrator. Drawing their service revolvers, they moved cautiously through the house, checking the bedrooms adjacent to the room where Gert was found. One room was ransacked, with dresser drawers open and objects scattered about. Nothing seemed out of place in the second bedroom.

Retracing their path through the house, they entered the bathroom nearest to Gert's body, where they discovered two throw pillows and a towel in the bathtub. The pillows and towel appeared bloody, and the bathtub had a faint reddish-brown ring.

Finally they checked the living room, where the sliding glass door was open. Convinced there was no one else in the house, they holstered their weapons and exited through the front door. They quickly radioed for assistance from the crime scene and homicide units. By the time the next squad car arrived, Asencio and Carter had the exterior of the house taped off to prevent contamination of the crime scene.

Within minutes, neighbors had begun peeking from their windows. Rumors spread quickly. Over the course of the next few hours, two dozen different officers arrived at Arroyo Way to question neighbors, gather evidence, and examine the body. The street was closed to traffic. The nightmare of urban life had come to another quaint and tranquil enclave.

Detectives Joe Brockman and Robert Frechette arrived on the scene by eleven, along with the coroner, Nat Gossett. Brockman and Frechette felt safe in their assumption that the victim was indeed Gertrude McCabe. Like the other officers, Brockman and Frechette were shocked by the frail nature of the victim. Despite having seen dozens of homicides, the two veteran officers found it difficult to believe that anyone could brutalize such a helpless old woman.

An examination of the crime scene revealed several things about the perpetrator. Although the front door was locked, there was no sign of forced entry. That indicated the victim might have known the perpetrator and let him in, locking the door behind them. The rear door, which had a heavy dead bolt with a key still in it, was closed but not locked. Whoever killed Gertrude might have been granted entry via the front door, then unlocked the back door and slipped away.

Brockman and Frechette continued their investigation. The two pillows and towel in the tub were still damp and bore obvious blood stains. The pillows, based on the size of the remaining stains, apparently had been used to cover Gertrude's face during the attack, probably to muffle her screams. Then the killer had filled the tub with water and left the pillows and towel to soak, hoping to destroy any evidence of blood. The tub had drained since the murder, leaving the reddish-brown ring.

On the sink was a pair of plastic gloves. They were much too large to have belonged to McCabe. Whoever killed her had planned thoroughly enough that they thought to bring a pair of plastic gloves to avoid leaving fingerprints. That hinted strongly of premeditation.

Sergeants Bud Harrington and Bill Santos of the crime scene unit arrived to take photographs and collect evidence. They followed a path they believed the killer had followed, photographing every item in the house, with particular attention to the den, where the body had been found. They photographed the ransacked drawers and desks, and the bathroom with the pillows and towel in the tub and gloves on the sink.

They dusted for fingerprints but were not very lucky. Although the killer had apparently used gloves to prevent discovery, he need not have worried. Less than a dozen partial prints were found in the entire home, none of which appeared fresh.

Yet Brockman and Frechette found one physical clue in the bathroom. Although a consistent layer of grime covered the walls and cobwebs filled the corners where the old woman could not reach, above the light switch in the bathroom was a fresh, clean swipe. Brockman figured the height of the cleaned area as approximately eight feet. The killer had to be at least six feet tall to wipe that high on the wall.

They were able to make an additional assumption. The drawers had been pulled from several desks and dressers, their contents scattered as though the perpetrator had just opened them and flung them across the room. The disarray had "bogus burglary" written all over it. Burglars are notoriously lazy. They do not dump drawers on the floor or fling their contents about the room. They would have to bend over and look for things, and burglars traditionally do not get on their hands and knees to look for anything. They go through drawers, flinging out unwanted objects until they locate something of value.

What's more, nothing seemed to have been stolen. Coroner Nat Gossett, the only person to touch or closely examine Gert's body, had already pointed out two expensive, if blood-soaked, diamond rings on her fingers. On top of

McCabe's dresser, clearly visible, was a glass jewelry box. Through the glass could be seen a gold charm bracelet, strands of pearls, a diamond watch, and several other items of silver and gold. Dust patterns on top of the jewelry box indicated the intruder had not opened it.

Her purse, hanging in plain sight from the doorknob in her bedroom, contained two hundred and ten dollars in cash. Later investigation turned up an unlocked strongbox on the closet floor nearby, plainly visible from anywhere in the room. It contained an additional four hundred dollars in cash.

No burglar would leave such obvious bounty as diamond rings and untraceable cash to ransack through clothing drawers.

Brockman and Frechette felt strongly that burglary was not the motive, which pointed toward the motive being personal. A few other clues added to the suspicion that Gertrude McCabe had known her killer. A cable-knit sweater hung over the edge of the couch with a book beside it. The book, *Fatal Vision* by Joe McGiniss, a 1983 best seller about the Jeffrey MacDonald/Green Beret murder case, had a small envelope for a bookmark on page 342. The sweater had probably covered Gertrude's legs as she read. When someone appeared at her door, she had likely set the sweater aside, marked her book, and gone to answer the door. Since blood evidence began in the entryway and the initial head wound appeared near the rear of her skull, the attack probably had begun as soon as she turned her back to the assailant.

The marked book also helped narrow down Gert's time of death. Two days before, she had been seen raking leaves late in the morning and had spoken to Juanita Lennon shortly before noon. Police soon found out that Gertrude watched a number of soap operas daily from twelve-thirty to three, so the murder probably took place afterward. Detectives determined that the light from the window failed about four o'clock and Gert could not easily read after that time without a light.

The murder victim was interrupted from her reading between three and four o'clock, opened the door to greet someone she never expected to assault her, and was bludgeoned in the back of the head as soon as she turned her back.

The question now was: who among the people who had known Gertrude McCabe was capable of committing such a heinous crime?

Chapter Three

At five o'clock that afternoon, Jane Alexander, who had been anxiously pacing her living room all afternoon, telephoned Gertrude McCabe's house in San Jose and pressed Detective Harrington for more information. He patiently explained that he had no additional news and that his investigation had just begun.

When Jane insisted she was driving to San Jose, Harrington told her not to do so. In the background, though, Jane could hear another officer speaking to Harrington. The officer told Harrington that unless someone stayed at the house to keep people away, he would have to assign two uniformed officers from the night shift to stand duty outside the house. The officer said he would prefer not to take a patrol car off the street for the entire night.

Harrington relented. He told Jane that she could come if she would stay in the house and follow police instructions. She quickly agreed.

Within a few minutes, she had packed a small bag and she, Tom O'Donnell, and their German shepherd, Duke, were en route to San Jose. Jane talked incessantly during the two-hour journey. Any attempt to calm her anxieties was futile.

While Jane and Tom drove, the police in San Jose were finishing up the first part of their investigation. Guffy Removal Service arrived at the McCabe house and removed Gertrude's body in a green plastic bag. The sight shocked and dismayed neighbors, particularly Juanita Lennon next door, who watched in horror, fearing that a maniac was loose on the streets. As Gertrude's body was loaded into the ambulance, she vowed to sell her house and move.

When Tom and Jane arrived at 165 Arroyo Way at seven that evening, they were met at the front door by Sergeant Harrington. Once inside, she met homicide detectives Brockman and Frechette, who offered their condolences.

As they entered the hallway by the front door, Jane looked to her left and saw a large brown stain on the carpet in the den. To officers, she appeared in a state of disbelief, asking repeatedly, "How could someone do such a thing?"

Brockman led Jane and Tom to four needlepoint chairs arranged in front of the living room fireplace. Jane pestered the officers for information on the murder, but they responded that they had none to offer.

"But what was the motive?" she asked repeatedly. "This is not the fanciest house on the block. Practically every house in this neighborhood is bigger and more expensive. She didn't have an enemy in the world; she was kind to everyone."

Veteran officers, Brockman and Frechette showed warmth and compassion to both Jane and Tom, who they assumed was her husband and called "Mr. Alexander." Yet all the detectives could tell her was that they did not believe it was a burglary. "We found cash, diamond rings on her fingers, and jewelry on her dresser. No burglar would pass those things up, especially the cash. The other evidence points to a simulated burglary. Since there was no forced entry, we think she knew the assailant and willingly gave him or her entry."

Jane asked them to confirm what she had learned from the *San Jose Mercury News* reporter. Slowly, Brockman verified the report. "She was bludgeoned, beaten, and strangled. It appears she may have been stabbed and tortured."

Jane continued to have questions, but Frechette and Brockman politely refused any further comment. She offered to go to the morgue and identify Gertrude's body if necessary. Tom O'Donnell interrupted and offered to make the identification for her, attempting to spare Jane further pain and anxiety. He mentioned how distraught Jane had become when she heard that Gertrude was attacked so violently.

At first the detectives accepted Tom's offer, but after a brief consultation they said it would not be necessary. Gertrude had identification and photos of her around the room that had convinced the detectives that Gertrude McCabe was indeed their victim.

After verifying that Jane and Tom would spend the night in the house, Frechette said detectives would return in the morning to continue gathering evidence. Tom did not like the idea of spending the night in a bedroom less than twenty feet from where Gertrude was murdered. He felt it would be frightening and disturbing to Jane, but she insisted.

Brockman and Frechette then made three additional requests. They asked Jane and Tom to save any facial tissues that they might find. They would not explain why. Second, the investigators asked them to keep an eye out for Gertrude's check registry. They explained the unusual request. They had found

Gertrude's checkbook, but the registry—the record of the checks she had written—was missing. To detectives it was a tiny but potentially significant detail: no one separates the records of the checks they have written from their checkbook.

Frechette and Brockman were looking for clues to support their emerging suspicions. They felt the check registry might hold the name of a disgruntled workman or someone with whom Gertrude had had a business disagreement. After receiving payment, he or she might have returned, killed Gertrude in anger, faked a burglary, then removed the check registry to conceal their identity. In addition, he or she would also have to destroy the check Gertrude had written. If one of Gertrude's last checks was not returned to the bank for cashing, it might confirm their suspicion.

The investigators' last request was for Jane and Tom to stay out of the front bathroom, where the bloody pillows, towels, and the plastic gloves had been found.

Jane consented and thanked the officers for their kindness and efforts. At approximately nine o'clock Sunday evening, the officers left, marking the first of many unusual events that would plague the investigation throughout its course. They left Tom and Jane alone at the crime scene, a crime scene that had not been fully processed. The fact would not sit well with subsequent investigators.

Dazed by the day's events, Jane found clean sheets in the hall closet and made up the bed in the extra bedroom. Tom spread newspapers over the dry bloodstains on the carpet in the den. Then he fed their German shepherd, Duke, and gave him his evening walk.

Though exhausted, they stayed awake for a couple of hours. They were jolted by an evening news report that showed a tape of the house where they were sitting. The report reiterated the scant details, conveying the shock felt by neighbors over the savage murder of eighty-eight-year-old Gertrude McCabe. "Police report there are no suspects," the reporter concluded.

At 11:30 PM, they went to bed. Tom fell asleep, but Jane tossed and turned for hours.

♦ ♦ ♦

By then, Coroner Nat Gossett had finished the preliminary examination of the body. Piece by piece, he began to reconstruct the crime.

The first thing he noticed when he turned Gertrude McCabe onto her back were the cuts in the front of her sweater. When he examined the body more closely, he found nearly two dozen stab wounds in her neck, face, and chest. None of them appeared to be very deep; the loss of blood from the stab wounds had been insignificant.

The blood on her matted hair had been caused by blunt-force trauma to her skull. Someone had hit her with a thin, round object, a club or perhaps an iron pipe, something that left no splinters or residue. Whatever the object was, it was hard and very smooth. Even so, the wounds appeared to be almost glancing blows. They had not even knocked her unconscious, as was evident by the scraped knees and carpet fragments under her nails. She had tried to crawl away from the assailant after the initial blow to her head. Whoever had inflicted those wounds on Gertrude seemed, on cursory examination, to be either physically weak, small of stature, or very timid.

Using long forceps, Coroner Gossett removed what appeared to be a brown, blood-soaked piece of paper wadded in Gertrude's mouth. He carefully unfolded it, noting its a distinctive blue-and-white floral design. It also bore a faint smear that later proved to be lipstick. Detectives Brockman and Frechette noted that it matched a tissue found next to Gertrude's leg.

The coroner turned to the cable around her neck. It was a bicycle lock: a thin steel cable wrapped in clear plastic. The attached padlock had been wrenched down so tightly that the cable had embedded itself in Gertrude's neck. From the broken blood vessels in her eyes and the open mouth, the coroner determined that she had suffocated to death as the result of strangulation.

Homicide detectives always keep one or two pieces of information out of their reports and thus from the media. In case they find a witness or extract a confession, that information is used to confirm the identity of the killer. They know he or she did not read it in the newspapers; only a killer or accomplice would be privy to that particular detail. Detectives Brockman and Frechette determined that the tissue as well as the bicycle chain and the lock, the exact cause of Gertrude McCabe's death, would be their hidden fact.

◆ ◆ ◆

Chapter Three

Jane Alexander had a very difficult time falling asleep. Only at approximately 4 AM did she drift into a tortured, shallow doze. She was awakened, alone, shortly thereafter by the sound of running water. At first she thought that Tom was taking a shower.

Duke was asleep on the floor next to her, his head resting between his paws. She called out to Tom. As she was getting out of bed, Tom came down the hallway and told her to stay put.

She asked him why he was up. He explained that Gertrude had left a can of orange juice on the sink, and somehow it had exploded. The sound had startled him, and he had gone to investigate.

When he saw the mess in the kitchen, the fastidious O'Donnell had stopped to clean it up. The sound of running water Jane had heard was from the kitchen sink. Since it was beyond the crime scene, it had not tainted any area of interest to the police.

For the rest of the night she was unable to sleep. Something inside was killing her.

Chapter Four

The morning papers were filled with the story. "Member of Pioneering San Jose Family Slain," reported the *San Jose Mercury News*. "Gertrude McCabe, 88, Beaten, Stabbed to Death in Her San Jose Home."

The article quoted Lieutenant Donald Trujillo, chief of homicide for the San Jose Police Department. "You have an elderly woman, slightly built, probably weighing less than a hundred pounds and living alone. She could have been anybody's grandmother. If you wanted something from her, she would not resist. Why did he or she or they have to brutalize her in such a fashion?"

Trujillo reported that a task force from the robbery, burglary, and homicide units was already forming. The age of the victim, the longstanding stature of the McCabes, and the inexplicable violence had roused the entire department, indeed the entire city. Crime Stoppers offered a one thousand dollar reward for information on the case.

On October 24, 1983, at 10:00 AM, Sergeants Harrington and Brockman returned to the house on Arroyo Way to continue collecting evidence. While the officers worked, Jane looked from the picture window in the den and saw several news vans arriving. Tom O'Donnell, who had made a habit of rescuing Jane from emotionally trying circumstances, intervened again. He went outside and politely informed them that Jane was too distraught to speak. Tom explained that the two women were very close and that Jane considered Gertrude a surrogate mother. Tom also told them the police were diligent in their efforts and reiterated what Lieutenant Trujillo had also said in the papers. "We know of no suspects. We have no idea who did this."

Inside the house, the investigators debated the conflicting theories of how the crime occurred. It might have been someone Gertrude knew and permitted entry to the house. Then again, an intruder might simply have walked in the open doors and Gertrude surprised him, though the location of the assault—within a few feet of the front door—made them favor the former theory.

The varied methods of assault—the blow to the head, the multiple stabbings, the suffocation—might indicate a drug addict or a psychopath. But

Chapter Four

neither would stop to clean the crime scene, and an addict would not have left cash in her purse and diamonds on her fingers. Plus, the superficial wounds also discounted this theory.

Why would anyone fake a burglary and leave so many obvious things to steal? Why would a perpetrator be calculating enough to bring plastic gloves and then leave them behind? Was the intention burglary or murder? That led the investigators back to the missing check registry. Could a disgruntled workman or merchant have been so incensed over a dispute that he would brutalize an old woman? They finished processing the scene at midday, still unsure what the evidence was telling them.

For her part, Jane began to search through Gertrude's papers. First she found her will. It named Gertrude's cousin Irma as executor. Jane muttered aloud that she was not happy about that fact, "Irma never told me this." The will also declared that the remainder of the estate be divided equally between Jane and Irma.

Then Jane found two passbooks, one in her name and one in Irma's, for twenty thousand dollars each. Gertrude had opened a savings account for each of them as a gift.

Jane called her cousin, who was still distraught by the events, and asked what funeral arrangements should be made. Irma stated that Gertrude wanted to be cremated. That also surprised Jane, but Tom found a pamphlet from the Neptune Society—a cremation service—indicating that Gertrude had indeed intended to be cremated.

Shortly thereafter, Jane telephoned Detective Frechette at the San Jose Police Department with a confusing piece of information. She had found Gertrude's check registry in the corner of one of her dresser drawers, leaning flat against the side. Frechette was surprised by the revelation. He felt his officers had made a thorough search of the premises and not found the registry. He thanked her and immediately drove to Arroyo Way to retrieve it.

By five o'clock that afternoon, Tom had reminded Jane that she had not eaten anything since the day before. Jane tried to get something out of Gertrude's refrigerator, but the sight of her late aunt's food made her ill.

Tom insisted on taking Jane to Original Joe's, a landmark all-night restaurant in downtown San Jose. He ordered both of them a drink, hoping it would help Jane calm down. Instead, while sipping her drink and picking at a slice of French bread, Jane started to cry and could not stop. She vowed to go to the end of the earth to find Gertrude's killer. She asked Tom for his patience

16

and understanding, explaining that anger could not begin to describe how she felt. Tom did not know what to say.

♦ ♦ ♦

Police investigators began to piece together a portrait of Gertrude McCabe. Two shining examples quickly emerged. Two years earlier, she had given her car to a friend who desperately needed it to make a living. Twice a week Gert would walk a mile and a half to a grocery store then take a cab home with her purchases.

Detectives honed in on the probability that Gertrude knew her killer. Neighbors provided the first slim leads. She was in the habit of cashing checks for neighbors after banking hours, a fact that roused police suspicion about a possible motive. But why then had the killer fled without a dime? Had they stopped to clean up the crime scene and been scared off just before taking their plunder?

They also learned that Gert had a habit of hiring workmen—plumbers, gardeners, and carpenters—from ads in the *San Jose Mercury News*. Her habit of inviting strangers into the house to make repairs troubled all of her neighbors. It would also establish the first line of investigation.

A nurse living on the same block reported seeing a woman of Hispanic descent drive onto Arroyo Way across from Gertrude's house, wait for a period of fifteen minutes, then drive down the street, turn around, and park in front of another house. The woman even got out of the car and paced; she appeared to be waiting for someone.

They also learned that several months before the murder, Gertrude's house had been burglarized. Though she had told several neighbors, she had failed to report the incident to police.

An interesting fact came to light. Whereas Gertrude had religiously tended her own backyard, her beloved peonies and daffodils, she had always employed a gardener to mow the small front yard. Police learned that within the previous year Gertrude had fired a gardener who had failed to show up for several weeks without informing her.

Detective Frechette found canceled checks written to a gardener whose last name was Pineda. They located his phone number in Gertrude's book. Frechette promptly paid a visit to Pineda and his wife.

Pineda was not the man who had been fired, Frechette learned. He had replaced the man who had been fired. Pineda and his wife, who sometimes translated for him, wrote his contracts, and handled his small business affairs, answered Frechette's questions freely. They seemed legitimately shocked and dismayed by Gertrude's death.

Frechette asked the Pinedas if they would give the police fingerprint samples and agree to be photographed for his evidence files. The couple readily agreed. The ease with which they answered his questions and offered to cooperate made him believe that they were not his suspects. A solid alibi later confirmed his observation.

Investigators did locate the gardener who had been fired by Gertrude for his tardiness, but he too was eliminated by a solid alibi.

Another lead they turned up seemed more promising. Juanita Lennon told Officer Asencio that she had seen a man and a woman of African American descent inside Gertrude's house a week before the murder. Juanita knew of Gertrude's proclivity for hiring cheap laborers from the newspaper, but she thought it odd that the pair was inside Gertrude's house: she almost never let strangers enter.

Juanita also told police that two painters had been working on her house the day the pair arrived at Gertrude's. Police located one of the painters, who confirmed Juanita's story. The painter said he was suspicious of the pair when he saw them. The man was much older than the woman, he said, and when they left Gertrude's house, he clearly heard them talking about the expensive antique furnishings. The pair drove a white van with no markings on it, which struck him as unusual. Tradesmen's vans are often a form of rolling self-promotion.

They found a scribbled phone number on a notepad. In the *San Jose Mercury News*, police searched the "Handy Persons" section and found a matching number. It belonged to a man named Virgil Jackson.

Detectives Brockman and Frechette paid a call to the apartment manager in the complex where Virgil Jackson lived. She told them that Virgil was fifty-three and his wife, Sheryl, was twenty-seven. They had moved from Poughkeepsie, New York the previous year. Other neighbors in their apartment complex claimed that Virgil was on the lam from bad check charges in New York.

Neighbors had also reported several violent confrontations between Virgil and Sheryl, stating that he had beaten and choked his wife. Patrol reports verified that police had responded to 911 calls at the Jackson apartment on several occasions, and Sheryl's daughter had reported that Sheryl slapped her in the face so hard she once lost a front tooth.

Adding to the picture, the manager told police Virgil and Sheryl had been late on their rent several times. That month, late in October, they still had not paid the rent, claiming they were broke and that Virgil was waiting for some money that would be arriving any day.

Virgil also had a close friend who had visited him several times and had been seen brandishing a handgun, frightening other residents.

Brockman and Frechette made a call on the Jackson apartment and found Sheryl at home. They advised her that they were conducting an investigation into the death of Gertrude McCabe, and she agreed to speak with them inside her apartment.

She confirmed that Gertrude had hired them to change light bulbs and fix the sliding door. She described Gertrude as a pleasant old lady, that she paid them for their work, and said she might need some painting in the future.

On the day of the murder, Sheryl claimed she had taken her child to school and spent the afternoon watching soap operas with friends. She went to her job at a local pizza parlor at five and returned late that night. Virgil, she said, was at work for a local heating and air conditioning company.

When asked to recount their prior lives in Poughkeepsie, Sheryl said they had operated a residence care facility for handicapped adults. Many of the patients were wards of the state. She further claimed that she and Virgil had closed the facility and moved to San Jose to be closer to Virgil's children.

Within a day, the Virgil Jackson story started heating up. Brockman called New York State Social Services and found that the Jacksons had not left New York for familial reasons.

Brockman was on the phone an hour later with the Jackson's apartment manager. He learned that Sheryl had gone to her immediately after he and Frechette had left. Sheryl had been in a panic, talking about McCabe's murder and telling the manager she wanted to sell her possessions and move that night.

"A little old lady we did some work for is dead, and I think Virgil might have done it." Virgil, she continued, had been having nightmares and crying in his sleep all week. He had been dealing heavily in drugs recently and spending too much time with his friend Mike Jones, the man who had brandished the gun.

By 2:00 PM that day, Brockman and Frechette paid another visit to Sheryl Jackson. "We feel you have not been completely truthful, and there may be something you want to tell us about," said Brockman.

Sheryl began sobbing. "There was something I wasn't completely truthful about. When I came home from work last Saturday night, I expected him to be asleep. It was about two-thirty in the morning. He told me he'd heard about the murder of that lady on the radio. He didn't have any emotion. It gave me quite a chill up my spine."

"Last Saturday night? You mean two-thirty on Sunday morning?"

"Yes."

That grabbed their attention. The murder wasn't reported until just before ten o'clock Sunday morning. How could Virgil Jackson have known about the crime on Saturday unless he was involved?

"I'm real scared of him," said Sheryl. "If he knew that I was talking this way about him to you, he would probably try to hurt me bad."

"Has he ever tried to strangle you?"

"Oh, yeah, that's his favorite sport, and I've got the scars to prove it." Sheryl showed the officers scar tissue and striations around her neck. Virgil, she explained, had even told her his "theory" about how Ms. McCabe was killed.

"He said it was probably someone that knew her," recounted Sheryl. "Virgil said someone who came in the back sliding glass doors because they didn't close properly. It was probably someone who thought she was out of the house, someone who came to rob her. He had to kill her because he didn't want to be recognized."

Sheryl became agitated as her husband's words took on a more ominous tone. "Virgil, he's been real strange. I woke up and heard crying the other night, and there he was in the living room, crying and mumbling in his sleep, with two pillows on his head. It was his birthday Tuesday, and he just said he wanted to shave his mustache; he was tired of the way he looked. I thought that was weird."

On the afternoon of Friday, October 21, her husband came home before four-thirty, showered, changed clothes, and was doing his own laundry. This too was unusual, she said. He usually didn't behave that way after coming back from work.

Sheryl Jackson went voluntarily to the San Jose Police Department to be fingerprinted. She was asked if anything was missing from her house, and she mentioned a small magnifying glass in a leather pouch that her husband normally carried. She hadn't seen it for a week. When one was produced from an evidence drawer, Sheryl examined it closely and said she felt it belonged to her husband. A police search of Jackson's apartment turned up a pair of leather house slippers with brown marks resembling bloodstains. They also seized a copy of a newspaper, dated Tuesday, October 25, which had an article about the McCabe murder.

"Mrs. Jackson," asked Sergeant Brockman, "did your husband kill Miss McCabe?"

"I don't want to answer that. But I think you have enough to arrest him, don't you?"

Virgil Jackson was interviewed at the policy department at 6:40 that evening. He said that he heard about the murder on the radio Monday morning and later read an article about it in the *San Jose Mercury News*. "I was wondering when you would get around to talking to me," he said. "After a couple days, I started wondering if you wouldn't call at all."

Jackson was extremely nervous during the interview. This was not surprising, since investigation officers began with questions about his history of crime and violence. Jackson confirmed a previous arrest for assault on his wife. He also confirmed several arrests on the East Coast for fighting and getting rowdy.

"Have you ever been accused of theft?"

"No," said Jackson. But when pressed about the problems with the board-and-care facility in New York State, he acknowledged an investigation. "Everything was cleared up before we moved out here," he said.

An alibi was difficult for Jackson to establish, since he had trouble remembering his schedule. He had worked through the entire weekend, he said. On Friday, he thought he was probably with a friend removing a heater from a house in Oakland, returning home at 4:00 PM. But he could have been pouring cement in San Jose with another friend, since he did that for a day as well. The police couldn't decide if Jackson was simply confused or trying to hide the truth from them.

"There are probably things you can't remember," Jackson was told. "Think carefully about your situation."

While Virgil Jackson was left alone, police contacted a friend of Sheryl Jackson's by telephone. The friend had spent Friday with her, and that evening her husband had gone with Virgil Jackson and his daughter to pick a pumpkin from a local pumpkin patch.

"All the problems you see there, that's just a takes-two-to-tango thing. She beats up on him; he beats up on her. Family violence, that's all it is. Virgil would never do it to anyone else."

Chapter Four

Meanwhile, Sheryl Jackson had called the San Jose Police Department to find out how the interview was progressing. She was asked how certain she was Virgil had told her about the murder on Saturday night.

"I would stake my life on that fact," she said.

"Could you relate the occasion of being told of the murder to some other event in your life? Did anything happen the following morning?"

"Well, I read about the murder in the newspaper the following morning."

The investigator was surprised. If Sheryl had read about the case the morning after her husband had spoken of it, it must have been Monday or Tuesday, not Sunday morning.

"Did you read about it in the newspaper we removed from your apartment?" This was the paper dated Tuesday, October 25.

She said she did.

"Well, if it's Tuesday's newspaper, I must have learned about it Monday night. He had been working that night, heard about it coming home on the radio. He doesn't work on Saturday nights, not ever."

The detective thanked Sheryl again for her cooperation.

Virgil Jackson had consented to a search of his white 1965 Ford Econoline Van, and forensic investigators had converged on the downtown San Jose intersection where the van was parked. The vehicle had been sealed for several hours while Jackson was at the station. Jackson returned to the scene to witness the search.

Investigators discovered an envelope with Gertrude McCabe's name, address, and directions to her home. Jackson confirmed that it was used to find McCabe's house on his handyman call. Also found was the small magnifying glass in a leather pouch, very similar to the one found at the crime scene, with only a slightly different bend in the handle. Jackson was asked to submit the shirt he was wearing for forensic examination. He said it was the same shirt he had worn the Friday before.

Further inquiries proved that Virgil Jackson was, in fact, pouring cement until late in the afternoon on Friday, October 21. Nothing linked him to the case except his wife's suspicions. The police had no choice but to release Jackson.

Two months later the couple separated.

After an initial burst of optimism that the case would be quickly solved, the police were back to square one.

Chapter Five

"We thought we had the guy, but it didn't pan out, Mrs. Alexander." Sergeant Harrington conveyed the news by phone to Tom and Jane just before they came to San Jose on a return trip. This time they removed some of Aunt Gert's effects and gave unwanted items to the Catholic charity of St. Vincent de Paul. Jane wondered aloud what to do with the countless books in Gert's house, most of them mysteries. She herself had never been a mystery fan and had never heard of the dozens of authors Gert followed diligently. Jane decided to keep a few of them to see if they would hold her interest.

Jane had been calling the San Jose P.D. on a daily basis, asking the officers for progress reports. To police investigators, her persistence was a possible warning sign.

When people who have a guilty conscience are questioned by the police, they often do one of two things. The first category turn away, try to hide in plain sight with a litany of "I don't know," and "I don't remember." As soon as someone says, "I don't remember," to a simple question, cops get very interested.

The other type is the person who pesters, who seems overly concerned, obsessed with details, who can't keep quiet. This second group are people hoping their fervor will be taken as such and mask their true intentions: avoiding suspicion and detection. On the other hand, they may be relatives obsessed with gaining justice.

"Are you absolutely certain he is not the killer?" Jane asked.

"We brought him in and printed him, but he had a solid alibi. We checked it all out. We had to let him go. We are pretty convinced Virgil Jackson did not murder your aunt."

"Someone on that street must have seen something," she said. "They all know each other; they all watch when strangers drive down the street. Didn't anyone tell you anything?"

Sergeant Harrington was as patient and accommodating as Frechette and Brockman had been. "We're still looking at plenty of other characters in the neighborhood, door-to-door salesmen, craftsmen, and transients," said

Chapter Five

Sergeant Harrington. "We are not stopping, Mrs. Alexander. When we see an old woman killed like that, it gets under our skin."

"You're back to square one, right?" said Jane.

Harrington refused to comment further, but Jane knew the answer. The first few days of an investigation are crucial, and the more time that passes the less likely it is that the crime will be solved. You could learn that watching TV crime dramas. The Gertrude McCabe case was already in its second week.

"Don't give up hope," Harrington continued. "Miss McCabe had an address book filled with people who had done work for her over the years. We feel there might be something in it. We won't stop until we have pursued every possible avenue."

When Jane hung up the phone, she turned to Tom O'Donnell, who had been sitting nearby. She was enmeshed in fear and anxiety, unable to eat or sleep. All she talked about was Aunt Gert's murder.

"Jane, why don't we just get away from all this?" he said. "What do you think of going somewhere, maybe going to Bermuda for a week or two? We need to get away. We could ride bicycles around the island, bake in the sun. The cops are going to handle this. You know they are going to solve the case."

"You're out of your mind, Tom," said Jane. This was getting to be a sore subject between them. "I'm not going to leave the country until they get the animal who did this thing. How could I enjoy myself? Besides, I hate the heat."

So they stayed home, and Tom watched as Jane slipped further and further into a state where she was unable to function. Normally ebullient, articulate, and interested in everything about her, she abandoned even her oldest routines.

Although she normally read several books a month, she was now unable to read for more than a few minutes. Even television seemed to irritate her. The news was full of murders, as always. Tom tried to take her dancing or to dinner, or for casual social calls on friends. She resisted all his efforts.

Gertrude had been a soap opera aficionado. Now, whenever Tom tuned in one of her favorites, Jane would quickly leave the room. The latter was particularly daunting to Tom, as he shared Gert's passion for daytime soap operas and watched them religiously. They had both followed many of the same series for years and the shared interest had made them more than casual friends.

When Jane and Tom would visit Gert in San Jose, the conversation would inevitably turn to the plots and intrigues that were the focus of network fare. They would dispute the qualities of different characters. Jane once said she disliked the character James Steinbeck on *As The World Turns*. Gertrude defended him by saying, "After all, Jane, I have known him a great deal longer than you have, dear."

Again and again Jane talked of her aunt, how spry she had been, how generous. After Tom broke his foot playing tennis on July 24, 1983, Aunt Gert loaned him an antique cane that had belonged to her father. "Tom, you're going to need this when you stop hobbling on your crutches." Gertrude had said. "But I want it back. It was one of my father's favorites."

That visit would be the last time Jane saw her aunt alive.

Daily she was becoming more obsessed with the progress of the investigation. Periodically, the San Jose newspapers reported tidbits about the investigation: citizens were outraged, police were always "hopeful" and "examining all possible leads," which meant they were getting nowhere.

Finally, Jane realized the strain was clearly getting to Tom, too. "Maybe we should go somewhere in the car," she said. "It wouldn't hurt to get away a couple of days. A drive to Tahoe or something, someplace we can take Duke."

Jane struck on the idea of visiting her friends the Harts, who had a home in rural Idaho. They could ride through the High Sierra in late autumn and stop to see a few friends along the way. In Idaho they could hike and read, relax, and enjoy old friends. They could try to forget the horror of Gert's death and the maddeningly slow pace of justice.

"First we should go down to San Jose and get the money Aunt Gert left in the account," Tom noted. "We might as well do it now, before going on this trip. You have to wrap up the loose ends sometime."

Tom O'Donnell had been taking care of the financial details of Jane's life since the beginning of their relationship. Jane had been married to a banker for thirty-four years, and never much cared for working with figures. She disliked the chore of balancing household accounts, although she had reluctantly taken up the responsibility following her husband's heart attack in 1974. Tom, however, seemed to enjoy the task. He was a man who paid attention to details, including financial details. She gratefully handed that responsibility over to him.

Jane knew Tom was right. The bank account Gertrude had left in her name had to be addressed at some point. The couple drove to San Jose. While Tom waited in the car, Jane stood in line at the San Francisco Federal Savings and Loan.

Chapter Five

It took a few minutes for a cashier's check to be drawn. As the teller examined her signature card, the bank manager approached her at the teller's window.

"Mrs. Alexander, I was so sorry to read the news about Miss McCabe."

"Did you know her?" Jane asked.

"Yes, for many, many years. She was already a longtime customer when I started here."

He escorted Jane back to his desk, and the two began discussing Aunt Gert. He had been very impressed by Gertrude's intelligence, he said, and the way she embodied the spirit of the early Santa Clara Valley.

"She was very genteel," he said. "But not shy or in any way aloof—just the opposite, in fact. She was outgoing toward everyone. Everyone knew her and adored her. It's just horrible that somebody would do that to her."

Jane was grateful for the manager's kind words. It was true that Gert lived her life on the assumption that people were honest and could be trusted, at least until they proved otherwise. What an irony that Gert would die in her own home, having very likely opened the door to the person who killed her.

"Do they have any suspects?" asked the banker.

As Jane shared her frustration about the state of the investigation, she suddenly became aware that Tom was standing next to her. She was startled. "What are you doing here?"

"I was just wondering what was taking you so long," he said, smiling. The bank manager apologized then got up to see if the teller had cut the cashier's check. By the look on Jane's face, Tom could tell that she was upset at the interruption.

"I just came in to see if I could help," he said. "I'm sorry."

Jane gave the check to Tom when she got in the car. They stopped at Aunt Gert's house, which was then being cleaned by someone hired by Cousin Irma. Jane refused to enter. Tom spent a few minutes inside looking things over, and reassured her that things would be okay.

The next day, Jane and Tom drove up to the Sierra Nevada mountains in eastern California. They stopped for a night at the hundred-year-old Murphy's Hotel, a favorite Sierra resort. The next day they passed through Reno, Nevada, where they had dinner with friends Barbara and Jim Storm. The conversation revolved around one subject: Gertrude's murder. Throughout the journey Jane found herself grateful for Tom's solicitude and for the small courtesies of hotels that allowed Duke to stay in the room.

After four days her spirits seemed to rise. She called Sergeant Joe Brockman from Boise and was told that although no arrest had been made, the police were confident they now knew who had committed the murder. Unable to elicit further details, Jane thanked Brockman and hung up.

"I think she was probably out back raking leaves and came in and surprised the burglar," said their hostess, Marti Hart, over dinner that evening.

Whenever someone has an unsolved tragedy in their family, everyone has a theory on how it happened. The Harts and their neighbors, the O'Learys, all transplanted Californians, were happy to assist in examining every possibility.

"There are more and more crazies on the streets these days," suggested Bill O'Leary. "Couldn't it have been some kind of psychopath, a serial killer? Those nutcases seem to show up in California about this time every year, looking to escape the cold back east."

"Psychopaths don't clean up after themselves," said Jane. "This guy washed out the pillows in the bathtub."

"Well, everyone has someone they have crossed," Sherman said. "Anyone can make an enemy these days."

The intense, emotional conversation went on for some time before Tom pulled Marti Hart aside. "I don't think we should spend the trip talking about the murder," said Tom. "The whole purpose of coming here was to get some rest and to get Jane's mind off the tragedy."

Marti agreed. "We'll put a lid on it, Tom."

The rest of the visit was spent relaxing in a small trailer outside the Harts' home. Tom seemed exhausted and spent most of his time immersed in Robert Ludlum thrillers, his favorite reading material. For the first time since the murder, Jane was able to get a full night's rest. It would provide only temporary relief from her anguish.

Two more phone calls to the San Jose Police Department revealed that they had not yet apprehended their newest suspect.

When they returned home, Jane learned that San Jose officers had been overly optimistic in their first assessment of the suspect. He was an itinerant salesman or laborer tramping through the neighborhood allegedly looking for work. Some residents reported he was selling candy door-to-door; others claimed he had been seeking yard work. Everyone who saw him was suspicious of his appearance. When police finally identified him, they learned he was an ex-con on probation for robbery. But exculpatory evidence soon convinced them he was not the killer.

Chapter Five

Using Gert's address book as a guide, they had tracked down and interviewed almost every workman who had set foot on her property. They interviewed laborers for a glass company and a floor-covering service, a stove repairman, a painter, a tree trimmer, a newspaper boy, a linoleum installer, a laundry deliveryman, a gutter installer, and an upholsterer.

Detective Frechette, checking for similar cases, noticed that two previous burglary victims had been members of the American Association of Retired Persons. He called the local chapter AARP, which was reluctant to give their member list to anyone. He did learn that Gertrude McCabe was not a member, so the killer had not met her there.

By December 1983, police were stymied. They had checked every lead and interviewed every possible witness. Yet they had not a single tangible clue or viable suspect. On television, the most complex crimes are solved in sixty minutes minus the commercials. In real life, a shockingly high percentage of homicides are never solved.

Throughout those months Tom O'Donnell was a model of patience and understanding, constantly trying to comfort Jane. She would rise in the middle of the night, sit in the living room, and look out on the lights in the valley. She didn't cry. She didn't shake. Tom would get up and sit with her. "You need your strength," said Tom. "Please don't get sick on me."

On one of her nightly vigils he said to her, "Jane, you have to accept that they may never find the killer."

She barely waited for him to finish before she replied. "Wrong, Tom. You're absolutely wrong. You know me better than that," she said. "I will never rest until that animal pays for it. I'll never quit."

By December, Jane was still calling the police twice a week, still asking the same questions. Do you have any news? Any suspects? Is anyone really working on the case?

With every day that went by, with every new murder in a city with a growing crime rate, Gertrude's case moved one more notch down the ladder. "Cold" cases gave way to "hot" ones. Homicides with fresh clues and solid suspects took precedence over murders whose leads had been exhausted, whose suspects had all been cleared. With each new violent crime, with each fruitless search, Gertrude McCabe got one step further from justice.

Chapter Six

Christmas is the most important holiday of the year for Jane Alexander. She starts her shopping in March and begins wrapping gifts in October. She makes a box for each of the twenty-one people on her list, into which she places dozens of small items, each individually wrapped. It is a custom she started in the early 1970s as a kind of care package for the children of Erin and Jim Rohde when they went to Hawaii one Christmas. As Jane's own grandkids were born, preparation of "the boxes" became an increasingly elaborate production that filled an entire room in Sleepy Hollow. This year her largesse extended to the men working on Gertrude's case.

On December 13, she and Tom paid a visit to homicide detectives at the San Jose Police Department. At Tom's suggestion, they brought four bottles of brandy as Christmas gifts for Sergeants Brockman, Frechette, and Harrington, and Officer Santos.

"Is there anything new at all?" Jane asked. Although the questions had become tiresome to all of them, Brockman offered a polite and elaborate version of "no." "We're examining every possibility, and there are many aspects to the case."

"What about the photos of the crime scene? I'd like to see them," she said.

"Jane, the photos are extremely graphic and unpleasant," he said. "You don't really want to remember your aunt that way." She did, she said, and asked when she might be able to see them.

"Perhaps in a year, but frankly, some of the photos are so inflammatory that we might not be able to show them to the jury."

Jane's diplomacy faded. "What do you mean the jury can't see the photos? That animal butchers an old woman and the jury can't see what he did to her?"

"That will be up to the district attorney." Brockman knew that engaging her in a debate about the photos would be futile, so he deftly let the issue pass.

"We're a long way from taking this to the district attorney, aren't we?" Jane asked.

"There is no statute of limitations on murder," Sergeant Frechette replied. "It doesn't matter how long it takes. Murder cases are never closed. Whatever it takes, we will get him."

What the detectives failed to mention was that each of the lead investigators would soon be off the case. Sergeant Frechette had accepted a security job at IBM and would be off the force at the end of the month. Sergeant Brockman was looking at an imminent promotion that would take him out of homicide.

Days later, with the holiday boxes dispatched to family and friends, the couple made a return visit to the Sierra Nevada haven of the Murphy's. For four days they read books, took long walks in the rain, and watched football on TV. On Christmas Day, Jane wrote in her diary, "I'm happy, Tom's happy, Duke's happy." But when they returned a week later in time for a Sunday 49ers party at the Rohde house, friends were unconvinced. Not since the death of her husband in 1977 had she looked so emotionally drained.

Aunt Gert's house on Arroyo Way had been left unheated that winter, and several essential repairs had been left unattended. It was an unusually rainy winter, and when Jane and Tom arrived at the house on January 6, 1984, to meet the lawyer handling the estate, they were shocked to find a corner of the living room ceiling had collapsed due to water damage. The sight made Jane furious. She knew that Aunt Gert would have been devastated.

As executor of the estate, cousin Irma should have been attentive to the house. *She never could do anything right,* thought Jane. Already unsteady of foot and with her memory failing, Irma had suffered a tremendous shock with the news of Gert's murder. She had grown immediately suspicious of everyone, and had rejected the offer of Jane's friend Hugh Fine to move in and paint and repair the house for free.

Irma had instead hired a lawyer out of the Yellow Pages, John Carroll, to oversee the disbursement of the estate's proceeds. Irma had insisted that anything Jane wanted had to be "purchased" out of the proceeds of the estate, including items that Jane had given Gert as gifts. She rankled Jane considerably, and the two were no longer on speaking terms.

On this day Jane and Tom were meeting John Carroll and an antiques dealer to evaluate Gert's possessions and to discuss putting the home on the market. It was a trying day.

"It must be very painful to visit this house after all that has happened," said the smiling dealer even before Jane had crossed the threshold. "I'll give you two thousand dollars for the contents of the house, and spare you the pain of having to see these things again. Your cousin has already agreed."

Jane was nonplussed. "The oriental rug you're standing on is worth twice that," she snapped.

Jane wanted several things belonging to Gert, including a snuffbox collection and a half-dozen chairs Gert had needlepointed herself. As Tom and Jane were walking through the house examining items, the antiques dealer and John Carroll started discussing Gert's murder.

"As if it wasn't enough to beat and stab the poor woman, he had to finish her off by strangling her with a chain around her neck," said Carroll.

"Chain?" Jane said in disbelief. "What's this about a chain?"

Carroll stopped. "Oh, I'm sorry. It wasn't a chain. It was a bicycle cable."

"What are you talking about?" asked Jane.

"Miss McCabe was strangled to death by one of those cables they use to lock bicycles to a rack."

"How do *you* know that and I don't? Who told you that?"

Carroll looked embarrassed. "The police told me. They knew I was a lawyer representing the estate, and they just sort of offered it. I'm sorry, you didn't know that?

Jane completely lost her cool. "I knew she had been strangled, but I assumed the murderer had used his hands. No one told me he used a bicycle chain around her neck." She was too angry to say more.

Learning new information about Gertrude's murder from a perfect stranger sent Jane's mind reeling. The police had stonewalled her on information, but offered strangers intimate details of Aunt Gert's death. She wanted to punch Carroll in the mouth. She wanted to tear into the San Jose P.D. Enough was enough.

Her first impulse was to call the San Jose Police Department and demand to know why things were being kept from her. They had not let her see the photographs, and they were not candid about the true cause of Gert's death. What else hadn't they told her?

But the phone in the house had been disconnected, and it was late in the day. Tom's common sense prevailed. He told her the detectives were probably unavailable, and it would do no good to call them in a rage.

Chapter Six

So she swallowed her anger and finished selecting furniture and objects that she wanted to keep for herself and her children, things that were precious to Gert and that Jane could not bear to see in the hands of strangers.

"I see you've tagged all the good things," said the antiques dealer in irritation.

"So what did you expect?"

The next day, while Tom flew to Los Angeles to visit an old friend and business associate named Harry Carmichael, Jane stayed at home, seething. Unable to reach anyone at the San Jose Police Department, she spent the weekend writing questions to ask the officers when they returned to work on Monday.

During those two days a profound change began to come over Jane Alexander. She would no longer accept at face value what the police had to offer. She would no longer accept their kindness and civility as a substitute for progress. She was determined to know everything related to the case. She had a right to know, she told herself; a victim's family has a right to know. Gone was the woman whose persistence might have been misread by police and passive observers as the workings of a guilty conscience. The seeds of a crusader had been planted by the offhand remarks of an insensitive lawyer.

On Monday evening, while Tom was still in Los Angeles, she phoned Sergeant Brockman. She demanded to know why John Carroll had been told about the bicycle cable around Gertrude's neck when she had not.

Brockman wanted to know how she found out.

"John Carroll told me at the house. He didn't know you hadn't told me."

"Carroll is a lawyer and an officer of the court. I had no legal reason to withhold the information from him.

"Joe, I am livid and I'm telling you so. What else haven't you told me?"

Brockman finally came forth with the truth. "The cable was locked around her neck to ensure that your aunt would die," he said. "The cable looked very old, encased in plastic. Have you ever seen anything like that in your aunt's house before?"

"No," said Jane. "What use would a thing like that be to Aunt Gert? She never owned a bicycle that I know of. The killer must have brought it with him. Why would he do that?"

Brockman had no answers.

After hanging up the phone, Jane was alone with her rage. This new piece of information did nothing to help solve the puzzle. If anything, it merely made the crime more heinous. In her mind Jane pictured the old lady on the floor, struggling to remove the chain from her neck, gasping for air as the lock held it tightly in place and the killer stood over her watching as she suffocated.

When Tom got home, Jane recounted the day's events, and he became more upset than ever. "You're becoming a pest with the police," he said, "and you really ought to cool it. If they have any information, they will call you. Give them some space."

Jane was taken aback. There had scarcely been a harsh word between Tom and her since he moved in with her in 1980. The plodding nature of the investigation was taking its toll not only on her state of mind, but on their relationship.

"Tom, I'm so sorry. I can't sleep, I can't function, I can't think of anything but getting this animal for what he did to Aunt Gert. This animal may have destroyed her life, but he's not going to destroy mine.'

Tom tried to break her out of her depression, but the once simple pleasures of life they had enjoyed for years—jogging on the fire road with Duke, entertaining friends, attending the weekly 49ers parties—failed to offer any reprieve.

She had reached the most horrible state a murder victim's loved ones can reach, the place where the horror continues to grow and hope fades by the hour. A place of ignorance and desperation, a place where it is impossible to find any glint of light. Something had to happen or Jane was going to go crazy.

Chapter Seven

The official line is that no homicide case is closed until it is solved. In reality, there is a point of investigative exhaustion when detectives find their time better spent on fresh cases with viable leads.

In January, 1984, San Jose investigators were already at a dead end in the Gertrude McCabe investigation. They did not have a single suspect or even a piece of physical evidence that would link a suspect to the crime. There were no witnesses, no fingerprints, hair, or fiber samples. The McCabe murder case had already slid into the unofficial "cold file."

Then step one of what Jane would eventually call "the miracle" occurred. It would be a lengthy and circuitous process, fraught with heartbreak and setback, but it was finally set in motion. A new investigator came along to help crack the case.

Sergeant John Kracht had been a police officer for nineteen years when he started as a homicide detective. He had investigated fraud for many years and had built an unequaled reputation for diligence, hard work, and uncanny insight. His tenacity was the stuff of legend, and tales of his exploits preceded his arrival in the homicide bureau.

Everyone on the force knew the story of his dogged pursuit of a vicious motorcycle gang. So incensed were the gang members by Kracht's relentless efforts to put them all behind bars that they planted a bomb under his car in the driveway of his home. He miraculously escaped injury when it exploded. It never even slowed him down; in fact, it made him more determined.

Kracht didn't look intimidating. A balding, thickset man of moderate height, he had a rumpled look about him. He was nondescript to the point that his colleagues swore he could sit in an automobile on stakeout and become almost invisible.

He was also legendary for his skills as an interrogator. This was puzzling both to friends outside the department and to many within. How can a man be a brilliant interrogator if he hardly ever talks? In San Jose, he was known as the quietest man on the force.

His first day in homicide was no exception.

"Sergeant Kracht, how about taking a crack at the Gertrude McCabe file?" said Sergeant Brockman.

Joe Brockman had already passed the lieutenant's examination and within weeks would be promoted out of homicide. Until then, Kracht would be his partner and learn the ropes. Brockman handed Kracht the stack of fifty-two police reports filed on the McCabe case since the day her body was discovered. "Read these through and let me know what you think," he said. "See if it reads like a whole lot of nothing." Kracht just nodded.

No matter what skills or reputation a detective brings to homicide, he is rarely given a fresh case to work. This is true for several reasons. By studying preexisting files, the neophyte gets a chance to learn how the department works, how evidence is collected and reported, and what investigative tools are available. A fresh homicide might be easier to solve, but a cold case is a better learning experience and presents fewer risks to the department. An inexperienced investigator can do scant harm to a case that stands little chance of being solved.

Kracht spent several days reviewing the evidence. His first job was to make sure every available lead had been thoroughly covered. To that end, he reviewed the interviews with Virgil and Sheryl Jackson, making sure that all pertinent questions had been asked and that there was no wiggle room in their stories.

Jackson wasn't the only potential suspect who had been investigated. Another one who caught Kracht's eye was the drifter Michael John Sperling. Kracht read with interest the conflicting reports that Sperling had canvassed the neighborhood for gardening work, had been selling candy, or wore a heavy overcoat in sunny San Jose. The files identified Sperling as a recent parolee whose last offense was being caught with burglary tools in a suburban neighborhood similar to that of Gertrude McCabe's.

On December 26, 1983, Frechette and Brockman had put out a watch bulletin on a 1966 Cadillac belonging to Sperling. The car was stopped in San Jose on January 6, and the suspect was booked for delinquent traffic fines. The car was searched, but nothing was found except a few dozen brochures for the Servamatic Solar Company, which marketed window-replacement units via door-to-door solicitation.

Sperling consented to being questioned at the police headquarters. While there, the reports said, Sergeant Bud Harrington borrowed a key ring in Sperling's possession and compared two keys with the bicycle lock found around Gertrude McCabe's neck. They didn't fit. Sperling never knew he was under suspicion for anything more than running too many red lights.

Now Kracht had his own questions for Sperling. He contacted the dean of students at San Jose Bible College, where Sperling had listed his residence. Although he had been enrolled in "Basic Faith" on Tuesdays and Thursdays and "Life of Christ" every morning, Sperling had only attended those classes for a week.

Another bulletin was put out for his car, and he was stopped again on January 20.

This time, Sergeants Brockman and Kracht met Sperling at the vehicle itself, where they took a more direct approach. They asked if he would sign a consent form to have both his vehicle and his bible college room searched for evidence relating to the McCabe murder.

Sperling quickly consented. "I haven't killed anyone," he said.

The search revealed nothing, so Brockman and Kracht went to work on Sperling himself. From the start the suspect seemed almost relieved to answer questions about McCabe's murder. It was scarcely the attitude one finds in a guilty man. Kracht surmised he might have been happy that, once he answered questions, he would not be in violation of his parole.

Throughout the interview Sperling readily offered detailed answers to the questions. He provided an alibi for the time of the murder and gave references of family and friends. His employer even vouched for his work record. Though he had a criminal record, nothing indicated any propensity for violence.

Throughout, Kracht did little talking but let Brockman ask the questions. After a few hours, Kracht was convinced that Sperling had nothing to do with the murder of Gertrude McCabe.

After just a few weeks in homicide, John Kracht was at a dead end in a case that was leading the department in dead ends. It did not faze him in the least.

◆ ◆ ◆

Apart from almost nightly insomnia, which Jane had never suffered before, life started to resume a familiar pace by February 1984. Tom and Jane haltingly resumed their cycle of social engagements in Sleepy Hollow. Tom did give up playing the commodities, an activity that had kept him occupied for hours each day, scrutinizing the ever-changing market. He said it had become volatile. The home "tick" machine he had rented the year before was returned to the leasing agency.

Since moving to Sleepy Hollow in 1980, Tom had dreamed of starting a lucrative home business. He had tried a number of ventures without success. One day, a promotional package from Yurika Foods came in the mail. Yurika Foods products, meals in small packages requiring no refrigeration and with a five-year shelf life, were designed for anyone who did not like to cook, particularly sportsmen and people with boats. Yurika Foods was a multi-level marketing concept similar to Amway and Tupperware. Individuals promoted and sold the products through their homes, and one couple Jane and Tom met claimed they were earning more than thirty thousand dollars a month.

Tom saw this as an excellent opportunity. The company was young enough that he and Jane could be high on the distributor's ladder. He spoke of enlisting a number of his European and South American contacts as distributors since those markets had yet to be tapped.

Jane and Tom threw themselves into the new enterprise. Within weeks they were hosting Yurika Foods parties for friends in Sleepy Hollow and traveling throughout the San Francisco Bay Area giving presentations. Jane would spend hours making Yurika Foods bread, muffins, gelatin, and spaghetti while Tom gave his sales pitch in the living room. They soon made new friends, including Vaux and Bob Toneff, the latter a former lineman for the San Francisco 49ers.

In early March, Tom suggested they take another trip together, this time to the Seattle area. It would be a "working vacation." Three of Jane's six children lived in and around Seattle, as did Tom's brother, whom Tom had not seen in seven years. They hoped their family and friends might sign on to the Yurika Foods program. On March 12, just before they left, Jane received her first call from Sergeant John Kracht in San Jose.

He was soft-spoken and polite. "I've been assigned the McCabe case and would like to drive up to San Anselmo to meet you," he said.

"We're leaving for a trip to the Pacific Northwest, but if it's very important we could cancel it," Jane replied.

"Oh, no, I just have a lot of routine questions. When will you be back?"

Jane told him. Kracht suggested that when she arrived in Seattle, she call him collect.

Jane was at the home of Tom's brother when she called the detective back. Kracht wanted to know the names and ages of Jane's six children, where they lived and what they did, and a bit of the McCabe family history.

He asked about Aunt Gert and her trust. He also inquired into the death of Jane's husband, Al Alexander, and about Tom and his profession. Jane told of Tom's Swiss trust, which was close to maturity. She thought Kracht sounded very nice and concerned, and she thanked him for taking an interest in the case. The conversation had already lasted an hour and twenty minutes when she asked, "Do you have any new leads?"

"Not much," he said, "but I look forward to meeting you when you come back to California."

Tom, sitting beside her, had overheard Jane's portion of the conversation.

"What did the detective ask?" he inquired.

"Well, you heard what I told him. Can't you guess what he wanted to know?"

It was the first time he had shown any interest in a detective's inquiries. Normally, talk of Gert's murder put him off.

The disposition of the McCabe estate was very much on Kracht's mind. On March 12, 1984, he met with Irma Clark's attorney, John Carroll. Kracht wanted to know how much money was in the estate and how it was being disbursed among Gertrude's relatives.

"Given that you are an officer of the court," said Mr. Carroll, "I don't see that I *shouldn't* be sharing this information, but there are things that Miss Clark isn't too happy to talk about regarding the McCabe family tree."

"How is that?" Kracht was intrigued.

"You know that the McCabes are a fine, upstanding family. But I understand that Jay McCabe—that would be Gertrude McCabe's late brother, the man they named the San Jose auditorium for—fathered a child out of wedlock. An illegitimate daughter. Not that 'illegitimate' is an appropriate term under the law today, but those were different times. This was a potential scandal."

"Do you think that is important to this case?"

"Well, my client, Miss Clark, certainly thinks so," said Carroll. "Gertrude McCabe's money came from a trust left by her brother, Jay. If the murder of Miss McCabe arose out of some sort of vengeance or blackmail, it might be profitable to identify the child and her descendants."

Carroll felt he had to speak to Irma Clark before he could divulge more information. Kracht thanked him, though he thought this an unlikely lead. What sort of murder would be committed to avenge the injustice of fathering and abandoning an illegitimate child, particularly since the man responsible had died sixteen years before? Irma Clark's suspicions seemed based on some archaic bias.

True to his promise, however, John Carroll sent John Kracht a full account of the McCabe family tree, including gossip dating back more than half a century. Jay McCabe had fathered an illegitimate child with an "actress type," and he had secretly provided for her throughout his life.

Carroll wrote out his theory in a long letter to Kracht the day after the detective's visit:

> If we suppose that someone contacted Gertrude McCabe and wanted some money; and perhaps said that Jay McCabe was related by blood, and this person felt that some relative was entitled to some assets and property (we would be speculating entirely, of course, while thinking along this line); if some unknown person contacted Gert a few months before her death wanting money, perhaps Gert would have said, truthfully enough, that Jay's money went to the Bank of America in trust ...

> I have heard speculation on more than one occasion that this homicide may have been committed by a person who was angry—possibly out of vengeance. Did the murderer come to Gert's home in the summer of 1983 and try to get money from her? Then did she turn to the bank trustee in an attempt to find out if there was any money available legally for an heir of Jay? When the bank told Gert "no," did she then, on the date of this incident, tell that negative answer to this unknown person?

It continued:

> I am sure that you have Jane Alexander's address and telephone number in San Anselmo, California. I don't know

39

much about her, but understand that she was married and she and her husband had six children. I do not know what happened to her marriage. Death of husband? Divorce? My understanding is that she lives in a very nice home "on top of a hill" and lives with a man whose name is Tom O'Donnell. Jane was concerned years ago about McCabe's estate. How did Jane Alexander get her money, and where? It was indicated to me that Tom O'Donnell may have something to do with "investments," including gold, and that he has spent some time in Africa. When my "personal property expert," Ms. Pat Madden, of Canterbury Auction Sales, talked to him about some gold artifacts, he had ready access to a device that weighed the gold, and he seems to know the value of it from day to day.

Jane Alexander is one of the beneficiaries of the Gert McCabe will. Jane Alexander might be extremely upset and disturbed if she knew that this information and these speculations were being put down in this letter and provided to you. Of course all of these sentences of mine may add up to zero. On the other hand, I am sure you know that Jane Alexander and Irma Clark have been wanting to bring at least some amount of pressure to bear on the San Jose Police Department to the end that (1) you continue to work on this case and solve it and (2) the San Jose P.D. not forget about this case. It certainly would be unfair to the San Jose P.D. if we were to pressure you to work on the case and yet not provide to you information which could conceivably lead to a murderer with a motive of trying to reach some of the assets and property of the McCabe family.

Although John Kracht would spend several months researching the McCabe family tree and would eventually discover that all of the speculation about the granddaughter was false, the letter from John Carroll did serve to correct one misunderstanding. Until then Tom O'Donnell had appeared in several of the initial San Jose police reports under a different name: Tom Alexander. Police had assumed he was Jane's husband; no one had bothered to ask if they were married.

Yet this detail did not help much. After reviewing the McCabe files, he knew that a fresh approach to the case was needed. He decided to get help from the FBI.

The science of behavioral profiling was not new in the early 1980s, but the use of the FBI's Behavioral Science Unit by local police investigators was. John Kracht had attended a seminar on the subject earlier that year, just after switching into the homicide division. One of the things that had stumped the prior investigators was the motive. If the FBI could give him a psychological profile of the killer, Kracht reasoned, it might help him establish a motive.

He methodically gathered a portfolio on the McCabe case to be sent to Quantico, Virginia, for evaluation. The FBI required a number of items. Among them were extensive photographs of the crime scene, as well as aerial photographs showing the various possible escape routes for a murder suspect. Kracht had already commissioned these photos on March 7, 1984. A thorough description of the victim and her habits was necessary. The dossier sent to the FBI included meticulous accounts of how Gertrude McCabe answered ads in the newspaper, hired door-to-door service providers, and kept large amounts of cash on hand.

There was also a chance that the peculiar *modus operandi* of the crime—the garroting with the bicycle lock, the Kleenex in the mouth—might trigger a response in the FBI computer. If this was a serial killer, the crime might match another somewhere else in the country.

By the time Kracht sent off the material to the FBI on March 28, 1984, he had investigated everyone from homeless derelicts to juvenile cookie salesmen. He had examined the records of several hundred known assailants in the San Jose area, none of whom provided a match to Gert's address book. No suspect had been linked to this quiet suburban street, or to this particular senior citizen, or to these particular circumstances. Quite simply, Kracht was nowhere.

Chapter Eight

Shortly after their return from Seattle, Sergeant Kracht called Jane again to make arrangements for a meeting in Sleepy Hollow. He asked to see Jane's records on Gert's financial affairs. A lunch date was set for April 16, 1984. Sergeants John Kracht and Steve Ronco made the seventy-mile trip from San Jose.

By chance Tom's attorney, Victor Sessell, was visiting from South Africa and had been a houseguest for several days. Sessell had advised Tom O'Donnell years before on a business affair in South Africa, and the two had remained close friends. At lunch Tom turned the group's chatter to tales of diamond and currency smuggling. Throughout the 1970s, as the apartheid regime of South Africa maintained its grip on power, strict currency export controls had been established to staunch the flight of capital out of the country. Many wealthy families circumvented the controls, though, and moved large sums out in order to establish a nest egg in Europe in case the apartheid regime collapsed.

A number of ingenious schemes were set up to transfer wealth into Swiss bank accounts. Tom bragged about having grown wealthy from his involvement in I.D.B., or "illegal diamond buying." In this scheme, a wealthy South African family purchased unregistered diamonds that had been mined illegally, had them smuggled abroad, then traded them for cash in Antwerp or some other international exchange. The money was then deposited in secret Swiss accounts. Wealthy South Africans often employed couriers to do work on their behalf, because the practice was highly dangerous. For his effort in transporting and selling the stones, then setting up the accounts on behalf of wealthy families, Tom O'Donnell received a commission after each visit.

While Tom regaled all with his animated tales, Kracht sat impassively, studying him as he spoke.

After lunch was finished, everyone sat down for the interview in the living room. Sergeant Kracht posed his first question. He was not one to waste words.

"Mrs. Alexander, what is your income?"

The question caught her by surprise. She glanced at Tom, who handled the financial matters. "I get sixty-seven dollars a month from my late husband's pension," said Jane. "Since his death I've also been collecting Social Security and that adds another two hundred seventy-five dollars."

Jane didn't see the relevance of the question. "Tom handles the finances," she said. "Perhaps you should ask him."

"As I explained, I'm retired from my previous business in Africa," Tom said. "My own assets are in Europe, in a trust that will mature later this year. We're going in the fall, and plan to spend a month in Ireland along the way," he said.

Kracht did not respond to this information, but instead turned his attention to the McCabe estate and Gert's finances.

"Did Gert ever give you any money?"

Jane said her aunt had been very generous with her, just as she had been with everyone else in her family. She had always been willing to share her modest wealth. When Jay McCabe died in 1971, Gert inherited all of his estate save for fifty thousand dollars that went to his brother. She promptly had given Jane a check for ten thousand dollars. She had also given Jane's husband, Al, and each of their six children a check for one thousand dollars.

"I borrowed twenty thousand dollars from her in 1982," said Jane, "which I was unable to repay before her death. I doubt she would ever have asked for it to be returned."

Again, Kracht did not show any reaction.

"Did she talk about her plans, what she wanted to do as she grew older?"

"Gert was thinking about selling her house and perhaps moving into a retirement home. Of course, that wasn't just around the corner, but I think she did mention it the last time we saw her. When was that, Tom? End of August?"

"August, yes, yes it was," said Tom. He was never good at remembering dates. He often used Jane's diary to help keep track of such things. Jane recorded even mundane daily details of her life in her diary.

Kracht asked about the McCabe family history. Jane had no idea Kracht had heard the story already, and she spoke of Jay McCabe's illegitimate daughter. The details corresponded exactly with what the detective had heard from John Carroll. Jane admitted that she had wanted to dispute the fifty thousand dollar paternity payment in his will, then dropped the claim when she realized the girl was the descendant of Jay McCabe.

"Aunt Gert never knew any of this, of course. But to tell the truth, she wasn't very please about Jay McCabe's will in the first place." Although Gert's inheritance was a trust worth about two hundred fifty or three hundred thousand dollars, she received only the interest and dividends and could not touch the principal. It was still more than enough money for her to live comfortably the rest of her life. Upon her death, the principal from the trust would go to several Catholic charities and the City of Hope.

Jane explained how Gert believed members of the Catholic diocese had coerced Jay into signing over the principal from his estate during a period when his mind had become enfeebled by age and Alzheimer's disease.

"Gert thought about disputing the will herself, and years ago she asked me if I would do if for her after she died. I said I might do it, but Jay McCabe made another mistake by putting the estate with the Bank of America. The money was converted into bank shares, and these fell to half their value with some bank reorganization just a few years later. So the Catholic Church will get what was left of Jay's estate."

"And what will you get, Mrs. Alexander?"

"Gert had other assets. I suppose, after the house is sold, something close to one hundred thousand dollars. I haven't given it much thought."

"The same as cousin Irma?"

"Yes."

"Would cousin Irma dispute the remainder, the portion that is supposed to go the Catholic charities?"

"I doubt it. I don't know what cousin Irma wants to do. We're not taking anymore."

Kracht took notes and listened intently. He had begun to entertain the idea that Gertrude might have been killed by someone who would benefit financially from her death. But he was puzzled. What use would killing Aunt Gert be to anyone if the bulk of her estate was set to go to charity? Moreover, Jane Alexander did not seem particularly interested in Gertrude's money, and neither did Irma Clark. Judging by Jane's' house in Sleepy Hollow, their comfortable lifestyle, and Tom's soon-to-be-realized trust, it seemed that none of Aunt Gert's heirs had any immediate reason to be concerned about money.

For her part, Jane Alexander liked Sergeants Kracht and Ronco, and she was pleased they were still working on the case six months after the murder. "Anything I can do to help, please let me know," she told them as they left.

"I will be calling you," Kracht replied.

Jane and Tom continued working on Yurika through the month of May. Their second check from the company came that month; it was a paltry $200.16.

Jane wanted to quit, but Tom was determined to press on. The couple attended rallies in Pasadena and Los Angeles, and continued their recruitment parties.

Jane was looking forward to having a break in the fall, when she and Tom would finally travel abroad together. The trust itself was located in Switzerland, but this would be a trip mixing business and pleasure. The two planned to travel across Europe by car. They would also spend a month in Ireland roaming and exploring their respective ancestries. She would be far removed from the obligations of the Yurika business and the unresolved questions surrounding Aunt Gert's murder.

Jane and Tom took a trip to Los Angeles in May 1984 and paid a visit to Tom's friend, Harry Carmichael. Upon their return, Jane received another phone call from Sergeant John Kracht.

"Do you think you could come to the lab in San Jose and take a look at some lipstick on a Kleenex? It was found at your aunt's house."

Jane thought back to that fatal Sunday, when she and Tom had stayed in Gert's house. Police had asked her then to look out for any stray tissues. She was not sure how lipstick could help identify the killer.

"Of course, I'll come tomorrow if you like."

On May 15, Tom and Jane left Sleepy Hollow for the San Jose Police Department crime laboratory. They were met by Sergeants Kracht and Ronco, who gave the couple a brief tour of the facility. The lab had been newly renovated at considerable taxpayer expense and offered state-of-the-art testing and storage facilities.

What Jane didn't know at the time—and Kracht would become aware of only years later—was that the facility had come a few months too late to be of help in the Gertrude McCabe case. Blood samples from Aunt Gert's body and from the pillows washed out by the killer in the bathroom had been stored in an overcrowded temporary refrigerator that contained samples from dozens of other cases. In December 1983, the McCabe samples had been removed from the fridge to make room for newer items. Left at room temperature for several days, they had deteriorated badly and had been contaminated with bacteria. When they would be tested years later against blood from a prime suspect, they would offer inconclusive results.

But it was lipstick that was Kracht's concern that day. A lab technician retrieved the lipstick-stained tissue, which also had dark-brown bloodstains on it. He spread it before Jane and Tom on an evidence tray.

"That's not Gert's, absolutely no way," said Jane. "Actually, it looks like mine."

Jane reached into her purse and retrieved her own fuchsia-colored lipstick. She took a piece of paper and made a sizable smear. "See?" she said to Kracht. "That's much closer." He took the sample and planned to have it tested later.

Kracht studied Jane's face, wondering how she would react to the revelation that her lipstick seemed a perfect match to the lipstick on the tissue that had been stuffed down Gertrude McCabe's throat in an amateurish attempt to silence her while she was being murdered. Jane's face revealed nothing.

"John, while we're here, I'd like to take a look at the bicycle cable."

"No problem with that," he said.

A lab technician went to retrieve the evidence. When it was unwrapped, however, Jane felt a shock. A large clump of Aunt Gert's hair remained entangled in the lock and cable. It had been pulled out of her scalp by the killer as the cable was twisted around her neck.

The sight of it immediately sickened Jane. "I can't stand this," she said. Rage welled up in her.

"I'm very sorry," said Kracht, genuinely embarrassed. "I forgot about this. I shouldn't have shown it to you."

The visit ended abruptly. Jane cried for most of the two-hour journey back to Sleepy Hollow.

"Jane, the chances of catching this person are really very slim," Tom said. "I am really very worried about your health through this. You have to *let go*."

"Tom, I have a lot of confidence in Sergeant Kracht. I think he's a different kind of cop," she said.

Silently, however, she made a vow to try not to talk to Tom about Aunt Gert anymore. Her obsession with the subject was wearing him down. If her silence could buy peace of mind in their relationship, so be it. She would carry her anger inside her. She would keep her continued efforts to herself as best she could.

She was not sure what the day had meant, what the lipstick on the Kleenex had meant. But she was right when she told Tom that Kracht was a different kind of cop.

He would not reveal the emerging theory just yet, but he had gotten his first clue in his first homicide, and there would be no stopping him. The wheels were turning, and a real suspect would soon appear in his sights.

Chapter Nine

Jane received a letter from John Carroll on June 12, 1984, regarding the McCabe estate. "I wanted to let you know that your second cousin, Irma Clark, has accepted an all-cash bid on the house in San Jose for one hundred thirty thousand dollars. The disbursement of the estate should occur within three months."

Jane was shocked at the low offer, which was at least eighty thousand dollars less than what many said the house was worth. Irma couldn't seem to do anything right, she thought; now she was giving Gert's house away. Irma had ignored Jane's repeated requests to heat the house through the winter, and there was still substantial damage in the living room from months of heavy rain and humidity. No wonder the house had attracted little interest. On the other hand, the murder had not helped sale prospects. California law requires that potential buyers be informed of violent crimes committed on the premises before a sale is made. Jane resigned herself to the fact she could do nothing. At least this chapter would now be closed.

As the summer progressed, the Yurika Foods presentations began to slow down. Jane and Tom spent more and more time working in the yard at Sleepy Hollow. Tom cleared weeds while Jane was absorbed in her vegetable garden.

It was like so many other summers. In the cool downstairs kitchen, Jane would make quarts and quarts of soup, which she would freeze for the winter months. Some of her routine was returning to normal, but Jane thought it strange that she could not read a book anymore. She used to devour a book per week. Somehow, her concentration had diminished to the point that she could not concentrate for more than ten minutes. It frightened her how much Aunt Gert's death had affected her emotional well-being. She prayed that the terrible anxiety and the continuous feeling of impending doom would fade. More than anything, she prayed for a break in Gertrude's case.

Chapter Nine

On June 18, the FBI Behavioral Science Unit delivered their psychological profile of Gertrude's killer. The report, written by Special Agent Ron Walker, did not seem at first glance to promise much, since it was little more than three pages long. There were many disclaimers, including a statement that the information was based only on probabilities and that the actual murderer might not fit all the descriptions contained within. Nevertheless, Sergeants Kracht and Ronco read the pages with rapt attention. By the end, it seemed almost as if a psychic had taken hold of the case and handed them the name of the murderer.

Walker began his report with a review of Gertrude McCabe's social station and her particular vulnerabilities. He noted that she was a low risk for violent crime, despite the fact that her neighborhood was near some economically depressed areas. Statistically, her use of unknown workmen raised that risk only slightly. It was her economic position and the possibility that she might provide an inheritance to someone which offered the most likely potential motive.

How did Walker surmise this? The crime scene and the mode of killing told him. Because Gert's injuries were so varied and, for the most part, non-lethal, they pointed to an inexperienced killer. "There is an almost total *absence* of violent trauma that is generally associated with homicide in which the types of assault are as varied as those on this victim," said the report. "This absence of violence correlates to an absence of anger and rage/hostility on the offender's part and tends to indicate that the offender's motive was other than emotionally based. The overall impression of the trauma to the victim is one of a *deliberate* and *methodical* attempt by the assailant to ensure the victim's death."

Further signs of planning could be inferred from the fact that the murderer brought weapons, including a striking instrument, a cable lock, and a bladed weapon. The cable lock was left to ensure the victim's death, thus confirming that the murderer intended his result. The other weapons were removed from the scene, showing rationality and planning on the part of the murderer. The effort to "stage" a robbery was a clear attempt to mislead the subsequent investigation.

This was probably the first time the perpetrator had ever murdered, since the assailant underestimated the effort it takes to kill someone with a blow to the head. But the report emphasized that the sex of the assailant could not be determined. "Of particular interest is the ineffectual stabbing attack targeted at non-vital areas of the victim's body. It is noted that this type of targeting is frequently seen in cases where the assailant is female. It also is indicative of a lack of criminal sophistication on the part of the offender." Furthermore, the report stated, given the age and size of the victim, a female assailant was capable of subduing her. The report also mentioned the facial tissue with the floral pattern, which was more likely to be carried by a female than a male. The existence of lipstick on the tissue further supported the notion of a female killer.

The blood-soaked pillows, which the murderer had removed from the couch next to the victim, were probably used both to smother the cries of the victim and to hide her face from the assailant. This was yet another clue that the murderer knew his victim. The killer used the pillows not to hide his or her own identity, but to be shielded from the anguish of watching Gertrude die.

Despite the initial conjectures the San Jose Police Department had made about possible torture, they had gotten the story backward. Her death was slow and painful because the murderer had trouble stomaching the act.

That the assailant cleaned the pillows and the bathroom of incriminating evidence, and possibly washed him or herself, indicated that the assailant had to travel some distance after leaving the scene, very probably by car. The killer did not want to carry any evidence with him in case he was stopped for an unrelated reason.

Ron Walter could identify no particular type of killer. Nothing indicated that a particular personality committed the crime. But he could draw a few conclusions:

The assailant was educated, and likely to be at least a high school graduate.

The victim was known to the assailant.

The assailant did not reside in the immediate area but traveled to and from the scene by motor vehicle.

The perpetrator was inexperienced or unsophisticated in crime, particularly in the commission of violent crime.

The motive was not emotional but monetary.

The age, sex, and relationship to the victim could not be determined. "A female offender should *not* be ruled out, nor should closely or distantly-related relatives be discounted."

No remorse or guilt from the act would be shown by the assailant.

The perpetrator was quite possibly interviewed by police during the course of routine investigation. "If so, the assailant would have appeared calm, relaxed (perhaps *too* relaxed), and willing to cooperate with police."

"The assailant may interject him/herself into the investigation under the guise of providing additional information or to check on the progress of the investigation."

The report confirmed Kracht's hunch about the murder. After meeting Tom and Jane but once, Kracht had a sense that they were key to solving the case. The FBI profile pointed to the real possibility that the killer was one of Gertrude McCabe's intimates. But the profile also opened up new possibilities. Could a woman have committed the crime?

"This criminal profile contains information of a confidential and sensitive nature," the report concluded, "and should not be disseminated except to those with a legitimate investigative or prosecutorial interest in this matter." Kracht took the notion very seriously. If Jane Alexander and/or Tom O'Donnell, or anyone close to them, was involved in Gertrude's murder, Kracht would be well served not to let them know of his suspicions or the FBI profile.

From that point on, Kracht's ears and eyes would be open for any chink in Jane Alexander's or Tom O'Donnell's armor. One slip might well crack the McCabe case wide open. He was prepared to catch one or both of them.

"Hello, Jane. Do you think you and Tom could come down to San Jose?"

Jane told Kracht she was pleased to hear from him. She might have felt differently if she had been aware of his suspicions and the FBI profile. It was Monday, July 9, 1984.

"Why, sure, John. Do you have good news?"

"Well, we've been going over our evidence from the crime scene, and we've found several sets of prints that we haven't identified. We now realize we never took your fingerprints for elimination purposes. We don't have Tom's, either. Would it be too much trouble to visit our lab again?"

Although Jane readily agreed to the request, she didn't hide her annoyance. More than eight months had passed since the murder. How could they have waited so long to take *fingerprints*?

"John, this sounds like sloppy police work. How could you get this far in the investigation and ask for something so basic? That's beyond me."

Kracht had no answer for her. He knew, of course, that fingerprints would provide little help in solving the murder of Aunt Gert. No prints had been found in the bathroom or on any of the important evidence. Even if one of the nine partial prints found in the house corresponded to Jane or Tom, they could have been made on any one of their many visits to Arroyo Way. Their fingerprints were actually useless.

Kracht's real motive was to expose Jane and Tom to the increasing heat of the investigation and study their reaction. This was the beginning of a cat-and-mouse game. The fingerprinting was an excuse to bring them back to San Jose, where he could apply some pressure.

"We can come down Friday," said Jane, after conferring with Tom. "We would like to take you and your partner out to lunch afterward. Would that be all right?"

"Very nice," Kracht replied.

On Friday the thirteenth, Jane and Tom drove from Marin County and arrived before noon.

"I'm sorry you had to make another trip to San Jose," Kracht said when he greeted them. "I hope you understand how important this is to the investigation."

"Anything to get to the bottom of this," said Jane.

Jane, who had not been fingerprinted since her service in World War II, was surprised to find out just how messy the procedure was. The lab technician wanted prints of all ten fingers and both palms.

"I suppose you'll be asking me for a nose print," she joked. When finished, she was covered to her wrists with black goo. She marveled at how difficult it was to wash off.

What Jane didn't know, however, was that she had been carefully observed throughout the procedure. She had shown no signs of nervousness or hesitation. When Tom O'Donnell gave his palm print, however, he protested that he was unable to spread his hand flat, due, he said, to his consistent use of a weed whacker. The technician quickly grabbed his hand and slapped it on the paper. A careful note was made of this behavior and passed on to Kracht.

"Did you see our new fingerprint computer the last time you were here?" asked Kracht. "It can identify prints with just a few ridges, and can make sense of partials in a way that's never been possible before."

Again the reactions of Jane and Tom were noted. Jane was impressed with the new machine and said so. If Tom had any reaction, he didn't show it.

For lunch, Tom O'Donnell took the two detectives to the dining room of the Hotel St. Claire, one of the city's most venerable institutions. The Hotel St. Claire had a McCabe family connection. For many years Jay McCabe had made Suite 317—in honor of Saint Patrick's Day—his official residence.

During the meal Jane again asked if there were any new developments in the case. This time Kracht was more forthcoming.

"We've received a very interesting personality profile of the murderer," he said. Jane was intrigued as Kracht explained about the FBI's Behavioral Science Unit and how their services had recently been offered to local police departments across the country. "The FBI says the suspect drove from out of town, cleaned up the crime scene to protect his identity, and was known to your aunt," said Kracht.

The detective once again scrutinized Tom's and Jane's reactions. He was convinced his quarry sat before him and that it was only a matter of time before someone made a misstep.

"Someone who knew my aunt?" asked Jane. "I can't imagine who that would be."

"There's a good chance it won't be long now before we catch the killer, maybe three months," said Kracht.

"Three months?" Jane could hardly contain herself. "May I read the profile?"

"I'm afraid you can't. It's confidential."

"Come on, John, give me a break."

Kracht smiled. It was something he occasionally did so he would not have to divulge more details.

Despite Kracht's refusal, Jane left the meeting in buoyant spirits. As they drove north toward Marin County, Jane couldn't stop talking about this latest revelation.

"We're going to have a wonderful trip to Ireland this fall, because that murdering pig will be in jail," she said. "Don't you think, Tom?"

"Wonderful," he said.

Chapter Ten

Through the last two weeks of July, 1984, Tom was occupied with their finances. It was not a pretty picture, Jane found out.

Already that month there had been a problem. The principal on a two hundred thousand dollar second mortgage was due in full to the Woodson Mortgage Company on August 24. This was a major inconvenience, Tom told her, since he could not draw on his 1.2 million-dollar Swiss trust until it matured in October. When she took the loan, she had relied again on Tom's trust fund if there was a problem. So Tom had been working hard to roll over the two hundred thousand dollar mortgage for another year. In early July he had told a much relieved Jane that he had succeeded.

Although the long-term financial picture looked rosy, and the arrival of Aunt Gert's estate promised additional monies, there would be a cash squeeze in the next few months. Tom needed money not only to cover the monthly two thousand seven hundred second-mortgage payment, but also for day-to-day household expenses. He also needed to pay for the plane tickets to Europe.

A lucky break came on July 23, Jane's birthday, when they returned from lunch and found a new credit card in the mail. Since the mortgage payment was due the next day, both Jane and Tom took this as a sign things would be working out. Tom took the card and drew the full three thousand dollar advance.

In the first week of August, Tom established a ten thousand dollar line of credit at West America Bank for Jane. Aunt Gert's estate was named as collateral for this debt. Tom was pleased that Jane's credit report omitted mention of the two hundred thousand dollar Woodson loan. Her record showed only that she owed a total of forty-two thousand dollars for the original mortgage on her four hundred fifty thousand dollar house. All other bills were currently paid. As a result she appeared to be a good credit risk.

That week Tom visited a dentist and a doctor, who examined him for a lingering pain in his foot. "No point putting up with this in Europe," he told Jane. "I don't want anything holding us back."

At 8:30 AM on August 6, 1984, John Kracht called. He wanted a copy of Jane's telephone bills covering October 23, 1983, as well as that month's telephone bill from the Martell's house, where Jane had been contacted with the news of Gert's murder.

Jane then went with Tom to the bank and signed the loan papers for the ten thousand dollar line of credit. A teller disbursed five thousand dollars in cash to Jane in one hundred dollar bills. The teller also supplied a cashier's check in the amount of five thousand dollars. This Jane signed over to Tom in the car, to be deposited into their household account later that morning at Marin Savings and Loan. She also gave him the fifty one hudred dollar bills.

Tom needed the cash to pay for the European plane tickets later that morning. He and Jane parted company for a few hours while Tom attended to the bank and travel agency business. They met again for lunch at Joe's, a traditional steak-and-seafood restaurant on fashionable Fourth Street in downtown San Rafael, Marin County's largest town.

The temperature that day had climbed close to one hundred degrees. Accordingly, Jane ordered a shrimp cocktail. Tom, on the other hand, had a liver-and-onion dinner with vegetables and french fries. Jane was surprised that Tom ordered such a heavy meal, given the heat. The two drank wine and chatted excitedly about their trip to Europe.

Tom paid the check with the American Express card that Jane still kept in her late husband's name. It was the only credit card in the household that did not allow a cash advance, so they used it solely for meals and occasional expenses.

The heavy lunch was not the only unusual thing. Tom had been planning their trip, handling Jane's financial situation, and pursuing his Yurika marketing business. He was constantly writing on a yellow legal pad. Jane had seen him scribbling away several times and asked what he was working on.

"A Yurika marketing proposal," said Tom. He planned to send it to his son in Montana.

"Tom, your handwriting is so terrible," said Jane. "I could type it for you if you like."

"No, it's not worth the trouble. I just need to work out my thoughts," he said. Jane did not press the issue or ask for details.

Also peculiar was his heightened concern about the dog. One evening he made a show of feeding Duke, explaining to Jane the elaborate recipe he followed. He picked up a large aluminum pan, opened a can of dog food, poured out four cups of meal, and added two cups of water.

"Look, this is the way Dukey likes his dinner, nice and wet. See how I fixed it?" Tom said, smiling.

Another odd note had been struck the night before. A light burned out in the laundry room, and Jane mentioned it while the two were having a drink. "Sometime when you have a minute, could you put in a new light bulb?"

Tom got up, found a ladder, and began changing the bulb right away.

"You don't have to do it now, Tom."

"I'll do it while I'm thinking about it. See? All set."

"Tom, you're crazy," she replied.

Hugh Fine, still pursuing his dream of becoming a chiropractor and staying with Tom and Jane while studying for exams, returned home the next evening at about six to find Tom in the office, wearing shorts. Jane was at the typewriter in a robe.

"Aren't you going out tonight?" Hugh asked. He knew they had a Yurika meeting scheduled that evening in Santa Rosa.

"I'm not feeling well," said Tom. "Jane's going to go with Vaux."

Tom had been concerned about the steering in his car, so he asked Jane if she could have Vaux drive her to the meeting. Jane dressed and was picked up at about 6:45 PM. Around that time Hugh offered Tom a drink. Tom demurred, saying he was going to lie down because of an upset stomach. In the living room, Hugh absorbed himself in copying videotapes for his chiropractic review.

Around seven-thirty Tom emerged fully-clad from the bedroom, a single bag in hand, his face drenched in sweat.

"Goodbye, Captain," he said to Fine. "Take care of things around here. I've had an emergency call. I've got to go." Tom abruptly shook Hugh's hand and went out the door.

"What emergency call?" Hugh thought to himself. He had not heard the phone ring. Hugh hardly had time to rise from his chair before the car was pulling out of the driveway.

Around 8:50 PM, while Jane was still at her meeting in Santa Rosa, the telephone rang at the house. Tom O'Donnell was on the line. He told Hugh he had left behind an envelope addressed to Jane's friend and lawyer, Jim Rohde.

"Hugh, please don't read anything," said Tom. "Seal the envelope and get it down to the San Anselmo post office immediately. It has the proper amount of postage on it."

"Okay, Tom," he said. "But *what* is going on?"

"You don't want to know, partner."

"But I have to know something, Tom. Jane is going to be coming home soon, and she's going to be all over me like a blanket. I've got to tell her something."

"You tell her she will hear from me within forty-eight hours," said Tom.

"So you're going to call back Thursday about this time?" asked Hugh.

"Just tell her she'll hear from me within forty-eight hours," he repeated.

"Okay."

"I also want her to have the car," he said. He explained that it was parked in the lot at the San Francisco Hilton near the airport and told Hugh the keys could be found under the mat.

Around ten o'clock, Tom called again. He told Hugh he had written on the last two sheets of paper of a five-by-seven yellow pad he had left on his desk in the office. He asked Hugh to retrieve the pad without looking at what was written on the pages and to take them back to the phone.

"Okay, Hugh," he said when Hugh returned. "Now tear them up and flush them down the toilet."

Although it was like a scene out of a thriller, Hugh did not question Tom. Hugh did as he was told without reading what was written on the pages. When Hugh came back on the line, Tom burst into tears.

"It's a disaster, Hugh," he sobbed. "To leave Jane and Duke and the house—it's a tragedy, a terrible, terrible tragedy, but there's no choice, no choice at all. I have to go with these people and I can never return."

"Who are these people, Tom?"

"I can't tell you. It's my past catching up with me."

"Tom, can't we call the authorities?" asked Hugh. "This thing can't be so bad."

"How come you're so naïve? I am trapped," he said. "I either do what they ask, or Dukey gets it and then Jane gets it."

Tom went on to say he had thought of going to Los Angeles and losing himself in the city, but he felt his enemies would eventually find him. And Jane would be in danger. Tom was leaving, he said, to save her life.

"Can't you stay in contact?"

"I will try my best if circumstances will permit, but don't ask me when it will be, because I don't know. I will not talk to anyone but you, and if Jane answers, I'll hang up. If we got on the line with one another we couldn't talk rationally. We would be too emotional." When Tom hung up abruptly, Hugh just stood there staring at the phone in shock.

Jane instantly knew something was wrong when she returned at eleven and saw Tom's car missing from the driveway. She thought immediately of the hospital. Had Tom's stomach ache been something more serious? Had Hugh taken him to the emergency room? She entered the house with Vaux Toneff to find Hugh fully clothed and asleep in the back bedroom. She woke him and asked where Tom was.

"Tell Vaux to go home."

"Why? What's wrong?"

"Do as I say, get Vaux out of here."

"What's wrong?" asked Vaux.

"I don't know," Jane replied, "but it's obvious Hugh won't talk as long as you're in the house." Perplexed, Vaux said she would leave, but that she would not go to bed until she heard from Jane. Jane promised to call her when she found out what was going on.

After she left, however, Hugh had very little to say.

"Tom had an emergency and had to leave," he said. "He went to the airport and left the car for you. He'll be in contact within forty-eight hours."

Hugh did not mention the envelope that he had mailed to Jim Rohde that evening and said nothing of his two previous telephone conversations with Tom. Claiming he had no more details to offer, Hugh quickly went back to bed, leaving Jane in a state of confusion.

"Vaux!" Jane said over the telephone. "We need to go to the airport and find Tom!"

Chapter Ten

Jane explained the situation. Both women realized that finding Tom was futile. It would take another hour to reach the airport. His plane had probably already left. Vaux suggested Jane check to see what Tom had taken with him.

For the next two hours Jane searched the house. She checked the drawers in Tom's office and the closets, including those in the spare rooms, making a mental list of all that was missing. Tom had taken clothes for warm and cold weather, including his leather coat, tennis shorts, sweater, and shoes. Curiously, he had taken no suits. In the downstairs family room, she was shocked to discover that his voluminous files were missing—eight filing cabinet drawers full of papers, canceled checks, and personal records. All gone. They must have been too heavy to take with him, but where could they be?

She searched the wine cellar, the workroom, the garage, but found no trace of his papers. Tom certainly could not have burned his records without leaving residue or significant evidence. What had happened?

Jane leaned against the Ping-Pong table and stared at the bookshelves. It seemed so unreal. She spent the rest of the night reviewing what had seemed to be an ordinary day: the visit to the bank, the lunch, the casual late afternoon. An emergency? What could it possibly be?

The next morning, Jane and Hugh drove to San Francisco airport to retrieve Tom's car. Although Jane grilled him on the way, Hugh gave up no new information. Finally she asked Hugh a more pointed question.

"Do you think Tom is ever coming back?"

"No," said Hugh.

"Why do you say that?"

Hugh would give her no answer. When they found the car, Jane spent a quarter hour searching it. She was sure that Tom must have left a letter. She looked under the floor mats, in the glove compartment, in the trunk. Nothing. Jane was beginning to panic. Hugh obviously knew more than he was telling her, and she was growing angry at his reticence.

Later, Vaux and Jane searched the home one more time, adding more items to the list of things that had disappeared. They found the name of a bar on a sheet of paper but could find no record of it in San Francisco. Several friends called that day, including the Rohdes, but Jane didn't mention Tom's disappearance. What could she say? How could she explain something like this, with so few details to offer?

Although Hugh had known Jane for twenty-five years, he was acting in confidence to Tom. He had certainly never planned such a thing, but he had been won over by the urgency and pain in Tom's voice. Jane had always considered him a loyal friend. But Hugh felt he was helping Tom escape those who were threatening him and protecting Jane from what Tom had said were threats against her.

He knew how much Tom loved Jane, and believed he would never hurt her. He and Tom had become close friends, and Hugh had not hesitated to destroy Tom's notes to protect Tom's trust in him. For several critical days he remained silent.

The next day Jane got a call from her friend Sandy Sullivan, who was manager of the local branch of the Marin Savings and Loan. As casually as she could, Jane asked if she had seen Tom.

"Yes, on Tuesday," she said. "He came into the bank and cashed a five thousand dollar cashier's check. Jane, is something wrong?"

Jane was shocked to hear this news. Tom was supposed to have put the five thousand dollar check into her account. That meant that Tom had left not with just five thousand dollars in cash but ten thousand. When Tom had come into Marin Savings, she was told, he had asked specifically for Sandy Sullivan. Because it was a household account in Jane's name alone, Tom could not have withdrawn any money. But this was a signed cashier's check, not specifically earmarked for deposit. As a friend, Sandy Sullivan didn't question him. "Large bills please, sweets," Tom told her.

Jane cut the conversation with Sullivan short. "I need to get back to you later."

Clearly Tom had not gone to the travel agency at all the morning he left. He had obviously needed the money for some other purpose. When Vaux arrived, she and Jane discussed what this meant, but could make no sense of it.

Later that day, around five o'clock, Jim and Erin Rohde showed up at the door. Jane immediately knew something was wrong. Erin's face was ashen, and she was shaking her head in disbelief. Jim Rohde was carrying the manila envelope that Hugh had mailed for Tom.

Rohde explained there was a letter to Jane. There was also a letter to the Rohdes, as well as letters to Hugh, and Brandon O'Donnell, Tom's son in Montana. Jane opened the envelope and began reading the lined yellow pages that Tom had been working on for days before he left. She immediately began to cry.

> My dearest love,
>
> You are without a doubt the most beautiful person in the world and I love you so much, so very much, that to have to write this letter is killing me inside—our remaining years looked so good together. My life has been truly fulfilled by the simple fact that you have let me share with you my time. There is positively no way these last four to five years could be replaced with the fun, the laughter, the respect, the trust, etc. etc. etc.
>
> Now for the future—Jane, my dearest, I have to leave the USA, but I want you to do the following for me & for the good of Jane S. Alexander.
>
> First you must list your house immediately—I know how you feel, but unless someone like Jim (Rohde) may know someone who would give you unusual creative financing you will have to sell—pay off everything—you should have $100,000 to $150,000 clear—Jim will do his very best for you.
>
> There are several alternative ways—renting the basement, taking in someone—with proper creative financing to pay off the payback leaving you a good monthly income. Maybe you and a friend like Nancy Martell will work something out in the equity of the houses, still giving you a lawn & garden to work in. Oh how I remember the many, many days we toiled in the yard—it was so hard but now seems so beautiful—you working—me working & Dukey going back and forth between us—I'm so sick inside to have to do this to you no words can describe it but I know you will be feeling same and that bothers me so very much.
>
> You must have someone around you, Jane, please my loved one, let your friends help you. I know Jim Rohde will do the best he can for you financially so you can still be independent. But let people help you—allow them graciously—you have so much to give, to offer this world—please be strong, accept this happening without bitterness and live a good healthy & full life. Please try for me. I know it will take the ultimate effort for you, but if there

is anything good left in my life it would be to only know that you have lived thru this ordeal and would be enjoying the many years left in your life. That will give me daily comfort, remember that please. So when you are down & sad—you know I feel it too—so please, for me, pick up your spirits—knowing that I will feel that boost too and feel so much better.

Let me now explain to you, as I have done somewhat in Jim and Erin's letter, what has caused this almost unbearable situation.

You know most but not all of my past activities in Africa. I should say you know generally, not specifically, and this particular incident was one of my main reasons for leaving Africa. I was instrumental in putting together one of the biggest diamond transactions: I.D.B., illicit diamond buying, of course. It involved people in Europe, North Africa, and our area. Somebody informed, and an entrapment took place. Some wealthy powerful families were involved and some ended up doing six years or so in prison—I do not have to tell you the prisons there are not like the prisons here. Some that were sent to prison felt I was responsible for the entrapment and swore on their family names (and it did cause real hardships etc. for them & their families—too numerous to go into now—heart attacks, etc.) to find me and settle matters. Most people involved realized it wasn't me—I knew it wasn't me and from other information I've told you since, you know I was never a government agent.

But evidently they still believe I was the one—it is part of the risk you take when you involve yourself with I.D.B. If you remember, I guess it was three years after arriving here before I slept one night without my gun under the pillow and then only moved it to the nightstand beside me. I was feeling more and more confident as the years rolled by—a mistake, one of my past that should not have been taken for granted.

They have been watching us for some time—they know our routines & habits well—that deer on the fire road was killed for our benefit (we ran there). The big buzzard (bird) was placed at our driveway purposefully—they do not take claim about the recent "animal cries" we have been hearing lately at night but

I feel it is them. The early morning calls on the office phone I answered was them—a warning to me to hurry up and settle matters & get cash. They originally asked for $50,000 or our lives—then $25,000—I informed them $10,000 was the most, plus my cooperation to go with them. $12,500 was finally settled on—it is so ironic—I remember when after 4 years of searching for Kulik and found him in the Holiday Inn in New York—he was so scared and cried like a baby—I insisted on an immediate $50,000 or his life—then held tough for $25,000 and ended up getting $12,500 in cash and a lot of promises—now it is my turn—what a full circle, only the names and places change.

They receive a bonus if they get me to go back with them—they mentioned they wish to still use what talents may be left and contacts in Africa I have. Please please my love do not spend one penny or one thought or one minute trying to help me—it would not be good for you and Duke and it would terminate matters for me—just one hint that someone was trying to assist or help me (and they do have ears in Europe, Africa, and now here) would bring about very unfavorable reactions for all of us.

Now I guess we come to my second most cherished concern in my life. Duke—just the thought of him turns my stomach upside down and around etc. etc. etc. Try very hard, Jane, to make him understand—I know you will give him twice the love, if that's possible—but brush him, wash him, and that is all I can handle on this subject—only you & he knows how much I love him!

And now my loved one, thinking of you and me—we really do have so much to be grateful for. I remember when I first arrived here in 1978, I believe—you were in real bad shape—living in only the bedroom & kitchen—no spark—no life but just look at what all that has happened since then—we have had such really truly great times—I think about N. Dakota, Texas, Mexico—so many wonderful times together—enough to fill a lifetime, my sweet. The old adage is so true: "It is better to have love & lost than never have loved at all." I know I will be able daily to think of all the good things that have happened to us & give myself a lift. You and I were 99,999+ "ON" my sweet, remember the good times because there really wasn't 1% bad times between us in all the years.

Think of the good and how fortunate we have been—do not be bitter—do not be sad or depressed for long—you know that I will always love you & I will know & feel the same of you but let us know that God gave us this time & we are better people from it—so be strong & brave and when you get past the shock please be happy—you & Duke—do it for me—I will feel your thoughts & feelings every day and I'm sure you would not want me to be miserable & sad the rest of my life—I will have good thoughts for you daily to pick up from me - so you do the same for me—as I will need the positive thoughts—make it an "affirmation" for me daily & I will do the same for you & think of our good times—will miss you but love you & Duke.

God bless you, my love—
Tom

P.S. Do you remember a few mornings ago the office phone rang at 5:30 I answered—it was them threatening your life if I didn't hurry up with the cash etc. About an hour later you woke up with a startled action—you had just been shot in the stomach—you were so frightened and I held you for ten minutes close to me. It was so horrible but real—they phoned— I'm thinking about it & you have the actual dream.

Sometime during the reading of the letter, Sandy Sullivan arrived at the house. She had been concerned about the phone conversation with Jane earlier in the day. Her husband, Ed, joined her a few minutes later. Suddenly it was a cocktail party that had gone horribly wrong: Jane, Vaux Toneff, Hugh Fine, Jim and Erin Rohde, Ed and Sandy Sullivan, all sitting around on chairs and couches, all trying to make sense of the letters. The yellow legal pages were being passed around the room. The magnitude of the situation was just beginning to dawn on the silent guests.

After a few minutes Hugh spilled forth his own startling news. Tom had actually left this envelope in the house two days before. Hugh recounted the phone calls from Tom and his trip to the post office to drop the packet in the mail. "I did what Tom needed me to do," he said.

Jane was furious. How could Hugh not have mentioned this before? How could he not have mentioned a packet in the mail?

"You let me sit here for *forty-eight hours* and said nothing?" She had been crying for two days, not eating, not sleeping, and Hugh had said nothing.

"I didn't know what the letter said," Hugh replied. He then confessed that he had destroyed the two pages in the yellow legal pad without reading a word of them.

At this point no one believed him or the whole absurd situation. Hugh again recounted the story of Tom's departure, the evident distress in his voice, and the sweat pouring off his brow as he walked out the door.

"Well, he probably stuck his head under the faucet," said Jim Rohde.

Jim and Erin Rohde had read Tom's letter to them in disbelief. It also contained the story of Tom's vengeful diamond smuggling cronies. Tom also wrote of Jane's impending financial problems and asked the Rohdes to take charge of Jane's situation. The last paragraphs of their letter read:

Well, my dear friends, you certainly have been good to me. I know Jane considers you her closest trusting friends—she will do what you think is best for her—lead her in the right way, she so deserves it. She can give so much yet to this world. Her mind is so fascinating to see function—it is true brilliance & a pleasure to be around.

> May God bless both of you forever—have nothing but good health & enjoyable living. I cannot thank you enough for what you will be doing for Jane.
>
> Tom
>
> Enclosed is the title to the Chrysler that I have signed for Jane to have. It needs a smog check—Andy at Chrysler is aware of it—$20 + $6 and that certificate plus a check for $62 should be mailed to the DMV by the 19th or 20th, due on the 24th of August. DMV paper is in accounts payable bin.

Jim Rohde, Jane's advisor for more than twenty years, felt an obligation to help in the crisis. But he was also getting angry about Tom's presumptuous requests and a little skeptical of his motives. Rohde and Ed Sullivan began going through files and drawers in the office in search of the monthly bills that Tom had mentioned in his letter. As was his habit, Tom had filled out checks to credit card companies and other accounts, each of which was ready to be mailed on a particular date. Rohde quickly found a Woodson loan payment check for two thousand seven hundred dollars.

The attorney stormed back into the living room. "Jane, what's this?"

Jane explained the two hundred thousand dollar second mortgage, which had never been mentioned to Rohde. The guests listened in a state of shock.

Rohde was angrier than Jane had ever seen him. "How could you have done such a stupid thing without consulting *me*?"

Jane explained that Tom's 1.2 million-dollar trust was security on the loan and that Tom had asked her not to discuss the second mortgage with him. Rohde was furious that Tom had coerced her into keeping it a secret. Ed Sullivan tried to intervene, saying that he had known about the trust and the loan from the beginning. It didn't help, however. Rohde instantly accused Tom of pulling a scam on Jane. The evening was going from bad to worse.

"Where *is* this trust?" asked Rohde.

"I don't know. Some place in Switzerland."

"Do you have any trust instruments, or any papers pertaining to this trust?"

"No."

"Where was this trust drawn?"

"I don't know."

"Do you have anything in writing pertaining to this trust?"

"No."

Rohde was getting angrier and angrier. Suddenly he took a different tack.

"Jane, what is your mother's maiden name? I need it for identification purposes, since I have to cancel your stolen credit cards."

"What do you mean? Tom didn't steal my credit cards."

"Does he have them with him?" he asked.

"Yes, of course."

"Then they're *stolen*!"

In a blaze of anger Jim Rohde retreated into the office. Vaux Toneff—who hardly knew the Rohdes—told Jane she had to leave; the situation was too upsetting.

Chapter Ten

How could Tom O'Donnell have done this? Everyone there knew him and liked him. They could remember his good humor, his easy grace, his marvelous anecdotes. Now these stories took on an eerie quality of vengeful South African diamond smugglers, kidnapping and extortion, dead animals on the lawn, and death threats against Jane and the dog.

The evening disintegrated as guests voiced their opinions. There were those who believed what Tom had written, such as Jane and Vaux, those on the fence like Ed and Sandy Sullivan, and those who refused to believe any of it, particularly Jim and Erin Rohde. No one knew what to make of Hugh Fine. It was all too much to digest.

Hugh did remember to tell Jane that Tom might call the house, but only to speak to him. Tom would hang up on Jane, he said.

"You're going to answer the phone from now on," said Jane.

"I could record the calls with the tape recorder I use for class," he said. His feeble offer of assistance did little to assuage Jane's anger.

She had hardly eaten anything in more than two days, since she had returned home and found Tom's car missing. That Monday night, after reading his letter, Jane was so drained she fell into bed without even taking off her clothes. The pain in her heart was almost unbearable. First she had lost her husband, then Gertrude, and now Tom. The round of heartbreak had gone from bad to worse.

The next morning, August 10, Jane began calling everyone she knew who might have some knowledge of Tom's whereabouts. She began with Tom's close friend in Los Angeles, Harry Carmichael, reading him the letter over the phone.

Harry was perplexed. "I can't imagine where he went," he said. "I don't know anything about these people, and he hasn't called me, Jane."

"Will you call me immediately if you hear from him?" she asked.

"Of course."

Jane then phoned John Mackey in Las Vegas, another close friend of Tom's. The two had worked together in the 1960s.

Mackey expressed his concerns. "Not a word from him," he said to Jane. "But I'll call you if I hear a thing, I promise."

Mackey and Carmichael seemed genuinely puzzled by the situation. They agreed it was out of character for Tom to leave like this. Yet they both reminded Jane that Tom had a lot of ghosts in his past and was bound to have crossed a few people in his life. Both men expressed concern for Jane's well-being and said how sure they were that he would never have done this had there not been some overwhelming reason.

Jane reached Tom's brother Neil in Seattle, as well as Tom's son Brandon and nephew Jack in Montana. All were upset and confused by the news. She contacted friends in Wisconsin, Florida, and Nevada.

Jane began to feel as if Tom had disappeared from the face of the earth. She could not help wondering if he was still alive. Could these diamond smugglers have taken the money and knocked him off? How was it that he would not or *could not* contact anyone he knew and loved?

On that day Dr. Gary Boero, a neighbor just up the hill, came to the house and read the letter. He said very little but left Jane a check for one thousand dollars. "I'm sure you'll need it," he told her.

Jane had not thought to check her own accounts. She found out that her checking account had less than $100 and that the money market account Tom had used for his commodities trading had less than twenty dollars.

The Yurika business account, which should have had a balance of five hundred dollars, had been emptied. Tom had visited several banks the day he left, taking an additional two thousand dollars. Although he had been scrupulous in making out checks to be paid for various bills, there were not enough funds to honor a single one. She was flat broke.

Jane called John Carroll, the lawyer handling Aunt Gert's estate, and asked for an advance on the disbursement. With permission from Irma Clark, she was forwarded a check for five thousand dollars. Jane felt she needed the money not so much to keep food on the table but to find Tom. Clearly, he needed help wherever he was. A little bit of money might make all the difference.

She could not imagine that her life, so horribly wrenched by Gertrude's murder, could get worse. And when it did, with Tom's disappearance, that the horror could go any deeper than that.

Little did she know that the nightmare had just begun.

Chapter Eleven

For several days Jane debated with friends whether she should call the police. Would they take Tom's disappearance seriously? Would they be able to find him? Vaux Toneff was friendly with Bernie Del Santo, the police chief in San Anselmo, and recommended Jane call him. But the letters had strongly warned against the danger of police involvement, hinting of recriminations from Tom's diamond-smuggling cronies. Hugh Fine in particular thought police involvement was a bad idea.

Despite skepticism and opposition from several friends, Jane was unwavering in her belief that Tom O'Donnell's past had somehow caught up with him and that he was in serious trouble. While others complained that he had taken her money, all she cared about was Tom's safety.

"We never had a bad day or an unkind word between us," she said repeatedly. Indeed, after her life had been shattered by the death of her husband, Al, it was Tom who had rescued her. It was Tom who had brought her out of a terrible depression, who made her laugh, who took her dancing, who cared for her and helped her in every way imaginable.

They had planned to spend the rest of their lives together. Jane refused to entertain any thought that O'Donnell's disappearance was related to anything but what he had claimed in his letters.

Jane frantically searched for any way to locate and aid O'Donnell. She and Hugh even entertained the idea of calling in favors from old political friends in Washington, particularly congressmen who might order a search of South African newspaper archives. If members of "wealthy powerful families" had served jail terms, if this diamond deal was as big as Tom hinted it was, surely there would have been a newspaper account of it.

Jane even made three trips to the Herbert Hoover library at Stanford University to search the archives of South African newspapers with Erin Rohde's assistance. For hours they stood at the research counters and turned page after page of Johannesburg and Pretoria newspapers. They searched publications dating as far back as fifteen years, hoping to find articles about elaborate diamond smuggling. Nothing.

Finally, Jane turned to the one official who had won her confidence. She phoned John Kracht. In a state of panic, all she could say was that Tom was gone.

"Did you two have a quarrel?" he asked.

"I would never call you over some domestic squabble," she said. "Tom is gone, he's in serious trouble, and I need your help."

Jane was too choked with emotion to say more. At the time she had never entertained the thought that Kracht considered her a suspect in Gertrude McCabe's murder. She knew he was a resourceful and dedicated police officer, and in desperation she turned to him for help in finding Tom.

"I have never in my life heard so many tears," Kracht said as he waited for her to catch her breath.

Jane passed the phone to Hugh Fine, who did little to clarify the situation. He explained that Tom had left, leaving behind several letters claiming that his life was in danger from vengeful former business associates. Hugh added he was fairly certain he wouldn't be returning. Kracht asked if Jane would like for him to drive to San Anselmo and talk to her. Hugh said he thought so. Kracht offered to call the next morning and arrange the visit.

By the next morning, however, when Kracht called, Jane was already having second thoughts about involving him in Tom's disappearance for fear of further endangering his life.

"Hi, Jane, how are you doing?"

Jane had been crying again, and still could barely speak through her sobbing. "I'm not doing very well, John," she said. "I appreciate your call, but I just don't want to see you, okay? Because in my emotional state, I forgot that you were first a police officer and secondly a friend. Hugh said that you and your partner would be coming here and that's an official visit and I can't talk to you ... I think you'll understand, I mean, I *hope* you'll understand. It isn't that I don't trust you, but that I *can't* trust you, because of the position you are in. I understand that you have an obligation and a duty, and if you hear things, you're going to have to act."

Kracht was most interested in the recent development. After the FBI profile and Tom's questionable behavior during the fingerprinting, he had become John Kracht's prime suspect. Now he had fled unexpectedly, claiming his life was in danger.

Chapter Eleven

From the moment John Kracht heard that news, he was convinced that Tom O'Donnell was guilty of the savage murder of Gertrude McCabe.

Jane's voice was barely a whisper. "I'm *sorry*, but I just can't put Tom's life in any more jeopardy than it is."

"I wouldn't do that, Jane," said Kracht. He could not help wondering if she was alluding to Gert's murder, had wanted to confess something but retreated.

"I know you wouldn't put Tom's life at risk, John. But you can't obtain information and just sit on it. Tom made it so explicit in his letter to not waste one minute trying to help him, because if I did, somehow they would find out and it would jeopardize all our lives. And I sincerely believe that and I can't say any more. I shouldn't have called you in the first place, but I guess I was just reaching out, trying to seek help from anyone and everyone, and I'm sorry I called, I really am."

Although Kracht believed the story was a concoction, he was hesitant to press Jane too hard. *Let her tell the story,* he thought. As every good detective knows, the longer a conversation is allowed to go on, the more information is likely to spill forth.

"Whoever these, uh, evildoers are, they must be pretty slick, huh?" asked Kracht.

"Oh, well, it's the underground, I'm sure. His past is catching up to him; it's been ten years. I could explain a lot to you, but I just don't feel I should. At least he's alive, and he's gone with them. And as Hugh said, he's never heard a grown man break down and cry like he did on the telephone. He said it was just the worst thing he'd ever heard in his life. And he acquiesced to go, and he went, because, I mean, we got the two dead animals."

"Two dead animals?"

"Yes," said Jane.

"What two dead animals?"

"A deer on the fire road about five hundred yards from the house. A doe with a bullet through her head. And Tom got a phone call to say that was the first warning. And then the big buzzard with an eight-foot wingspan was placed on the pillars outside the driveway."

"When did that happen?"

"Last week. It was there for about five days. I took the dog over to run, and there's no sign of the deer. Not only did they put it there, they took it away.

70

There's no trace of it. That's not a figment of my imagination. The buzzard was placed at the pillars by the driveway, and Tom and I threw it over the gully, threw it over the side."

"In general terms, the way I understand that—"

"John, *please* don't do anything."

"No, I won't."

"Please, *promise* me you won't do anything."

Kracht lowered his voice. "I promise you I won't do anything."

"Thank you."

"But I need to satisfy myself that you're not in any danger."

"I'm not afraid, John. I'm not in any danger. I mean, they *got* what they wanted."

"You told me you were in some jeopardy."

"*If* Tom didn't go with them, *then* I was in jeopardy."

"Explain that to me so that it will make some sense."

"Well, he told Hugh on the telephone that when he was first contacted, his first impulse was to run himself. But that he couldn't do that because if he ran, they would kill me, and they would kill the dog. And he *loves* this dog, he loves this dog like you can't believe. He told Hugh he was trapped, and he couldn't run and take me with him. We couldn't just walk off into the sunset. So he tried to negotiate, and in order to protect me, he said he was willing to go with them. He gave them twelve thousand five hundred dollars and his cooperation, whatever that means."

"Was this *your* money that went with Tom?"

"Yeah. But *that's* not the point, John."

"I know, I know it's not the point," said Kracht, making a mental note that Tom fleeing with Jane's money was *exactly* the point.

"I take it these people feel that they suffered some sort of injustice in the past," said Kracht. "And now, with Tom going with them, he is going to be able to rectify whatever it was he did."

"Yes. But he said he would never be able to come back. That even if he got away from them, he was in a catch-22 situation. And if he got away from them … John, you won't *do* anything, promise?"

"Of course," said Kracht.

"He said that if he did get away from them he could never come back, because they know where I am and they would always find me, and that I should start my life over. He went on and on. He wrote a letter to his son, and told him he could probably never contact him again. He asked me to call his brother, who has a heart condition and who broke down completely when I called him. They are very, very close. He mentioned everyone in the letter who was close to him or dear to him or meant anything to him. He wrote a letter to my attorney. John, promise me you won't call Rohde?"

"All right."

"And then he wrote a letter to Hugh, and asked him to be gentle with the dog, and asked him to stay with me and help me through this. All the letters were in one big manila envelope," said Jane.

"Do these letters sound like suicide notes?" asked Kracht.

"No," Jane said with exasperation. "He just *had* to go with these people."

Kracht soon elicited an account of the diamond-smuggling business and the sting that had put so many prominent South Africans behind bars. Kracht said he wanted to read the letters himself, asking for the names and addresses of everyone who had read or touched them. Jane asked Kracht to visit without his partner so that it would not be an "official" visit. Kracht agreed, after chuckling to himself about her naiveté.

On Monday, Kracht drove to Jane's home, arriving at noon. Jane had not an inkling that he was visiting for a reason completely different from the one she anticipated. Tom's disappearance from Marin County and alleged problems with foreign diamond smugglers were both beyond his jurisdiction. She never dreamed he was there hunting a murderer.

For the first time in months Aunt Gert's murder was not preeminent in Jane's mind. She was desperate to find help for Tom.

When Kracht arrived, she received him as a friend.

"This sounds very serious, Jane," said the detective.

"It really is," she replied.

After reading the letters, Kracht looked at Jane. "So what do you want me to do?"

"All I want to know is that Tom's safe," Jane said. "We need to find him."

Kracht couldn't have agreed more. He made no mention of the McCabe case. He believed O'Donnell fled because the murder investigation was leading to his front door, but Kracht was careful not to give Jane the slightest hint of his growing suspicion. While Jane was anxious to engage his help, Kracht knew this was a golden opportunity to dig for clues about O'Donnell's involvement in Gertrude's death.

"May I look in Tom's office?"

"Sure."

"If I find anything interesting, papers or records, would you mind if I took it back with me to San Jose?"

"Not at all, John. You can take anything you think is important, anything you need to find Tom."

Jane and John Kracht talked through the various money transfers that had occurred before Tom left—the loan, the cashier's check, the other withdrawals. Kracht decided that Tom probably did have twelve thousand five hundred dollars with him when he left, just as he said in the letter. Kracht pointed out, however, that if Tom gave his friends the twelve thousand five hundred dollars, that didn't leave him much to spend on his own.

Jane and Vaux had made a list of clothes Tom had taken with him, including winter coats, shorts, and a leather jacket. She took the detective on a tour of Tom's wardrobe. It appeared Tom had taken clothes for all seasons, including sports coats and dress pants, but had neglected to take any of his suits. Kracht searched the house room by room. Jane took him downstairs and showed him the empty file cabinets.

Kracht also had a look at the financial records Tom had left in his office. Though he mentioned nothing to Jane, he knew this was a trove that could yield potential clues to their activities on the day of Aunt Gert's murder.

"Jane, do you have any dental records for Tom? Has he seen a dentist lately?"

"Why?"

"Well, we can use that to help identify him, if we were to put out a missing person's report." The idea of obtaining dental records made Jane uneasy. That was, after all, the way corpses were identified. Kracht continued his thought. "With a missing person's report, I think it would take about four months to find him."

"Four months!" said Jane. "He could be dead in a week."

Kracht figured she'd want to find Tom faster. He knew a way to do that. "Well, you know the ten thousand dollars he took from you the day he left could constitute a felony charge, that is taking money under false pretenses. If you put out a warrant for his arrest, we could probably find him faster."

His gambit was instantly quashed. "I won't even consider it, John. I don't want him arrested, I want him protected. His life is in danger." Despite the fact that Kracht doubted everything O'Donnell had written in his letters, he had seen the kind of loyalty Jane Alexander displayed many times.

"Would you consider putting a trace on the phone, so that we could find out where Tom is if he calls?"

"No," said Jane, beginning to cry again. "I want him found, but not if it's going to endanger his life or get him arrested."

Kracht suggested a compromise. Why not tape her phone calls, so he could have a record of anything that seemed important or in any way relevant to Tom? Hugh Fine mentioned that he had the equipment on hand. Kracht said he would bring blank tapes on his next visit.

The detective spent almost six hours in Jane's home that day, listening and observing, comforting and consoling. He was impressed by Jane's cooperation. When he left, he took O'Donnell's letter and some records and receipts of Tom's financial dealings that he felt might be important in any potential prosecution.

He never mentioned the murder of Gertrude McCabe or voiced suspicion about Tom O'Donnell's departure. Though he had honed in on O' Donnell as the prime suspect, he was still not convinced that Jane Alexander had not been somehow involved. If not in the planning or execution, then as an accessory after the fact for hiding information about O'Donnell's culpability. For now, all he wanted was to stay in Jane's confidence. Through her he would have access to the life and activities of a fugitive from justice.

Chapter Twelve

A few days after Tom's departure, Jane asked her friend Marge Whelan if she would come up from San Francisco. Jack and Marge Whelan had escaped the city fog for many summers by weekending with Jane and Tom in Marin County. The two couples had become close, close enough that the Whelan's had lent Tom twenty-five thousand dollars earlier that year, after Gertrude's death. Tom had promised to repay the loan when Jane received her portion of Gertrude's estate.

When Jane found out about the loan, she was furious with Tom. Jane did not believe in borrowing money from friends. Immediately, she contacted the Whelan's and offered a lien on her home as collateral. The Whelan's gratefully accepted.

Halfway through reading a copy of Tom's letter, Marge threw it across the room. "That jerk is sitting on a Caribbean island, enjoying your money!"

"You're wrong, Marge. You know how much Tom loves me!"

A loud argument ensued. It was the first of many friendships that would be strained or destroyed in the weeks following Tom's departure. Although everyone was sympathetic to Jane's situation, only a few—Vaux Toneff and Hugh Fine among them—shared Jane's belief in Tom's self-proclaimed predicament.

The majority of Jane's friends believed that O'Donnell was a con man who had gambled away Jane's two hundred thousand dollars from the second mortgage by playing the commodities market. They accused him of cleaning out her bank accounts as he made his getaway.

As the weeks went by, Jim Rohde's contention that Tom had never had a trust fund became more and more obvious to everyone, even Jane. Her friends were torn between trying to knock sense into her and the desire to help her through her growing depression. Yet even the biggest skeptics, including Jim and Erin Rohde, never suspected Tom had left because he had murdered Gertrude McCabe.

August passed slowly and painfully, with no news from Tom. Jane's days passed in a fog. She found it almost impossible to shop, cook, or perform any of her normal routines.

Vaux Toneff had become her personal savior. Every morning, without fail, Vaux would call.

"Get up and put your feet on the floor," she would say. She brought food and kept Jane company, trying desperately to raise her spirits. Within a few months Jane lost twenty pounds.

Yet she was still intent on finding Tom and helping him if possible. She telephoned John Kracht every other day to ask if he had any news. With this new loss, Gertrude's murder faded into the background.

On September 11, 1984, John Kracht came to Sleepy Hollow to have another look at the financial records in Tom's office. This time he was more methodical, taking the canceled checks, phone bills, spreadsheets, and bank statements he considered potentially relevant to the Gertrude McCabe murder case. He was also hoping to discover some link between Jane and Tom and the events in San Jose.

For the first time he questioned Jane directly about her activities on the day of the murder. "Where were you on October 21, 1983?"

"Just a minute, John. I'll check the diary."

Jane went to her bedroom and recovered her large hardcover calendar ledger for 1983. More than two inches thick, the book contained space for three days' events on each page. John Kracht immediately recognized the importance of such a record as Jane explained her meticulous entries.

In 1980, Tom started to manage their financial and social activities, at approximately the same time Jane began to keep her diaries. Both Tom and Jane read and referred to the diary on a regular basis. She read Kracht the entry for October 21, 1983.

> Xerox and post office. Sent stuff to Idaho. Shopping for boxes. Watered plants. Lazy day, missed Tom. Tom called 10 PM Couldn't get back to LA from San Diego to get plane. Will stay with Harry one more night. Duke and I really disappointed. Lois called about her 49er game Sunday, it will be at the Martell's.

"So you see, John, nothing out of the ordinary that day," she said. "Tom was trying to straighten out the house loan down in San Diego. I was shopping for the Christmas packages I send every year to my kids and grandchildren."

"Do you remember where you went shopping that day?" asked Kracht.

To all who know her, Jane's memory is a phenomenon. Prompted by the cursory notes in her diary, she has the ability to recall copious details of almost any day. "Well, the packet to Idaho, that was a bunch of newspaper clippings and magazine articles. They would have been sent from the Fairfax post office," said Jane. "It's not here in the diary, but since Tom was away, I'm pretty sure I bought dog food for Duke, and that would have been from Lucky's across the street from the post office. I never go there otherwise. After that I went to JC Penney in Corte Madera to buy pajamas for my grandchildren for Christmas. Otherwise, I was probably at home most of the day. I spent some time in the garden, I remember that. It was just what it says here, John, a lazy day."

Although John Kracht was familiar with Jane's uncanny talent, having heard her recall the minutiae of Aunt Gert's life, this conversation gave him pause. How was it that Jane knew *that* day so well, October 21, 1983? It shouldn't have been special, thought John, for any other reason. Would Jane have made a point of remembering these details, perhaps even inventing them, to disguise a trip to San Jose?

"Jane, do you ever lie in your diary?"

She was affronted. "What kind of crazy question is that? Who would lie in their diary?"

Kracht just smiled. "So who is Harry, the man you mention here?" he asked.

For the first time Jane told him about Harry Carmichael, Tom's friend in Los Angeles. Harry was a great guy, said Jane, but drank too much booze. Yet he had a good marriage now, was kind to his stepson, and was always a thoughtful host when she and Tom were in LA.

"Do you have his address?"

"Tom left his address book, which for the life of me I can't understand. There must be something in it he doesn't want these people to know. I'll get it for you."

Nearly all the entries in the black, spiral bound folder were for foreign addresses. Tom had arranged his contacts alphabetically, according to the city in which they could be found. Under L, for example, could be found addresses in La Paz, Liechtenstein, Lagos, London, and Lusaka. Harry Carmichael's name was under Los Angeles. John asked if he could take the address book with him, and Jane agreed. "Do what you can to find Tom," she said.

"Well, how about those diaries? I'd like to take a look at them."

"No *way* are you going to read them. Would you want me reading *your* diaries? These are private."

Kracht did not press Jane on the subject. Only later, after other more mundane matters had been discussed, did he return to the issue.

"We can do it the easy way or the hard way, Jane. The easy way is that you give the diaries to me, and the hard way is that I get a court order and subpoena them. But the bottom line is I'm going to have them."

Kracht smiled at her. It was one of Jane's first lessons in investigative arm twisting.

She was furious. But the look on Kracht's face told her there was no way he would leave without her diaries. He promised to return them on his next visit.

Reluctantly, she handed them over. Although Jane did not know it at the time, she would never get her diaries back. The diaries would prove critical in the long pursuit of the murderer.

Kracht politely thanked her, bade her goodbye, and was heading toward the door, when he turned and asked offhandedly, "Jane, do you happen to have a receipt from the post office or Lucky's for the dog food you bought that day?"

Jane told him she had paid for the dog food by check. The check, she said, was in the box he already held.

He stopped and thumbed through October's canceled checks. Sure enough, dated October 21 and time-stamped at 1:52 PM was the Lucky's check, bearing Jane's signature.

Kracht knew that the coroner had fixed Gertrude's time of death at close to 3:00 PM Jane could not have gotten to her car and driven from Fairfax to San Jose and committed the murder in that span of time. He finished his thoughts by saying, "I doubt someone who was about to commit a murder would stop and buy dog food along the way."

In her distress over the loss of O'Donnell, the comment barely registered with Jane. Only months later would the significance of Kracht's comment register.

He had just cleared her, in his own mind, of the murder of Gertrude McCabe. She had never dreamed she was a suspect.

Shortly after receiving Jane's diaries, John Kracht met with Alan Nudelman, Supervisor of the District Attorney's homicide team, to discuss the particulars of the Gertrude McCabe investigation. While it is unusual to involve the DA's office before an investigation is complete, Kracht felt that he needed to consult a legal authority. After all, he was exploiting a friendship with a vulnerable woman who wanted nothing more than to be reunited with her estranged boyfriend.

Although Jane had voluntarily surrendered her diaries as well as her telephone and financial records, Kracht might well find himself in a position where these would be used against her. If he obtained incriminating evidence at this stage, would it be admissible? Could he be accused of obtaining information under false pretenses?

Even though Kracht was fairly sure that Jane had not participated in the homicide, he could not guarantee she was without knowledge of the crime, either before or after it was committed. Given her blind devotion, she still could be covering up for O'Donnell.

Kracht explained to Nudelman the circumstances of Tom's departure, mentioning the FBI profile that implicated a possible female suspect. This was Alan Nudelman's introduction to the case and to Jane Alexander. Nudelman was silent for a while.

"You're doing a good job here, John, but there is nothing better than a confession," he said. "This woman wants to tell you something. That's the ultimate prize. With just a little patience, you're going to get it."

The following day, Kracht issued a missing-persons report for Tom O'Donnell. The report noted that O'Donnell had with him a valid passport, credit cards, and identification in the name of a deceased person, Alfred Alexander, and that O'Donnell had a history of extensive foreign travel. Kracht attached a dental chart to the report, and for visual identification he included a photograph of Tom with Duke.

Weeks later, John Kracht received a response from Interpol with some interesting information about Tom O'Donnell. He had last lived in Switzerland in 1977, the report said, at the Nova Park Hotel in Zurich. While in residence, he had negotiated the sale of a diamond for a South African company. O'Donnell had been banned from reentering Switzerland for failing to pay taxes on the transaction.

Kracht had long been skeptical about the existence of Tom's trust in Switzerland. If the trust existed, it would be a way of tracing Tom. If it did not, it would help confirm a financial motive for killing Aunt Gert.

Using information he found in Tom's address book, Kracht made inquiries through Interpol concerning the "Greenfire Trust," which was managed by a Hans Bühler in Zurich. Kracht learned that Bühler's Greenfire Trust was a precious gem business. Bühler knew of no trust belonging to Tom O'Donnell.

Two days after Kracht heard the name Harry Carmichael for the first time, he flew to Southern California to meet him.

Carmichael was in his mid-fifties, a few years younger than Tom. He stood six foot six, and even though he tipped the scales at more than three hundred pounds, he didn't appear overweight. Instead, he was the proverbial larger-than-life figure who told humorous stories and bragged that the bulk of his career in the Marines had been spent in the brig. Carmichael had tried a hundred different businesses, most of them low-level, door-to-door schemes that he ran out of the back of his car.

Harry Carmichael and Tom O'Donnell had met more than twenty-five years before in Denver, when Tom was newly married to his first wife, Kay. Tom had interested Harry in his built-in home vacuum cleaner business. Harry had taken charge of field sales and service. The business failed, but the two men remained friends.

Carmichael was also an alcoholic who would consume prodigious amounts of bourbon during a binge. He interspersed his drinking bouts with long periods of adherence to Alcoholics Anonymous. When Kracht met him, he was living with his wife and son in a shabby apartment building in Van Nuys.

Kracht waited until Carmichael had just returned home from work before knocking on his door.

"How can I help you?" asked Carmichael.

Kracht introduced himself with a business card. Harry visibly shuddered as he read "homicide detective." He knew his friend Tom was in trouble; worse, trouble had come knocking on Harry's door.

Kracht asked if he was acquainted with Tom O'Donnell.

"Tom O'Donnell? He's been popping in and out of my life for a couple of decades," said Harry. "But I have to admit, it's been a while since I heard from him."

Kracht picked up on his nervousness. Yet Harry also seemed like the talkative type, and Kracht was happy to lend an ear. Harry invited him in.

"How'd you two meet?"

Harry talked about the vacuum cleaner business in Denver, exaggerating its successes. He spoke of Tom as a great father and family man. Harry told Kracht he was a pilot who had flown politicians all over the state with Tom and Jane.

Harry had the feeling he was impressing the detective, and he would eventually convey to Tom that Kracht was easily impressed, even gullible. Harry worked hard to convince Kracht that his friend was not the kind of man who would commit murder.

"Did Tom pay any visits to you in the last couple of years?"

"Sure, a few times. Early this year, January or February 1984, he came to try to refinance his house. We went to Merrill Lynch in San Diego. Then a couple times this past April, I think, Jane and Tom were both here for Yurika Food rallies. And some time a year and a half ago, a visit to another old business friend of ours, Harold Moen in La Jolla.

Harry was willing to recall everything but the visit on October 20, 1983.

Kracht then became more specific. "Mr. Carmichael, I'd like to question Tom in relation to the murder of Gertrude McCabe in San Jose. I'd like to clear his name if I can. But since he's not here to help do that, I need your help. Did Tom ever come down and stay just one night? Could that have been in late October 1983?"

"Can't remember, but he had his business here, so sure," said Harry.

"Did he ever rent a car?" asked Kracht.

Harry made a show of trying to remember.

"Did you ever rent one for him?"

"I suppose I picked him up at the airport once, helped him rent a car," he said.

"Could that have been a visit on October 20, 1983?"

"Hard to remember," said Harry. "The visits all blur together. I think he did come in once for a couple days. I helped him rent a car because he didn't have a credit card, and he came back and took us to dinner at the Granada restaurant."

"Do you know when you rented the car, what time of day it was?"

"I think the night he arrived," said Harry. "Tom wanted an early start the next morning. But that might have belonged to a different visit. I really can't remember."

"Do you have a receipt?"

"Nope, Tom took it."

Kracht changed tack. "What sort of business was Tom doing then?"

"Tom just tells you what he wants you to know," said Harry. "That's just the way he is."

"Do you remember the car rental agency?"

Harry remembered a small agency on Sepulveda Boulevard, across from a well-known furniture store, and gave Kracht directions.

"Mr. Carmichael, if you have any questions or if there is anything else you remember which might be of help in this case, I'd appreciate a call. And if Tom O'Donnell contacts you, I'd like to know about it," he said.

"Sure thing," said Harry. "Anything I can do."

Later that day, Harry Carmichael called Jane Alexander. "Why in the hell did you give that detective my address?" he said.

Jane was shocked to hear that John Kracht had gone to Los Angeles. "I didn't give him anything, Harry."

"Then how did he find me?"

"He's trying to find Tom, and he has Tom's address book."

"Damn straight he's trying to find him. He's trying to pin a murder charge on him, that's why. Do you have any idea how much trouble that will cause? You are putting his life in danger."

Jane was newly thrown into turmoil. Was she doing the right thing by cooperating with John Kracht? She couldn't believe Tom was in any way linked to Gertrude's murder.

"I'm sure John is only trying to find him to clear his name," she said. "I can't believe he thinks he's capable of murder."

"I know what the police are capable of, and they're ready to nail him to the wall," Harry said. "Don't say anything to that detective again, Jane. Do you hear me? *You will destroy Tom*," he said, slamming down the phone.

On his second visit to Los Angeles, a week and a half later, John Kracht tracked down the rented car. It had not been from a small independent agency, as Carmichael had asserted, but from Budget-Rent-a-Car.

A copy of the car rental agreement showed a curious sequence of events, one that would prove extremely important in the case. Harry Carmichael had reserved the car in advance, at the weekend rate of $21.95 a day, for pickup on the afternoon of October 20, 1983.

The car presented to Harry Carmichael the evening of October 20 was returned for unspecified mechanical problems at 8:01 the following morning, just after the office opened. A new vehicle, a brown Ford Fairmont, was issued to Carmichael at 8:14 A.M.

It had 40,544 miles when it was rented. When it was returned the following morning, it had 41,213 miles, for a total of 669 miles in just 24 hours.

When Kracht returned to San Jose, he sent another police officer on a long trip. He had him drive from Gertrude McCabe's house to Harry Carmichael's apartment, then to Gertrude's house in San Jose, and back to the rental agency.

The distance was 667 miles. Kracht figured Tom used the other two miles driving around the block several times on Arroyo Way, making sure the coast was clear for him to kill Gertrude McCabe.

Chapter Thirteen

Sergeant John Kracht continued to call Jane every week. He kept asking her to file fraud charges so that a warrant could be issued for Tom's arrest. Jane was adamant in her refusal.

Kracht was still doing his best to find Tom and save him from his diamond-smuggling adversaries, or so Jane believed. She and Kracht had developed a cordial, if somewhat wary, friendship.

"So why do you keep going down to Los Angeles to harass the Carmichaels?" asked Jane one day.

The date was October 17, 1984, and Kracht was paying another visit to Jane in Sleepy Hollow shortly after a visit to Harry and his wife, Mary. This time he had come to examine more of her financial statements.

"Harry doesn't understand why you're asking all these questions about Tom, because he doesn't really understand what this has to do with my aunt's murder."

By this point Kracht believed that Harry had something to hide. As per Kracht's instructions, Jane had been taping her steady stream of phone conversations with Harry. Kracht wanted to know why they were in such constant contact.

"Well, what is Harry saying now?" Kracht asked. "Does he remember any more about October 21, 1983?"

"He recalls Tom spending Friday night with him. That would have been the twenty-first because he and Mary took the rental car back the next morning. They went to a Mexican dinner on Friday night. Tom flew back here Saturday morning."

In Tom's papers Kracht had already discovered a receipt for the Granada restaurant where Tom, Harry, and Mary had dined. It was dated October 20, the night before the murder. Harry had remembered the meal, but he conveniently remembered it on the wrong evening, creating a false alibi for Tom.

Kracht said nothing of this to Jane, however.

"Where does Mary work?" he asked.

"Lockheed, or PRW, one of those big defense manufacturers. She does assembly work. She doesn't work Saturday."

This was another interesting detail for Sergeant Kracht. The plastic gloves found at the crime scene were unusual, the sort that were used in high-tech assembly. Kracht was in the process of tracing their lot numbers. Could Tom have borrowed them from the Carmichael household?

"How much of that Friday did Tom spend with the Carmichaels?"

"Harry didn't say."

"Well, it certainly sets one wondering where he was," replied Kracht.

"He didn't kill Aunt Gert, if that's what you're suggesting," said Jane.

"So what do you think happened here?"

"I don't know," she said.

Kracht started to dig. "Well, somebody knows who killed her. What do you think?"

"I've given up speculating. I just want the animal caught, and Tom's not capable of killing anyone," said Jane.

Kracht was careful not to antagonize her. All he wanted was to plant the seed in her mind that, despite her feelings, there was a distinct possibility that O'Donnell had committed murder.

"Jane, four or five months ago you never would have believed you'd be sitting in the position you are right now."

"You're very right, John," she conceded. "Did you find any evidence at the crime scene that would point the finger at Tom?"

"No, I can't say that," said Kracht.

"See, John?"

"But I'd like to resolve this one way or another, this thing with Tom, and it seems like Harry should know."

"Sure, if Harry was with him that day," said Jane. "Didn't he say he went with him to San Diego?"

"Yes," said Kracht.

Kracht had found records for another car rental in Harry's name from October 9 to 10, two and a half weeks before the murder. More than one thousand miles had been registered on the odometer.

Kracht now believed that on the October 10 visit Tom had driven to San Jose to do one of two things. It was either a practice run, seeing how long it would take him to drive to San Jose and back, or he had actually intended to kill Gertrude that day and was frightened off.

Perhaps Tom had taken the dry run with Harry Carmichael.

"Well, you took my diaries or I could get to the bottom of this," said Jane.

Kracht knew very well what had been recorded in Jane's diaries, and he had kept them deliberately. If she was covering for Tom, he did not want her adding or subtracting anything that might create an alibi for him.

"Do you remember what Tom took on his trip to Harry's? Did he take a lot of luggage with him when he left?"

"No, I think he just took his carry-on. It's just a small blue carry-on with a lot of zippers."

"Do you know what he took in it?"

"Probably a clean shirt and a few toiletries because he only intended to stay the one night."

"Remember how he was dressed?"

"No."

"I guess what I'm saying is, did he take a change of clothes? Did he come back with the same stuff he went with?"

"As far as I know. He called me Friday night and said he had missed his plane and had taken Mary and Harry out to El Granada and he'd come home the next morning."

"And when did you write that down, about the phone call on Friday night?"

"Well, on Friday."

"Did you write the entry right after the phone call? That night?"

"That's what I do every day, just before going to bed."

"So what did he tell you about the trip? Did you discuss it?"

"Well, he didn't go into details. Did you find the rental car?"

"Uh, no," said Kracht. He explained that the Ford Fairmont had been traced to a Budget Rent-a-Car office in Texas. It had logged more than fifty thousand additional rental miles since the murder and was slated to be sold. Countless cleanings had obliterated any blood or physical evidence that might have been discovered.

Kracht diverted the conversation to Jane's finances. It was a sticky subject, but he wanted to ascertain how seriously Jane had been bilked.

"Do you think he left because, well, he had already drained your resources?"

Jane became defensive. "It must have been something horrendous, something much worse to make him leave. Because I'm going to get out of this financial mess the way Tom and I would have done it together."

"What are you going to have left after all this?"

Jane hadn't given it much thought. Her attorney, Jim Rohde, was handling her finances, and she was focused on finding Tom.

"If my house sells for the price I'm asking, I could probably clear a hundred and fifty thousand or more after paying off both mortgages."

Kracht changed the subject.

"Jane, what's Tom's blood type?"

"I don't know."

"Did Tom go to the doctor while he was here?"

"Other than the dentist, sure, for his foot. I'll give you the name."

"What's your blood type, Jane?"

"O."

"How do you feel about me looking into this aspect of the case, the forensic evidence?"

"What do you mean, about who murdered my aunt? I want to know who did it."

"What if something turned up about Tom?"

"Well, that's absurd. It's so impossible that I would like you to pursue it, so that I can prove to you that it's not true."

"Well, I'd like to– "

"John, let me put it this way. Anything you want to do, anything is fine. "

"I want to search your house."

"*Pardon* me?"

"I want to search your house."

"For *what*?"

"I don't know. Tom's bloody clothing."

"Come on, John. Certainly, you can do anything you want. In no way do I believe that Tom had anything to do with my aunt's death. No way. Absolutely no way. What would be the motive?"

"Money."

"He had money here. He had no way of knowing how much was in Gert's estate." Jane was calm and direct. She felt that Kracht was doing his job but could not have been more wrong about Tom O'Donnell.

"Tom didn't know anything about the will or the trust?"

"I didn't know, so how could Tom have known?"

After a moment Jane came back to the search of her house. "So, John, do you want to look around here for yourself?" she asked.

"No, I want to have Sergeant Harrington do it. I'd like them to look at the clothing that Tom left here, piece by piece. But I'd also like them to look through everything else."

"Why would I object?"

"Because you are in love with Tom–"

"As much as I love Tom, if he had anything to do with my aunt's death, you find him. I'll make sure he gets the death penalty."

On October 24, 1984, Sergeant Bud Harrington and his partner spent six hours going through drawers and closets in Jane's house, checking the car, basement, and tool room. They examined everything belonging to Tom and photographed hundreds of books on the shelf.

They carted off dozens of seemingly innocuous objects. When Jane was asked if a particular sweater belonged to her, she nodded yes and did not give it a second thought. She fed the two detectives lunch and thanked them for their time and effort on the case.

By November 3, 1984, Harry Carmichael thought he knew why John Kracht was so anxious to see him again. Tom O'Donnell had passed through Los Angeles the Friday before, and Harry was fearful that they had been spotted together.

Tom was so stupid sometimes, thought Harry. He had used a credit card in Al Alexander's name at a motel near Harry's house. When the manager found out the card was stolen, he confronted Tom. Harry had been helping Tom carry his luggage into his room at the time. Although Tom checked out immediately, Harry was sure the police had been notified. The manager had seen the two of them together and could offer a description.

Now Harry was worried that he was going to be dragged into the whole mess along with Tom. He was convinced that Kracht had found out and that was the reason for the visit.

So Harry decided to tell him the story about Tom's visit to LA.

It was a lucky break for Kracht. Since there was no warrant issued for Tom, the word had not filtered back to San Jose. John Kracht knew nothing about the credit card incident, but Harry did not know that.

"Have you heard any word from Tom?" asked Kracht.

"Tom gave me a ring last Friday, said he would be passing through Los Angeles that morning and asked me about my schedule. I told him I was free and picked him up about noon. We drove to the Westminster Café and had lunch, and Tom told me about his having to leave Jane in Sleepy Hollow."

Carmichael then explained the incident at the motel.

"Tom decided he didn't want to stay there," he said. "He asked me to drive him back to the airport, so I took him back and dropped him off at TWA."

"Did you ask where he was going?"

"He wouldn't say."

"Did you ask where he had come from?"

"Wouldn't tell me."

"Did you ask why he left town so suddenly?"

Harry recounted the familiar diamond-deal-gone-bad story. "Tom wouldn't give me any details. He was afraid of getting me involved. But you know he's always been on the fringe of the mining industry, gold, and diamonds. I can remember deals he made in Texas, Nevada, and Bolivia. Wouldn't be surprised if he's caught up again in something like that."

Tom had fled, he said, before his old enemies could abduct him. He had worked out some sort of compromise through an intermediary in Europe, but Jane's life was still in jeopardy and Tom could not risk being in contact with her.

"Did you tell him about my speaking with you?" asked Kracht.

"I did bring it up," said Harry.

"And what did Tom say?"

Despite his earlier candor, Harry quickly slipped back into lying. Tom had been furious when he found out Harry had let Kracht into his house and had spoken to him.

"Not much," answered Harry. "Something like, 'My God, they can't still be thinking I had anything to do with Jane's aunt. I thought that was over and done with a long time ago'. He didn't seem to dwell on it."

"What did he look like?" asked Kracht.

"More or less the same. Same old Tom."

"Harry, did seeing Tom jog your memory for details about his previous visits?"

"Actually, it did. Tom was down a half dozen times in 1983. He would just go off alone and come back the next day. He'd always take me and Mary out to dinner at our favorite place, the Granada Restaurant."

"Seems like you had trouble remembering that the last time we spoke," said Kracht.

"I don't want to cause any trouble for Tom," said Harry, "but you see, there is something I'm sure he'd rather I not talk about. Three or four years ago, Tom was going to have dinner with a certain lady and he was going to be quite late. I dropped him off at a high-rise on Olympic Boulevard. He told me he'd call Jane sometime that evening to keep her from calling my place. 'Better yet,' he said, 'why don't you call Jane and tell her I'm taking care of business somewhere?' Jane's a lovely lady, but she doesn't need to know about these things."

On another occasion Harry said he had asked his wife, Mary, to lie for Tom while he was visiting the same woman.

"So he is a womanizer, Tom O'Donnell?"

"A womanizer? Not in the vulgar sense of the word," said Harry. "They have to be attractive women, with some intelligence."

"So," asked Kracht, "the phone call from your apartment on Friday, October 21, 1983, at 10:31 PM, was made by whom?"

"I called Jane to reassure her that Tom was okay," said Harry. "He just had some business to manage and would be back in the morning."

Kracht's case against Tom O'Donnell was getting stronger. Jane Alexander had already told him that Tom himself had called on that night. Harry was lying to provide an alibi for his friend. Still, he let Harry continue to believe this was a chance to clear Tom's name.

"Do you know where he was that particular evening?"

"Las Vegas," said Harry. "I know, because I gave him directions."

"Do you remember what you told him?"

"More or less. Go straight up Hollywood Way here to Interstate 5, then north to 14, which runs into Interstate 15. Tom left that morning, I think it was Friday, about 8:15 or 8:30 AM. Came back the next morning about 5:30 or 6:00 AM. My wife Mary drove Tom to Burbank, then picked me up where

I had returned the car. We both went back to the airport and waited for the plane with Tom."

"Why did he ask you to rent the car?"

"He didn't want it on his credit card, because of Jane," said Harry. "He didn't want her to know he was gambling."

Kracht asked Harry if he believed Tom's story.

"There must be some truth in it, because if his intent is just to get rid of Jane, there are easier ways. I mean, why go to all this trouble? All you have to do to get rid of a woman is just leave."

"If you want my theory," Harry went on, "I think he has been involved in some bad business deal, but he has magnified the problem just a little bit to get out of the relationship with Jane. That's not a nice thing to say about a friend, is it? And that's no way to treat a lady."

Kracht thanked Harry Carmichael for his time. Kracht might never have known about Tom coming to town if not for Harry's concern about getting into trouble himself.

Tom O'Donnell had not disappeared. He had not fled to South Africa or some exotic locale. He was still in the U.S. of A. That meant, sooner or later, John Kracht was going to find him.

Chapter Fourteen

Two weeks later, Kracht again arrived at Jane's home in Sleepy Hollow. This time he was in a different mood. He turned on a tape recorder almost as soon as he came in the door. "Jane, I'm going to have to read you your Miranda rights."

"John, are you crazy?"

She reached over and switched the machine off. Kracht turned it on again.

"You have the right to remain silent–"

"John, you have no right! I'm going to call my attorney."

"I think that's a good idea. You will probably feel better with him here."

Checkmate, thought Jane. The idea of being taken to jail in San Jose made her feel physically ill.

"John, what's this all about?"

"Jane, you have to be honest with me."

"Of *course* I'm honest!"

Jane noticed the recorder was still turned on.

Kracht said he had been back in LA to see about Harry Carmichael. "Jane, you know about Tom being there, don't you?"

"What are you *talking* about?" Jane was stunned. "You mean, Harry has seen Tom and he didn't call me?"

"That's right, Jane."

"I can't believe it! At least I know he's alive," said Jane.

"Well, would you give me a warrant for credit card theft? That would help."

"John, that's ridiculous."

Kracht was adamant. "He had twelve thousand five hundred dollars of your money three months ago, and he is probably running short of cash about now. The fastest way to get him is with a warrant."

"No way. He's not a criminal. I won't have him charged with a felony."

Kracht decided to change tactics. "So did Sergeant Harrington tell you about the evidence he found here in the house?"

"I know he took several things, but he never mentioned any evidence."

"He found a Kleenex here that was an exact match to the one found on your aunt's body."

Jane was so startled, she nearly fell off the couch. "Where did he find it?"

"In one of your garments."

"Which garment?"

"A blue sweater, if I'm not mistaken."

"That's just *impossible!*"

Jane immediately went to her clothes closets. She came back to tell John he must have been referring to a green cable-knit sleeveless sweater that had belonged to Aunt Gert.

"That must have been it, John, something that came from the San Jose house. So your detectives are mistaken."

John nodded. "That sure got your adrenaline going," he said.

Jane felt like hitting him. Reading her Miranda rights, then bringing up the Kleenex. *What a sick joke to play*, she thought.

Several hours later, after providing Jane details of his trip to Harry's house, Kracht left for the drive back to San Jose. Jane called her attorney immediately after he left.

"He must think that Tom and I killed Aunt Gert," said Jane.

"Well, John has been here and talked to me about it," said Rohde.

"Really?" asked Jane.

"He's just doing his job. Why don't you cooperate with him and give him the warrant to find Tom?"

For the first time in her life, Jane hung up on her attorney.

As soon as she hung up on Rohde, Jane called Harry in a fury. She had spent countless hours fruitlessly pleading with Harry via long distance to learn anything about Tom's whereabouts. Harry had been in touch with Tom the entire time.

"Harry! Why didn't you tell me Tom was in Los Angeles?"

"Tom asked me not to tell you I saw him," he said. "You would have been on the first plane down."

"How does he look to you?"

"Well, he's dyed his gray hair a reddish brown. He looks tired."

"Why is Tom not calling me?"

"He is too upset, and he has a lot of problems he doesn't want to involve you with. He really is on the run."

For the first time since O'Donnell left, Jane had her first twinge of doubt about both Harry and Tom.

"If you hear from him again, will you ask him to call?"

"Yes."

He's lying, thought Jane.

"And have him call John Kracht, so we can get this mess cleared up."

John Kracht called Jane Alexander the next morning at eight-thirty.

"Did you speak to Harry Carmichael?" he asked.

"Of course."

"Did you tape the call?"

"Yes," said Jane.

"Would it be all right if I heard the tape?"

"No, it wouldn't," said Jane. "I just don't trust you anymore, not after yesterday." She began to cry. "Will you mail my diaries?"

Kracht said nothing.

Jane hung up on him.

For Thanksgiving 1984, Jane refused all invitations from friends and family. She knew she would be terrible company for anyone. She was consumed by the war between logic and emotion. She loved Tom and knew he was not a murderer, but then why had he left so suddenly, saying nothing, leaving a note that almost everyone else felt was ludicrous?

She had begun to realize that his hasty departure was not spontaneous, as he had told Hugh Fine on his way out the door. The ten thousand dollar loan had been in the works for weeks. She realized now how evasive Tom had been when she offered to type the Yurika marketing plan, which was actually his getaway letters. They had taken days to prepare. He had given careful consideration to the clothes he took and destroyed any record that might have allowed the authorities to trace his whereabouts.

She was troubled by every aspect of his departure. Most of all, didn't their love and commitment count for more than this? How could he appear in Los Angeles and still not give her the call she so desperately wanted? It was an impossible puzzle for Jane. She wondered how Tom could love her yet so callously leave her in such pain.

By the end of November, Jane was in a very deep depression. The daily calls from Vaux Toneff were becoming more and more crucial to her survival. It was the only thing that got her out of bed in the morning.

Vaux was very worried about her friend. Sometimes it took several phone calls to rouse Jane from bed. Several friends joined in the campaign, encouraging Jane to get dressed every day, to go shopping for food. But more and more she refused to go out. Increasingly, as her friends became convinced of Tom's guilt, she cut off contact with them.

John Kracht knew that Jane's son, Scott Alexander, had lived in the house with them, although he had left before the time of Gert's murder. The detective called on the twenty-four-year-old at his job in an auto parts store in Mill Valley.

Scott Alexander admitted that he had never much liked Tom O'Donnell. "He was friendly to me just to win me over," he said. "My friends and I called him Leech, because that's what he was doing, leeching off of Mom. He was spending her money, eating her food, and living in a nice home for free."

"Why did your mom put up with that?"

"Mom's never had any reason to doubt Tom's word. My dad trusted Tom, too. And my dad was a good judge of character, so Mom put a lot of faith in that."

Kracht was careful not to question Scott about his mother's possible knowledge of the McCabe killing. It was too delicate a subject.

"Do you think Tom O'Donnell is capable of murder?"

"I don't think he has a conscience," said Scott. "I really don't."

"Why do you say that?"

"Years ago," Scott said, "Before he lived with Mom, he told me a story about killing a man in the desert and burying him. I don't remember which desert, or who the man was, but Tom was bragging about it."

"Do you think that's true?" asked Kracht.

"Let me put it this way. Whether he killed the man in the desert or not, it would make no difference to his conscience. Tom O'Donnell doesn't have one. He is the kind of man who makes lists and does everything on them. Today I'm going to get up, wash the car, drop the clothes at the dry cleaner's, kill the old lady in San Jose, pick the dog up at the vet, and take Mom to dinner."

"Do you think he killed your aunt?"

"Don't you?"

On November 27, John Kracht called Jane Alexander and asked her to take a lie detector test.

"What the hell for?" asked Jane, panicking. "John, I've been telling the whole truth as I know it. I think the problem has been Harry Carmichael, who keeps changing his story."

"So why do you keep talking to Harry?"

Jane had no answer for that.

"Well, Jane, would you take the test?" asked Kracht.

In California, polygraph tests are not admissible in criminal cases, except in rare situations where the prosecution and defense stipulate an agreement beforehand. But polygraph exams are frequently used by law enforcement officials as a kind of litmus test. They help establish a witness's willingness to cooperate in an investigation and to test the limits of what a witness might know. If someone refuses to take a lie detector test, it can be considered a tacit acknowledgement that they have something to hide.

The test also helps an investigator to narrow his focus. Though the test is not admissible in court to *convict* a suspect, it helps an investigator to *eliminate* a suspect who passed the test.

John Kracht was trying to smoke out Jane Alexander. Did she know more than she was letting on? Why was she so passionate about keeping Tom O'Donnell out of legal trouble?

"Certainly I'll take a polygraph, John. But I'm such an emotional wreck, I'll probably flunk."

With her agreement, a test was scheduled to take place two days later at the nearby police station in San Anselmo. John Kracht would come up from San Jose.

Jane called Harry Carmichael afterward. He went ballistic.

"A *lie detector* test? Tell those damn cops to go to hell! Tell them you'll sue if they don't get off your back!"

"Harry, I really don't know why they're doing this to me, but I have nothing to hide."

"I'll tell you why they're doing this. They want to frame you for this murder, Jane. You know that, don't you? That's the only reason they ever do these things."

The following night, Jim Rohde called Jane to ask about a car insurance question. She told him about the polygraph.

"Jane! Why didn't you phone me immediately?"

"Jim, it seems I bother you every day about something."

"Nonsense, Jane," he said. "But there are a few things you need to know."

Rohde told her that no one in the San Anselmo police department was capable of administering the test. It should be done by an outside professional. All of the questions should be provided to her in advance. If they were not, she should refuse the test and call him immediately. He added that he wouldn't come with her. "Even if you wanted me there, I would not be allowed in the room with the exam," he said.

Jane was in tears after the conversation. She was sure she wouldn't pass.

George L. Johnson, who worked for the Bureau of Investigation in Sacramento, was chosen to administer the test. He had been giving polygraph exams for the state of California for seven years in countless homicide cases. He had been trained in the US Army, serving a one-year polygraph internship and then a three-year stint supervising other examiners. Before that, he had spent years as a criminal investigator in the military.

It is no coincidence that most examiners have extensive law enforcement and investigational experience. If a person is found to be deceptive, it is standard practice to confront them with the results and then move immediately into an interrogation. For this reason the polygraph examiner must be thoroughly briefed on the details of the case beforehand.

There is an art to teasing a confession out of someone taking a polygraph test. Johnson had spent as much as seven hours in a room with a suspect, as a murderer doled out a story to him in bits and pieces. Johnson met for several hours with Sergeant Kracht before the test with Jane Alexander.

Jane arrived fifteen minutes early for her 11:00 AM polygraph appointment. She met John Kracht and Peter Graves, and then waited most of an hour alone in a squad room. She finally called for an officer.

"If I have to wait any longer, I'm going to go home," she said.

"The test administrator is coming from a state agency in Sacramento," Graves told her anxiously. "He lost his way, but will be here soon."

Jane, realizing that her impulse to leave might indicate a sense of guilt, sat down again. She didn't know that the examiner had long been present in the next room.

Jane was finally led into a small interrogation room with a one-way mirror. John Kracht entered and asked her to sign a statement that she was taking the test "not under duress."

"What a joke, John," she said.

Kracht didn't respond. He read Jane her rights. He informed her that although the lie detector test was inadmissible as evidence in court, if she confessed to any element of the crime during the polygraph or subsequent interrogation, her statements could be used against her independent of the test.

So far the police were following every rule Jim Rohde had prescribed for a fair examination. But she was still far from comfortable.

Soon afterward George Johnson entered the room and introduced himself. He began questioning Jane about her knowledge of the crime scene. Johnson then asked personal questions, concerning her children, birthplace, education, and the like.

"But when you take the test itself, you will answer yes or no to every question. Nothing more, nothing less."

Johnson then explained how the machine worked. He would be testing three different physiological responses. A device similar to a standard EKG machine would record Jane's heart rate from a cuff on her upper arm. Two cords, which Jane thought looked like bungee cords, were placed around her chest and stomach to record her breathing. On her left hand, attached to two fingers, he strapped a pair of metal plates. A small electrical current flowing through her hand would be measured for galvanic skin resistance. In general, when a person is untruthful, a higher level of electrical resistance can be recorded.

"I'm going to be giving you five or six different tests, each lasting just four or five minutes. You can move in between them, but during the test you have to remain completely still."

Johnson then showed the questions to Jane, reading them aloud as she carefully examined the list. She confirmed that she understood them. This is an essential element of a successful polygraph exam. Lie detector tests got a bad name in the 1980s when a number of fly-by-night operators began administering tests to corporate employees, and the practice was largely outlawed for pre-employment screening in 1987. There is a simple reason for this. An unreviewed question, even one as simple as, "Do you like chocolate chip cookies?" will register extreme deception if the subject feels surprised on hearing it.

Jane was again reminded to be still as the first series began. "Did you inflict any of those injuries to your Aunt Gert in October 1983?"

"No," said Jane. Tears began running down her face. It seemed she could hardly breathe, let alone answer the question.

"Were you physically present in your Aunt Gert's house when she received any of those injuries?"

"No."

"Did you conspire with anyone to cause your Aunt Gert's death?"

"No."

By this time Jane was crying so much that mucus from her nose began to run uncontrollably into her mouth and down her chin. She couldn't use a tissue because the test didn't allow her to move. The situation was embarrassing. She was conscious of the fact that John Kracht was probably standing behind the mirror, watching her. Jane stuck her tongue out at the mirror.

"Do you know for sure who caused your Aunt Gert's death?"

"No."

"Before 1970, did you ever seriously want to kill or severely injure another person?"

"No."

Before 1970? Immediately on answering no, Jane remembered an incident that had taken place in December, 1966. While working late in the campaign office of William Penn Patrick, a Marin County Republican who had challenged Ronald Reagan that year in the governor's race, Jane had been attacked by a maniac with a switchblade. "This is a message for Mr. Patrick," he had said just before slashing her chest and then her ear.

The perpetrator was never caught, and Jane had buried the awful memory. But the question brought it all back—the blood running down her face, what her attacker looked like. Jane remembered she had fought her attacker off, suffering additional injuries in the process. Indeed, she *had* wanted to injure him.

After the series was finished, Jane told the test administrator she had made a mistake. "On which question?"

"The one about wanting to do bodily harm to someone."

After Jane explained, Johnson showed her that the machine had registered six off-the-chart spikes after that particular response. It was a somewhat theatrical gesture on Johnson's part, showing that her deceit was registered. But it is good practice to show an examinee when they have failed on a question.

Next, Johnson administered a series of control questions, including questions on which Jane was asked to lie. He then repeated the series of questions about Aunt Gert's murder, this time in a different order.

After three of these short exams Jane was finished. She had cried through the whole process, yet she showed no signs of deception.

John Kracht greeted her afterward. "Now we have to find Tom," he said.

"So I passed?"

"Of course, Jane," Kracht said with a smile.

Kracht and Sergeant Graves joined Jane at her house for coffee, where the three listened to tapes of calls to Harry Carmichael. Kracht tried to convince Jane that Carmichael was not to be trusted.

"Harry says that he called you on October 21, Jane, at 10:31 PM. Is that true?"

"No way," said Jane. "Absolutely not."

"Is it true that Tom visited Los Angeles five or six times in 1983?"

Jane quickly checked a photocopy of her diary that Kracht had provided to her.

"Wrong," she said. "Just twice. October 10 and 21."

"Carmichael says he came down for about three or four days the second time."

"Wrong again. He was gone only two nights."

Kracht's scope of suspicion had expanded to include Harry Carmichael. He might well have been involved in the actual murder itself, or in the planning or cover-up. He asked her to keep him up to date on what Harry told her.

Then he bore in on Tom. "Jane, I think Tom drove the rental car to San Jose, killed Gert, and returned to Harry Carmichael's in LA. I think his visit on October tenth was a practice run. On the second trip, the mileage on the rental is 669 miles, which is just about perfect for a round trip between San Jose and LA."

"You're kidding," said Jane.

John Kracht did not smile.

Later that evening, after telling friends she had passed the polygraph, she gave Harry Carmichael a call. "So I passed," she said. "Surprised?"

"Yeah. They'll get you sooner or later, Jane. You should never trust the police."

Jane was in no mood to take advice. She knew he had been dishonest with her before, and she was in a confrontational mood. "So why did you tell the police that you called me on the twenty-first when you know damn well you didn't?"

"I'm only saying this to help Tom, since they're out to frame him."

"But this is a homicide detective, Harry. You can't lie to a homicide detective."

"The hell I can't!"

"Harry, why are you doing this?"

"To keep them from barking up the wrong tree, Jane. I'm saving them time."

"Well, John Kracht thinks the mileage on that car rental, 669 miles—"

"Jane, how could you be so stupid? You know it's more than 740 miles from here to San Jose! He couldn't have driven up in that rental car."

How did he know it was 740 miles?

"Harry, why don't *you* take a polygraph test?"

"No way, not unless they hand me a court order."

Jane taped the conversation. At least the next time she saw Kracht, she could prove that Harry was the liar.

Chapter Fifteen

For many weeks, Duke had been chewing a hole in his leg, and Jane finally took him to the vet in early December.

"Has a child gone off to college?" he asked. "Has there been a death in the family?" He told Jane this sort of behavior was quite common when the dog loses a loved one. Jane knew the answer of course, but did not feel like explaining.

Even the dog is suffering, she thought. *When will this end?*

Jane had remained in frequent telephone conversation with John Mackey, Tom's friend in Las Vegas. Mackey felt certain that Tom would not let Christmas go by without some kind of communication.

"Tom knows how important this holiday is," said Mackey.

"I think Harry Carmichael might have some way of contacting Tom; maybe he even knows where he is. Do you think you can call Harry and get something more out of him?" Jane asked.

"Harry's coming up to Las Vegas next week, so I'll see what I can do, Jane."

Partly because she herself felt word from Tom was imminent, she wanted to stay in Sleepy Hollow through the holidays. She turned down invitations from three of her grown children. She did not want them to see her in such a depressed state.

She was ignoring the need to sell her home and continued to let Jim Rohde juggle the little money that was left in her bank accounts. Most days, after taking Duke on a long walk along the fire trail above her house, she would sink back onto the couch and watch soap operas. She had never watched them before, but she took comfort in the fact that Tom and Gert had both enjoyed them. Sleeping at night was almost impossible. She would lie awake for hours, wondering about Tom.

That December she watched the broadcast of a television miniseries, *Fatal Vision.* She remembered that Gert had been reading Joe McGinnis's book when the killer appeared at her door.

During the broadcast she composed a long letter to Tom. Despite mounting suspicions about his involvement, she still loved and missed him desperately. Like a mantra she repeated to herself, "We never had a harsh word or a bad moment between us. How can a man that kind and loving be a cold-blooded murderer?"

In longhand, on a yellow legal pad, she told Tom she loved him and that despite his pride he should contact her. Call collect, wherever you are, she wrote. Whatever the problem was, it could be worked out. And call John Kracht, the homicide detective, she continued. You need to clear your name, she wrote, and put an end to this torment for both of us.

She mailed the letter to Harry Carmichael in Los Angeles. Then she called and pleaded with him to pass it on to Tom.

On December 19, 1984, Harry called from Los Angeles. He had received her letter, and also a letter from Tom O'Donnell addressed to her. He had mailed it to her that day.

"Good God! Where is he?"

"The letter was postmarked from Antwerp, Belgium, on the sixth of December. He wrote a note to me asking to destroy the envelope."

"Don't you understand that the police will want to see it?"

"To hell with the police," said Harry.

Jane was a nervous wreck, anticipating Tom's letter. When it finally arrived on December 21, she was at the post office waiting for it.

It was written on a yellow legal pad, like the departure letter. Just seeing Tom's handwriting was an emotional shock. She began to cry. She said a silent prayer of thanks that Tom was all right, then hurried home to read it.

> My dearest Jane,
>
> I take pen in hand with great hesitation. My instincts tell me not to write, but I know how much the Christmas season means to you, and you always give so much—just one of your many wonderful traits. I am in the land of the living, am in good health, and sincerely hope you are of same. Could really use some of your excellent diet cooking right now!
>
> I certainly hope you have received funds from Aunt Gert's will by now, and that Jim Rohde was able to help you get long-term financing on the house, or the market has been right for selling. You deserve it. I'm also hoping that the San Jose police

have found the person responsible, as I know it would make you feel so much better.

Jane, I have a feeling you are spending much time and money to locate me, but as I asked in my letter to you when I left (and I was sincere) please do not waste your time and money. Two reasons. First of all, with my background and experience in traveling, I am not about to be found unless I want to be found. Secondly, every time you contact someone you are helping my opponents have another lead in finding me. They are not after the loss of their money, they just want revenge. The immediate future is not very bright—I did not show up for the prearranged meeting, primarily because it was in their backyard.

As Jane read, the details of the letter began to have a strange effect on her. She had practically memorized every word in Tom's departure letter. He had previously stated he had left with his old diamond-smuggling accomplices. But now he was writing of never having met them.

I felt strongly that had I gone, I would have lost my freedom for about 12 years. I sent a representative with specific instructions containing certain facts which I felt would help prevent the chances of you being involved any further, and I pray that you have not been harassed. I offered to meet them on neutral grounds, but at this point there seems to be no room for any type of negotiation. So I have now constructed a rather creative but conservative plan of action. I will have to go to work for many long months and maybe years, in one form or another, in my old business. They will take $250,000 as a payment. They have set the parameters of this asinine game, but I have decided that I am not going to be the "hunted" for the rest of my life, to hide in fear is not the way to live. It has always been said one must have a goal in life to succeed. Well now I finally really do have one. To earn $250,000 for them is not impossible—I did it before & much more, in fact. I had that much taken from me by trusted friends!

Jane, I'm sure you feel I was very wrong in leaving you the way I did and I've certainly had second thoughts, especially for the first month or so. But with what I've been through the last couple months, I now know that I did make the correct decision. I could not possibly wish this kind of life on someone I love. They took four years to find me—and they make their own rules for this world with absolutely no regard for local, state, or any countries' authorities. I know what you're thinking, that we could have slipped away one evening, including Duke. And done what? Live as I have lived for the past five months—a telephone rings— you jump—a door knock—you practically panic—even hearing someone walking in the hallway increases your heartbeat. Think of these conditions in terms of years and years. You and I being cooped up in a small dinky room—no lawns—no gardening, no space—without Duke—you with your claustrophobia— no contact with family and friends. Living under the above conditions would put an almost intolerable situation upon us, even with our strong love. I feel every bit as badly as you do that we are not together. It is the loneliest feeling in the world. You know me very well, and you truly understand that I could not just stand by seeing and having you suffer from the lack of the little and big things. I will be traveling almost every day from one city to another city, from one country to another. Jane, could you actually see yourself sitting in a hotel room, overseas, day after day? Moving to different hotels every couple weeks or months, and waiting alone, weeks at a time, for me to come back from each trip? No, my love. Considering all factors, you really are much better off this way.

Something was wrong here. On the one hand, Tom seemed to say he was still in danger, running for his life, and afraid of these who were pursuing him. On the other hand, these same people had offered Tom a contract and he was returning to the same smuggling profession. Was he in business with these people, or was he running from them?

I do not know how to end this epistle, Jane. I would like to say wait, but due to the unknown time factor involved, I have to ask that you start thinking of a life without me. This situation could consume up to four or five years, maybe more. And considering the double risk elements—one, working in my old business, and two, my opponent's desires—I think it quite logical you should consider it. I have not been with a woman since leaving you, but considering the time element we are facing, we should both give it serious thought. I'm not saying this is the end for us. I'm only trying to be practical, and it sounds ugly and horrible. I have, I do, and I will love you for years. We have experienced something so beautiful that only very, very few couples will ever have them in their lifetime. If memories are any indication of perfection, we have had thousands of them in a very short period of time.

I would wish you a very Merry Christmas, but as with me, I know it can't be too merry. Get out as much as you can and try to enjoy the season.

All my love,
TOM

P.S. With every dog I see or hear, I can't help but think of that beautiful big puppy dog of ours. Give him a hug & kiss for me. In fact, several of them.

P.S., P.S. I will make a bargain with you—you stop contacting people and trying to locate me, and I will drop a line every so often to let you know how I am doing. O.K. IT IS A DEAL.

P.S., P.S., P.S., Please give my regards & season's greetings to my friends—if I have any left! If not, they can be consoled by the fact that I am living a very lonely and miserable life each day. I do miss them.

Jane finished the letter and began to read it again. But the more she read, the less sense it made. How did Tom know she had been "contacting people and trying to locate me?" Why was he on the run from people with whom he had struck a bargain?

And then there was the callousness. Give the dog hugs and kisses, he says. *What about my money?* she thought. The ten thousand dollars he took when he left? The two hundred thousand dollars that he lost in the commodities market and the pending loss of her house?

The letter, she noticed, was in pristine condition. How could it have come from Antwerp, bouncing around in mailbags since December 6? Had she known, she would also have realized that the lined yellow 8 ½" by 11" paper on which the letter was written is not a standard size in Europe.

"Tom is probably only an hour away from you," Kracht had once told her. She tried to push the idea out of her mind.

Jane spent several hours lying on her bed. She had not cried in several weeks, but this time it was like a river—and it felt like a death had occurred. The phone rang repeatedly, with friends anxious to hear what Tom had said. But Jane was unable to answer it.

After a while she took Duke and went on a walk for several hours. It was so close to Christmas. She remembered all those years she had spent with her husband, Al, assembling toys for the six children, coming home from midnight mass. She could remember putting the packages under the tree, filling the stockings on the mantel.

She came home to find the Rohdes at her door.

"Would you like to come for Christmas dinner?"

"No," said Jane. "I would rather be alone this year."

The Rohdes did not ask about the letter from Tom, and Jane volunteered no information. For a half hour, until they left, Jane was unable to speak of Tom's letter. Her pride was devastated. The Rohdes had been right all along. So had other friends.

It was true, thought Jane. *Tom O'Donnell had left because he had taken her for all she was worth.*

John Kracht called in the late afternoon to wish her a Merry Christmas. Jane was touched by his thoughtfulness, and she told him about the letter. She told him she now thought that Tom had left because of the money.

Kracht did not respond. Instead he moved to a topic he had raised before. "Have you given any more thought to that Kleenex, Jane? I have some news."

"What is that?"

"The lipstick found on the Kleenex at your house matches the lipstick on the Kleenex at Gert's house."

"How can that be?"

"Jane, I was hoping you could tell me."

Jane remembered her visit to the San Jose lab in the summer. She had seen the lipstick on the Kleenex, the one that had been stuffed in Gert's mouth. Even she had thought it looked like her own.

In a flash Jane realized what had happened. She had kissed Tom goodbye, he had wiped the lipstick off his cheek, and stuffed the Kleenex in his pocket as he departed for LA.

Tom, like countless others, had tried to plan the perfect crime. But he suffered from chronic hay fever and always carried Kleenex in his pockets. He never gave them a second thought.

A kiss had contributed to his downfall.

"Jane, I want a warrant for Tom's arrest for fraud on the ten thousand dollars he took. It's the only way I can find him. What do you think?"

"John, I need just a little more time."

It was the first time Jane hadn't said no. Kracht knew he had her, and he didn't push.

"Merry Christmas, Jane. Get out and see some friends."

When she hung up, she called the Automobile Club and asked the mileage from Los Angeles to San Jose. Harry had told her Tom could not have killed Gertrude because the round trip was over seven hundred miles. The call confirmed what John Kracht had told her. The distance was within a few miles of that reported on the receipt of the car Tom had rented the day of Gertrude's murder.

Until that day Jane had clung to any fact she could find to reinforce her belief that the man she loved was not a murderer. Now she was looking at the facts objectively. Tom O'Donnell had bilked her out of more than two hundred thousand dollars and then murdered her Aunt Gert, hoping to replace the money through Gertrude's estate.

Jane, you've been a damn fool, she told herself.

Two hours later she visited Vaux and Bob Toneff. She kissed Bob on the cheek, wiped the lipstick off with a Kleenex, and showed it to him.

"Someday there will be a book about Tom and me," she said. "How do you like my title? *Kiss of Death.*"

The next morning, Christmas Day, was cold and rainy. Jane made breakfast for her son Scott and his girlfriend, then said good-bye as they left to spend the day elsewhere. It was too wet to take the dog for a walk. Jane made a fire for herself. She stared at her tiny Christmas tree.

While most of America was unwrapping Christmas presents, Jane Alexander wandered around her empty Sleepy Hollow home. Over and over the same thoughts haunted her. "I caused that poor old woman to be butchered by that monster. I slept with him for ten months after he killed her. He used my money to commit the crime; he used my money to escape."

She had heard, of course, of vulnerable widows being bilked by con men. Now Jane shook her head in disbelief and wondered how she could have been so naïve. She now realized that O'Donnell's charm and braggadocio were the machinations of a pathological liar. And murderer.

This is a day for work, she told herself.

Jane searched the house for every tube of lipstick she could find. She went through the cabinets and drawers in the bathrooms. She searched through purses and the pockets of coats and sweaters. She went through her car and even dust-covered suitcases in the basement.

She was determined to find the actual tube of lipstick that made the mark on the tissue that had been stuffed into Gertrude's mouth.

She laid three dozen tubes of lipstick on her bedspread. On a white sheet of cardboard, Jane made a streak of color using each tube. Beside each streak she recorded the color and the name of the manufacturer. Lilac Champagne from Revlon, Coming Up Roses from Revlon, Angora Pink by Helena Rubinstein, on through the entire collection. It was as if Jane was creating Exhibit A for the future trial of Tom O'Donnell—a trial in which the lipstick might prove his presence at the crime scene.

When John Kracht returned from Christmas vacation, Jane sent him the chart and the lipsticks. She agreed to swear out a warrant for the arrest of Tom O'Donnell on felony fraud charges for the theft of her ten thousand dollars.

Once Jane had filed charges, she realized what a master con man Tom was, effortlessly blending fact and fraud. His knowledge of foreign locales was voluminous. He had to have been there. His deftness and wealth of storytelling details won over even the most skeptical of listeners. And who cared if he embellished a bit?

She remembered once when a coin dealer called from New York. Tom had sold him one thousand five hundred dollars worth of Jane's gold sovereigns two years before. The dealer wanted to know if Tom was interested in reentering the market.

The dealer asked her, "Do you still have Rin Tin Tin?"

Jane thought he was speaking about some kind of stock holding, perhaps in tin.

"Rin Tin Tin?"

"Yes, the dog, the famous TV and movie dog."

Jane could only laugh, much to the coin dealer's bewilderment. Tom had told the man that their Duke was actually Rin Tin Tin, and that they made their livelihood traveling across the country attending shows and fairs.

The man seemed uninterested in the fact that the last incarnation of Rin Tin Tin was on a television show more that twenty-five years earlier.

"But ... why would he tell me a story like that?" asked the caller.

"He was trying to impress you," said Jane. "Tom wants to be remembered. And you did remember him, right?"

Jane now realized that Tom lived inside his own mythical adventures, that he believed his own lies as befits a compulsive liar. He used a glib tongue to ease his way into people's pocketbooks. She wasn't the only one who had been taken.

Jane Alexander emerged from her shell of depression. On that lonely Christmas, she found strength from a lifelong belief in justice, one that was instilled in her by her uncle, Judge Louis H. Ward. His voice rang in her ears as she vowed Tom O'Donnell would pay for what he had done to Gertrude McCabe.

A remarkable journey began. It would take her on a quest for justice that no one, least of all she, could ever have imagined. Along the way it would impact the lives of thousands of other victims and profoundly influence some of the basic tenets of the criminal justice system.

Chapter Sixteen

Despite Jane's new fervor and John Kracht's meticulous reconstruction of the case, the District Attorney in Santa Clara County still did not feel there was enough evidence to charge Tom O'Donnell with first-degree murder. There was no physical evidence, no eyewitness, nothing that put O'Donnell at the crime scene other than the suspicious mileage on a rental car from the Burbank airport.

Since no arrest warrant was forthcoming from his own prosecutors, Kracht had to turn to the District Attorney in Marin County, outside his jurisdiction, for help in the one crime he felt would stick: fraud. He had clear evidence that O'Donnell had stolen Jane's ten thousand dollars.

The Marin County DA. was skeptical, though. "We think of this as a boy-girl spat," was the response in the Marin County DA's office. "If this money is really so important to you, why did you wait so long to file fraud charges?"

"Well, I believed his letters at the time," replied Jane, steeling herself against the painful truth. "Doesn't it make any difference that he is the prime suspect in a murder?"

By early January 1985, Jane had gathered evidence of Tom's financial activities just prior to his departure in order to prove that he defrauded her. She obtained a copy of the five thousand dollar cashier's check Tom had endorsed, as well as the cash-out slip Tom had signed for fifty one hundred dollar bills from Jane's account.

These two transactions totaled more than enough for a felony fraud charge. As supporting evidence, Jane also collected records from the various bank accounts Tom had drained. The morning of his departure, Tom had withdrawn $425 from the Yurika business account, leaving $34.31. Four days before, he had left a balance of $5.98 in the Homestead account, all that was left of the two hundred thousand dollars borrowed against Jane's house.

While the Marin County DA mulled over their decision, John Kracht revealed to Jane some of O'Donnell's past. Although Tom had written of a

South African diamond-smuggling operation, and of former business associates who had served six-year jail terms, inquiries in South Africa revealed nothing remotely corresponding to Tom's story. O'Donnell's connection to the "Greenfire Trust" in Switzerland so far seemed equally specious.

But Tom was involved in a money-laundering operation, according to one Interpol report. In the late 1970s, more than three million dollars were stolen in a heist from a refinery in South Africa. An accomplice, who was caught with more than two hundred thousand dollars, named Tom O'Donnell as the individual who was to receive the balance of the money in Switzerland. The allegation did not sit well with Swiss authorities. Tom was declared persona non grata by the Swiss government and denied reentry as of June 20, 1980.

As Kracht revealed more details of his investigation, Jane learned how Tom had pulled off the murder. She found out that the car he rented on October 20, 1983, had suffered mechanical problems, forcing Tom to turn the vehicle in the following morning for a replacement. If not for the first rental car failure, the police would not have such a precise account of Tom's mileage on October 21, when he drove directly to Gertrude's house and back. Because of the mechanical problem, Tom was unable to leave Harry Carmichael's house at 3:00 AM as originally planned, according to Harry's interview with Kracht. Instead, Tom had to return to the car rental agency when they opened, then drive all morning to San Jose, commit the murder in the late afternoon, and drive back to LA.

Had the first rental not failed, Tom may well have driven the five hours to San Jose, killed Aunt Gert by mid-morning, and returned in time for an early evening flight back to Northern California. He would not have missed dinner with Jane, forcing him to call at 10:31 PM from Harry's house, making excuses for an uncharacteristic failure to phone earlier.

Tom was forced to lie about having dinner with Harry and his wife at the Granada Restaurant and to spend another evening at their home. A near-perfect murder plan had been foiled by an unlikely mechanical problem in a brand-new car.

Jane proceeded to look over her diary entries for the days following Tom's return from Southern California. In retrospect, they told a curious story.

When he came back on Saturday, October 22, he made a brief phone call to his cousin Jack O'Donnell in Montana and then went straight to bed and slept for more than five hours. This was highly unusual. He had only been away on a business trip, supposedly looking into the refinancing of the home mortgage loan.

Tom and Jane were scheduled to have a dinner with their friends, the Sullivan's. Jane had trouble waking him from his long nap.

The dinner with the Sullivan's went very late into the evening. Tom and Ed Sullivan drank an inordinate amount—in fact, Tom drank more than he ever had in Jane's presence. He was so drunk that Sandy and Jane half-dragged him to the car. When they returned to the house, Jane had to call Duke in order to rouse Tom from the car.

"Funny evening," Jane wrote in her diary.

In retrospect, Jane could see why Tom had been exhausted. He had driven twelve hours and expended an unexpected amount of physical and emotional energy in murdering an eighty-eight-year-old woman. He had a poker face to maintain and a dozen lies to keep straight. He had to worry that friends would remember the details of the lies that would support his alibi.

It had been a very long day.

Perhaps he drank so much that evening, Jane thought, out of either fear or remorse. Or was it a sense of relief? He thought that the Gertrude McCabe estate would cover the two hundred thousand dollar second mortgage that he had lost in speculation. He had bought another chapter in the good life he was living in Sleepy Hollow. He had bought time.

Jane was shocked to take her first close look at the way Tom had juggled the money in her various accounts around the time of Aunt Gert's murder. They were desperately short of cash in October 1983, and Jane would soon have discovered it. There was only $124.88 in the household account to cover the two thousand seven hundred dollar mortgage payment due October 24. Tom was anxious to get his hands on some money before Jane became aware of the problem. No wonder Tom had taken the check registry from Gert's house—he wanted to scrutinize her finances for any large sums in case that might be available soon. No wonder he had been so overjoyed a few days later to find the passbook with twenty thousand dollars in Jane's name. No wonder he was so anxious to get to the bank to withdraw that money—in fact, the whole reason he invented the need for a "vacation" was to have an excuse to access that account.

Tom had missed the October mortgage payment of two thousand seven hundred dollars. When Jane later spoke to the loan officer, she remembered Tom coming in to apologize about the missing payment.

"He showed me the newspaper clippings about your aunt's murder," said the clerk.

"When you have to live through something of this magnitude, you just put everything else aside," Tom had told her.

The loan officer was so touched by Tom's concern for Gertrude McCabe, she waived the late payment charge of $154.

How could she have trusted him so completely? Jane asked herself. Had she really been so blind? Yet she knew the answer. Tom had fooled everyone, not just her.

Tom O'Donnell was a world-class raconteur, as good as they get. He was the life of every party. He had a vast repertoire of stories ranging from palaces in Paris to adventure in "the bush." He had been a smuggler, a mercenary, and a treasure hunter. He bragged that he was known throughout Africa as "the Silver Fox," and that he was always "one step ahead of trouble." He would look straight at his wide-eyed audience and tell them tales of being chased and shot at, and of swimming rivers while breathing through reeds.

One of his best stories, she recalled bitterly, involved aiding British commandos in former Rhodesia and helping them dig for treasure during the 1970s war for independence. "Communist insurgents," said Tom, "had built a runway over a cache of buried gold, 'the Rhodesian treasure,'" as he explained. Tom and his friends dug beneath the tarmac, ducking every few minutes to avoid the sweep of a large searchlight across the airfield. After three nights of sweat and stealth, they finally recovered the treasure. The communists never even knew they were there.

People hardly ever questioned the story. When one did, Tom would dip into his pocket and drop a large coin on the table, booty won in the face of death.

As the news spread that she had filed charges against him, she learned how others had fallen prey to Tom's charm. Just two weeks after the murder of Gertrude McCabe, Tom had told Idaho friends Marti and Sherman Hart about a cache of silver bars buried under a railway track in Mexico. He asked the Harts to invest five thousand dollars in a venture to recover the loot. After Tom was gone, Marti Hart called Jane and added another wrinkle to the Mexico story. She had just read an identical tale in a copy of *True Treasure* magazine she found at a laundromat. The treasure had been discovered years earlier.

Then there was that trip to Denver. Tom showed her a castle—a replica of a medieval European castle—surrounded by lakes and set amid a hundred-acre park. It was like a fantasy of mad King Ludwig, sporting turrets, parapets, and crenellations.

"I bought this from the man who built it," Tom explained. "I lived here with my ex-wife, Kay, and my son. I had to sell it when a flood destroyed my first business."

Tom proceeded to drive up the driveway and greeted a young girl, the daughter of the current owner. Tom recounted the minute details of the house, including windows opening on metal dowels, the working on an unusual water-pumping system, even the idiosyncrasies of the small-gauge train that ran around the property. Tom knew everything. But now Jane remembered how deftly he had avoided the girl's offer to meet her parents.

In the aftermath of her realization, Jane learned from Tom's sister-in-law that Tom had worked years before as the castle's caretaker while the owner was away. The thirty rooms of the castle were locked away from him, the furniture draped in heavy cloth. Tom, Kay, and their baby son used the kitchen, maid's room, and a small sitting room.

He had never really made an honest living. If there was a chance to make a quick buck, Tom would opt for a risky wager rather than an honest wage. The stories he told were someone else's. He lived a vicarious life.

Jane was horrified, humiliated, distraught. Her resilience was rooted in her Irish temper. Anger would pull her out of her emotional morass.

Almost a month passed after Jane presented her request for fraud charges to the Marin County District Attorney's office. More than a half dozen times she was told that the warrant was "imminent."

Although they would not admit it at the time, the Marin County District Attorney's office was reluctant to spend the money. It was the richest county in California, the only one with a civic center and jail designed by Frank Lloyd Wright, and a fraud case for ten thousand dollars was not worth the money to prosecute.

Lobbying by John Kracht seemed to have little effect on the situation. All of Jane's friends—including the Rohdes and the Tonneffs—pleaded with Marin County authorities to take action.

Finally, a sympathetic Marin deputy DA named Josh Thomas issued a warrant for Tom's arrest on Tuesday, January 29, 1985. A judge set Tom's bail at fifty thousand dollars. But it was a tainted victory. The warrant was issued only for California and would not be entered into the national computer. If Tom were found outside the state, Marin would not extradite.

Jane was disgusted. *No wonder there are so many criminals walking the streets,* she thought. "If you need money for extradition, I'd be happy to give you a thousand dollars," she said in exasperation.

A few weeks earlier Jane had decided to call Harry Carmichael, as a month had passed since they last spoke. She promised herself prior to the conversation to control her anger and not let Harry know how radically her feelings had changed.

Mary Carmichael answered the phone. She seemed nervous when she found out it was Jane on the line.

"Harry's not home. He'll be back about nine or ten PM."

"Will you have him call when he gets back?"

"Sure."

"By the way, do you happen to have John Mackey's new phone number? The old one in Las Vegas was disconnected over a month ago."

Mary Carmichael said she knew nothing about it. Clearly she was anxious to get off the phone.

A few hours later, Harry phoned Jane, who avoided any mention of fraud, warrants, or murder. She asked Harry for Mackey's phone number so she might wish them a belated Merry Christmas.

"We had dinner with John and Debbie at Christmas, up in Vegas," said Harry. "We stayed in a hotel up there, and left on the twenty-sixth. They're doing well."

That offhand remark stuck in Jane's craw. If Mary had seen the Mackey's just a couple of weeks before in Las Vegas, how could she not have the phone number?

Suddenly Jane knew that Tom had been there, too.

"Thank you, Harry. For everything."

Jane called John Kracht and told him of her suspicions.

On February 9, Sergeant Lyle Rice of the San Jose Police Department went to Las Vegas to attend an academy reunion. Rice had been one of the many investigators who worked in the early days of the McCabe investigation, canvassing and searching for suspects and witnesses. He had met Tom and Jane when they visited the San Jose Crime Lab.

At Kracht's request, Rice enlisted two Las Vegas police officers to accompany him on a "courtesy call" to John Mackey's house.

"Gentlemen, may I help you?"

Sergeant Rice had never met John Mackey, but he did recognize the figure sitting behind him on the couch, sporting a new mustache and dyed brown hair. Tom O'Donnell was barefoot and watching television.

Rice told him he was under arrest.

"Is it all right if I put something on my feet?" asked Tom. Rice accompanied O'Donnell while he retrieved his shoes, and the Vegas officers handcuffed him.

At the Clark County jail, O'Donnell wasted no time in telling his guards he was being hunted by international gangsters and needed a private cell. To his surprise, his request was denied. For the first time in his life, Tom O'Donnell was somewhere where his tall tales were not welcome.

Chapter Seventeen

J ohn Kracht arrived in Las Vegas the next morning and went straight to the county jail, where he met Tom in his cell. Kracht set up a small tape recorder and then read Tom his Miranda rights.

"Does this interview have to be recorded?" asked Tom. "I'd prefer that it not be."

Kracht, true to form, did not reply or try to defend the procedure. He just left the recorder on. Tom spoke about what he felt were the misuse of lie detector tests and recorded police interviews. Kracht simply let Tom continue. He knew that the more his suspect said, the more likely he was to convince himself that talking to the detective was the right thing to do.

The seeds that Kracht had planted with Harry Carmichael were beginning to sprout. Kracht had pretended to buy all of Harry's lies, and Harry had told Tom that Kracht was not too bright and would be easy to snow. He was the con man's dream. One look at John Kracht and Tom saw what Harry meant. The tall, strapping, debonair O'Donnell could not imagine the smiling, unimposing detective who sat before him was much of a threat.

After a show of hesitation, Tom said he understood his rights and waived his right to an attorney. After all, he had nothing to hide.

"You paid a visit to your friend Harry Carmichael in early October 1983," Kracht began. "Around October tenth. Harry said you had some business. What were you doing down there?"

"I was trying to work out the refinancing of a home loan for Jane Alexander," said Tom. "I had contacted a local Merrill Lynch office, and they had directed me to the branch in San Diego."

Tom was only too eager to expound on the subject. He knew from Harry Carmichael that the detective had probably checked out the story. Tom said that the Merrill Lynch office had merely given him a form to be filled out and mailed back. Though he had been hopeful about the trip, he had not met with any loan officer.

Kracht nodded in agreement, as if the story reinforced what he already knew. Of course, he did not mention that October 10 was Columbus Day, and the Merrill Lynch offices were all closed. He also did not ask why Tom had gone to San Diego to retrieve a form he could have gotten at the branch in Marin County, five miles from his house.

"Tell me about your next trip to visit Harry, later that month," asked Kracht.

"Well, you see, in the early 1960s I used to gamble in Las Vegas quite a lot, and I was quite successful," said Tom. "I have a system, card counting that was shown to me by a friend in Omaha who invented it. It works pretty well if you're not afraid of getting caught, which sooner or later will happen," Tom said. "So I drove to Las Vegas. I came to make some money."

Tom had had many conversations with Harry Carmichael about the investigation into the McCabe murder. Jane had unwittingly relayed a great deal of information to Harry, and on that basis Tom and Harry had together worked out an alibi that took into account the mileage on the rental car.

"I didn't want Jane to know what I was doing in Las Vegas. Not that Jane would mind that I was gambling. But we were somewhat low on money at the time. That was why I flew to Harry's and then drove on from there to Vegas."

"How much money did you have with you?" asked Kracht.

"Five hundred and fifty dollars," said Tom.

"Did you rent a car?"

"I could have rented one on my own, but Jane would have seen the credit card receipt and suspected I had driven to Nevada. So Harry rented the car for me."

Tom explained how the car had worked poorly and that he had changed the car for another rental on the morning of October 21, soon after the agency opened. His story fit perfectly with what Kracht already knew.

With Kracht's encouragement, Tom spoke more freely as the interview wore on.

He spoke in detail of the progression of casinos he had visited while in town.

"I drove first to Sam's Town, just on the outside of the city," said Tom. "I then went to the Nevada Hotel Casino, where I had a sandwich for lunch. I didn't like the place, so I drove back to the center of town and bought some gas. I bought it with cash, so Jane wouldn't know I was there."

Tom was treading water with this particular alibi. He knew the trip to San Jose had been much longer than a trip to Las Vegas, so his alibi had to take into account more than one hundred fifty extra miles on the rental car odometer.

"I spent a lot of time driving up and down the strip, looking for a place to gamble. You get hunches and feelings about certain places," Tom said. Cruising the strip seemed to have taken much of his day.

Later in the afternoon, Tom went to Caesar's Palace.

"Where did you park?" asked Kracht.

"In the regular lot. I avoided the valet parking, I never go for that," said Tom.

He then played blackjack for a period of time. From Caesar's, Tom went on foot to various casinos in the center of the strip. He passed through the Dunes and the MGM Grand. He spent considerable time at the Frontier, where he admitted losing track of time during the evening. About two-thirds of the way through his visit to Las Vegas, having lost most of his money, he took a break to have a drink.

He claimed to have met a woman whose name he could not remember.

"She was white, blonde, about thirty-two years old, five feet six inches, I'd say. Not overweight, about a hundred twenty-five pounds. She was dressed in a white ruffled long-sleeved blouse with black slacks. I bought her a drink and we spoke, maybe, three-quarters of an hour."

What Tom described was the standard uniform for women in a casino job. It was an alibi, yes, but Tom was careful to create such a general description that it could never be traced to anyone in particular.

"Did you call any other person in Vegas? John Mackey?"

"No," said Tom. "I didn't want word to get back to Jane."

"At what point did you make a call to Jane?" asked Kracht.

"If I did, I paid in cash. I didn't want her to know where I was."

Although Tom had rehearsed his alibi, he had left out the 10:31 PM call he made from Harry's house on the evening of the twenty-first. This was one crucial detail that Harry had forgotten to convey to Tom.

"What time did you leave Las Vegas?"

"I think between midnight and one AM," said Tom.

"The morning of the twenty-second?"

"That's right."

Tom followed the same route back from Vegas, he said. But he had made a wrong turn at one point.

"Could you show me the route on a map?" asked Kracht.

"Certainly," said Tom.

Two months before, with Harry's help, Tom had worked out a route to and from Las Vegas that would approximate the distance to and from San Jose. They had decided upon a "detour" which would account for the extra miles.

"On my way back, I took a wrong turn off of Route 58 here at Four Corners," Tom said. "I drove about forty or fifty files north on US 395, and when I realized I was going in the wrong direction, I turned back."

"Do you remember where you turned back?"

Tom remembered the name of the town he and Harry had decided on.

"Atolia," said Tom, marking the town on the map. "Right here."

It was a name that would haunt Tom many years later. Atolia was a ghost town. When a San Jose police detective later drove the route, he would find that the town was unmarked. There was no filling station, no overpass, and no sign that a town had ever been there. Nothing but tumbleweeds.

Worse still, Tom's story gave him too many miles on the odometer. Even if he had not cruised the strip in Las Vegas for hours, he would have clocked 687.4 miles for a round trip.

"Well, I think that just about clears everything up," said John Kracht. "Would you mind signing a search warrant for your possessions back at John Mackey's house?"

"No problem," said Tom. His relief was palpable. He knew there was nothing incriminating at the Mackeys'.

Tom had no idea what John Kracht had just done to him.

"Jane's going to go nuts, isn't she? I mean, she must have just lost her mind," said John Mackey.

John and Debbie Mackey were meeting Sergeant Kracht for the first time. Having been given authority to search through Tom's belongings, Kracht wanted to make sure the Mackeys had not disturbed anything in Tom's room.

"This whole thing is just crazy," said Mackey. "I mean, Jane let Tom invest her money, gold and silver, and the market collapsed. Tom felt very bad about it, but she knew the risks. So she shouldn't be pressing a case."

"Well, the warrant only covers the money that Tom took in the last twelve hours he was there."

"Oh," said John Mackey. "I didn't know that."

If the Mackeys knew few of the details of the warrant, they were even more in the dark about the ongoing homicide investigation. They had been out of touch with Tom in 1983 when the McCabe murder took place. Although they were certain he would never have been involved in such a crime, they were forthcoming in speaking to the detective.

Yes, Tom had flown out to Las Vegas the night he left Jane Alexander the previous August. Yes, he said he was being hounded by a ring of international diamond smugglers. Yes, Tom had been living with them, off and on, for several of the past few months. Yes, they had covered for him when Jane called, because that was what Tom wanted them to do.

Tom had spoken to them about the McCabe murder investigation and had said he was in trouble because he had rented a car to go to Vegas that day. He was concerned about being hit with a false murder charge. He had even asked the Mackeys' help in finding the blonde with whom he had had a conversation that night in the Frontier casino.

When Sergeant Kracht searched Tom's room, he quickly found the .32 revolver taken from Jane's house. Kracht also recovered twenty-eight credit, gas, and department store charge cards. Eight were in Tom's name, twenty in the name of Jane's late husband, Alfred Alexander.

Tom also had Al Alexander's Social Security card, birth certificate, and driver's license. When necessary, he was still passing himself off as Jane's late husband. He also had a Yurika Foods distributor ID and a National Republican Senatorial Committee card.

John Mackey had said Tom was flat broke and could not afford a lawyer. When Kracht searched his wallet, he found Tom had thirty dollars in cash.

Kracht also recovered Tom's passports, dating back to the mid-1970s. Indeed, he was very well-traveled. There were more than a dozen entries from South Africa, with excursions into Zambia, Angola, Botswana, Malawi, Ghana, and Zaire. He had been to Brazil and Bolivia, Sweden, Saudi Arabia, and Hong Kong. He had made more than twenty-five visits to London.

His last visit there was in the autumn of 1984, a few weeks after leaving Jane. He spent about six weeks in England and the continent, presumably living off the twelve thousand dollars he had taken.

"Without his address book, he had a very difficult time connecting to his old currency-smuggling contacts," said Mackey. "He said that was the worst mistake he made."

John Kracht telephoned Jane on Monday morning, February 11. She expected him to say that Tom O'Donnell was on his was to California. He was not.

"Nevada can't hold Tom unless they receive an extradition request from Marin County within the next forty-eight hours. If nothing happens, Tom is gonna walk."

"What do you mean, he's gonna walk? He'll be in Mexico in an hour."

"Well, there is nothing more I can do here," said Kracht. "I have no authority."

Chapter Seventeen

Jane spent a furious day calling on every legal and political connection she had. The local DA was not answering her calls, or anyone else's.

Jane and John Kracht spoke late in the day, as the detective was about to take a flight back to San Jose. "If the law refuses to act, then I'm coming to Vegas to take care of Tom myself," Jane said.

John Kracht did not know what to make of this. Was Jane implying that she wanted to kill Tom O'Donnell? Kracht called Jim Rohde, Jane's attorney, and asked him to cool her off. If she committed a crime, it would be Kracht's duty as an officer of the law to make sure she paid the price.

"Never, never talk to a homicide detective like that again," Rohde told Jane.

Finally, Jane was able to reach the California attorney general in Sacramento.

"He will be able to see you two weeks from tomorrow," Jane was told.

The hell with this, thought Jane.

That evening she decided to go to Vegas.

Jane rushed to San Francisco airport the next morning, only to find out it was fogged in. She was paged while waiting for an early afternoon flight. "Jane Alexander, please call the courtesy services desk." It was a message to call John Kracht in San Jose. She ignored it. Of course Kracht wouldn't want her to go to Vegas. She would call him when she got there.

She arrived at the Clark County jail at three o'clock and was denied entry to see Tom. She was told there was a rule about prisoners having just one visitor a week, and that Mr. O'Donnell had already had a guest. What Jane didn't know was that John Kracht had arranged this ruse with the Las Vegas jail. Under no circumstances would they allow Jane Alexander to visit Tom. When Jane finally called Kracht a few minutes later by telephone, he was very upset.

"You shouldn't be there, Jane!"

"John, what am I supposed to do?" said Jane. "Tom has an extradition hearing tomorrow. He is going to get out in a day unless something happens, and do you think you'll ever get your hands on him again?"

"There's nothing I can do," he said.

"Well, there's something I can do," said Jane. "I'm going to get him to waive extradition and come to California voluntarily. I need to talk to John Mackey. He's not home, but I know he's at the bar where his wife is a bartender. That's where he hangs out. What's the name of it?"

Kracht reluctantly told her. Within minutes Jane was in a cab heading downtown.

"Lady, you sure you want to go to that place?" asked the driver.

"Why?" asked Jane.

"Well, it isn't in a very nice neighborhood. There was even a murder there last year."

At that point Jane could relish the irony of the situation. She was now familiar with the concept of murder.

The bar where Debbie Mackey worked was in a dilapidated area of the city. Jane walked in and tapped John Mackey on the shoulder. He was so shocked that when he tried to stand he stumbled, and both he and the bar stool went over.

Debbie called out from behind the counter. "Jane! What are you drinking?"

"Jack Daniel's with a splash," said Jane.

"You got it," said Debbie.

John Mackey felt he had to tell the whole story of Tom's arrival on the night he had left Jane. Harry Carmichael had driven from Southern California to meet Tom. Although Jane could hardly forget the many nights she had pleaded with both of them for any word from Tom, she kept silent. She had a job to do.

She also had a tape recorder in her purse.

"Tom said something about being in trouble then, something about an international arrest warrant," said Mackey. "You have to know he was really upset about having to leave you, and about your money, too."

Yeah, right, thought Jane. *And you bought it the way I did.*

John Mackey said that he often tried to convince Tom to call Jane and alleviate her worry. "He wouldn't listen," said Mackey. "I don't believe his story a hundred percent, but what could I do?"

"It's not the money I really care about," said Jane, fighting an urge to tell Mackey off. "I'm more worried about Tom being able to clear up this matter about my aunt's murder. Do you think he is going to fight extradition to California?"

"I don't know, Jane," Mackey said. "Tom is broke and can't afford an attorney. He has sought a public defender, but because he is on a California warrant, he was told he could not get one until he was extradited."

So Tom has not even seen a lawyer yet, thought Jane.

Mackey continued. "I called a lawyer from the ACLU. They said these sorts of extradition procedures can take three months or more to fight. Do you think Tom would last three months in prison? I don't know. I don't know what to do."

Jane began to see an opportunity. Tom was so ignorant of the law, she might just be able to maneuver him onto a plane to California. In this city of poker-faced gamblers, Jane decided to bluff.

"I think I could forgive Tom," Jane said, "if he would only take a polygraph exam about my aunt's murder. I would drop all these other charges. I just want him to clear up this matter and get that case solved."

"I think Tom wants to clear it up, too."

Jane could see that Mackey was getting drunker as the evening wore on. She had to maintain control of her faculties, although she continued to let her glass be filled. When Mackey was distracted or went to the bathroom, she used the dim light in the bar to switch her glass with another table or pour drinks into the nearby aquarium. She wondered if the Jack Daniel's was poisoning the poor fish.

Mackey informed Jane that Tom was calling him collect at the bar at six o'clock to find out if Mackey had been able to secure a lawyer. Jane knew that Harry Carmichael prided himself as a curbside lawyer, and Mackey confirmed that he had been counseling Tom by phone. If Jane had any hope of convincing Tom to waive extradition, she would have to first convince Harry.

But Harry would never trust her.

"I tell you what," said Mackey. "I think it's a good idea if Tom just went back to California. I'll call Harry and check with him."

Jane felt like her heart would stop. "Please, John, don't tell Harry I am here in Vegas."

"No problem. Do you want to listen in on the conversation?"

Jane stood next to Mackey and listened in on the pay phone as he explained how he had failed to obtain free legal advice and that Tom could be in jail for months awaiting the outcome of the extradition.

Best of all, John Mackey represented the whole strategy as his own. "I am sure Tom and I could convince Jane to drop the ten thousand dollar charges," he told Harry. "All she cares about is her aunt."

A few minutes later, Tom called Harry collect from jail. Harry relayed to Tom his conversation with Mackey, and urged Tom to voluntarily return to California, where he could get free legal help.

Tom told Harry he would sleep on it.

Jane made the Mackeys an offer they couldn't refuse. Instead of staying at a hotel room, she offered to buy them dinner if they put her up in Tom's room for the night. They readily agreed.

She spent the night rummaging through Tom's belongings for anything that could be used in court against him. The only thing she found of any interest was a Help Wanted ad that he had circled in the local newspaper, seeking male escorts. He was obviously planning to spread his charms around, this time on an hourly basis.

The next morning Jane slipped discreetly into the back of the courtroom while Tom was brought in, chained to a dozen other prisoners and wearing an orange jail jumpsuit. She scarcely recognized him. His hair was a rusty brown, and he was drawn and thin. He did not spot Jane or Mackey in the crowded courtroom.

After going through a number of other cases, the judge finally asked Tom to stand up.

"Are you going to waive extradition, and return of your own free will to the state of California?"

Jane held her breath.

"Yes," said Tom.

The judge raised his eyebrows. "Do you understand what you are doing in agreeing to be extradited?" asked the judge.

"Yes, your Honor, I do."

The clerk then passed some papers to Tom for his signature. When he had signed and returned the papers to the judge, Jane quietly walked up and took the seat directly across the aisle from Tom.

Their eyes met.

He knew without a word being said that he'd been had. She saw the hatred in his eyes.

Jane knew then, without a question of a doubt, that he had murdered Gertrude McCabe.

Chapter Eighteen

It had taken sixteen months, but the principal suspect in the Gertrude McCabe murder was finally behind bars. Detective John Kracht had all but solved the case. It was only a circumstantial case against Tom O'Donnell, but with a few more loose ends tied up, he believed, the investigation could be presented to the Santa Clara County District Attorney for prosecution.

Meanwhile, the fraud charges pending in Marin County would buy some time. Fortunately for Jane, the deputy district attorney assigned to the fraud case saw it as much more than a "boy-girl spat." "I'm trying to widen the scope of the accusation against Tom O'Donnell," Josh Thomas told her. "I want to charge him not only with the ten thousand dollars he left with last August, but with the two hundred thousand dollar second mortgage you took out on the strength of his phony Swiss trust."

Thomas had already begun working on the O'Donnell case before meeting Jane. He had a good sense of humor and a mind for details. Most important, he could see how Tom O'Donnell's motives for fraud were also his motives for murder. Thomas had been in contact with the detectives in San Jose and was working quickly to prepare for the preliminary hearing in Marin County, when a judge would decide if the fraud case was worth taking to trial.

"Tom could spend years in prison on these charges alone," said Thomas. "But it means that you will have to take the stand, Jane, and tell precisely how he fooled you for so long. Are you ready for that?"

Jane could not believe her good luck. She wanted to tell the world what Tom had done. "I can hardly wait," she said.

Meanwhile, she was worried that Tom was going to post the bail of fifty thousand dollars. When his nephew Jack had called from Montana just a few weeks before, Jane had said nothing about Tom being in the Las Vegas jail. She did not want him springing his uncle. "I'll call you when I get back from my Vegas vacation," Jane had told him.

She need not have worried about Jack O'Donnell. When she spoke to him later, she found out that he had been trying for years to get his uncle to repay fifteen thousand dollars Jack had invested with him long before. In the late 1970s, Tom had been trying to promote US sales of African "picture rocks," pieces of sedimentary rock that, when cut and polished, looked like desert landscapes. Tom hoped to start a picture rock fad and grow rich from it. He had borrowed seed money from his nephew, yet the business went nowhere.

For Jack and Bonnie O'Donnell, who lived in rural Montana, fifteen thousand dollars was an enormous sum of money to lose. By the fall of 1983, Jack had needed a cash infusion to keep up payments on a second property. He had called Tom in the hope that he could return at least part of their investment; Tom promised seven thousand five hundred dollars by August, 1984. But he never sent anything. Jack and Bonnie O'Donnell lost their second property.

"I have a feeling Tom probably just put that money in his pocket," Jack said.

Jane, eager to help with the fraud investigation, knew that Tom had dated a number of women over the years, and for the first time she wondered if their experiences had been anything like hers. Jane had not spoken to Dorothy Von Beroldingen, a prominent San Francisco lawyer and politician, in more than ten years. But she knew that Tom had dated her in the late 1960s and early 1970s, and the two had had a significant falling out. Jane phoned Von Beroldingen in her chambers. She had since become a San Francisco municipal court judge.

"Jane," she was told, "Tom O'Donnell took me for more than eighty thousand dollars."

"Really?"

"I'd be happy to talk with you about it," she said. "I think Tom cured me of men forever!"

I know just what you mean, thought Jane.

Dorothy Von Beroldingen, then seventy years old, had had an extraordinary career in law and San Francisco politics. After eighteen years of a solo law practice handling business law, she had begun a career in politics in 1963, when she chaired a bond campaign for better street lighting. Impressed by her strong leadership ability, San Francisco Mayer John F. Shelley appointed her to the San Francisco Board of Supervisors—the third woman in history to serve on that body. While still managing her private law practice, she was reelected by voters for two more terms. Von Beroldingen became the first woman to chair the board's finance and budget committee, the third highest-ranking elected position in the city. For close to ten years, she was responsible for the fiscal health of the city, keeping the budgets balanced through her entire tenure.

At the height of her career, she had the misfortune to fall in love with Tom O'Donnell.

Jane and Dorothy met over cocktails. Jane explained the fraud case against O'Donnell, and asked Dorothy if she minded having their conversation about him taped. "It could be useful for the district attorney," she said.

"No trouble at all," said Dorothy.

The two women agreed that Tom was an excellent partner in most ways. He was intelligent, fun and kind, not to mention a considerate romantic partner, always attentive in the flower and wine department. Tom had excellent manners and knew how to act in social situations. The two women joked about how he dressed: always immaculate, in tailor-made suits and shirts.

"When did you meet Tom O'Donnell?" asked Jane.

"I met Tom in 1966, when he was working for William Penn Patrick in Holiday Magic."

"Do you remember his position with the company?"

"I think his card said he was assistant to the chairman, and he told people that he was international sales manger."

At the time Dorothy Von Beroldingen was the chief counsel to the company. She remembered Tom closeted in meetings with the CEO, attending a lot of sales meetings around the country. But Tom's specific duties were somewhat vague, and he lasted only a year and a half with the company. By that point he had moved in with Dorothy, and was absorbed by his own business enterprises.

"I'm trying to determine how he ever supported himself after that. Did he ever earn an honest dollar after Holiday Magic?"

"Not that I know of," said Dorothy.

"And did you support him?" asked Jane.

"Well, I paid the rent. I paid for the food, paid for his tennis lessons, and bought his clothes."

"Dorothy, you're as bad as I was," said Jane. "Except he no longer needed tennis lessons by the time he lived with me."

The two women shared a hearty laugh.

Von Beroldingen had paid more than incidental expenses. She had invested in Tom's own cosmetics business, as well as in his various gold and diamond ventures. She gave him between ten and fifteen thousand dollars for his Telecator project, an early attempt to match potential real estate customers to buyers using a primitive computer system. Tom traveled a great deal, visiting Africa on a regular basis. He was apparently working hard to make good on several old debts. But none of Tom's ventures seemed to yield an independent income.

Tom enjoyed dating a well-to-do woman with celebrity status. Von Beroldingen's position on the board of supervisors assured her frequent headlines, and gave Tom the chance to socialize with some of the most prominent figures in the city. Dorothy and Tom occasionally double-dated with Dianne Feinstein and her husband. Feinstein was also on the board of supervisors. She would later become mayor of San Francisco and senator from California.

By 1970 Tom's business debts amounted to more than sixty thousand dollars, but the financial setbacks were not a major issue in the relationship— after all, the two were deeply in love. They planned to be married on November 15, 1970.

Two months before that, Tom went to Africa to put together a diamond deal. Dorothy knew she would not hear from him for some time, as he would be "in the bush" and far from normal communications. As the day of the wedding approached, however, she began to grow worried. November passed with no word from Tom. Dorothy was frantic; she was sure something terrible had happened.

But she held out hope. Tom had borrowed a number of her credit cards, and various charges in hotels (the Dorchester in London, the Meurice in Paris, the President's Hotel in Johannesburg) still trickled in from Tom's stays of a few weeks before. She could not cancel the cards, for fear Tom might need them in an emergency. There must be some explanation, she reasoned, for Tom's silence.

Von Beroldingen sought help from a mutual friend, who had an extra key to the post office box Tom used for his business correspondence. Perhaps she would find some clue to his disappearance.

Dorothy found the box filled with personal letters.

"Jane, I opened them and they were from at least ten women in various ports of call. All of them expected him to arrive to marry them, and all of them had supported him at various time when he was in town."

Von Beroldingen was stunned. She telephoned one woman in South Africa, a woman named Marie, who claimed to be Tom's secretary. Marie told her Tom was in Lisbon, Portugal, and would be back in a few weeks. Sure enough, a few weeks later Tom began calling Dorothy—collect, of course. By this point Dorothy had refused to speak with him.

"Then began the stream of letters," said Dorothy. "'My dearest love, how can you do this to me? I can explain everything.' I ignored them. And I canceled the credit cards."

"I did not come forward and press charges against him …"

Dorothy did not finish her sentence. It was clear that she regretted not putting an end to Tom's scheming, which had caused problems for so many other women.

"Did you know he got to Carnell Rogers?"

"No," said Jane.

Carnell Rogers was an older African-American woman who had cleaned in the Von Beroldingen home for many years. Tom had befriended her. When Rogers received a ten thousand dollar life insurance payment on the death of her husband in 1968, she asked him how to invest it. Tom said he could give her twice the interest she could earn in a bank.

"So he ran off with her ten thousand dollars as well," said Dorothy, "and never repaid it as far as I know. Carnell was loyal for many years, and was sure he would come back with it. When I had to get rid of Tom's clothes, it was Carnell who came and took them from my apartment. She was holding them for Tom. Eventually, he sent a friend to her to retrieve them."

Jane was shocked to hear this. Neither of them knew if Rogers was still alive, or if she might be able to testify.

"I finally realized Tom isn't immoral, he's amoral," said Dorothy. "He can lie as easily and convincingly as anyone you might ever meet. He has the most persuasive manner in the world, and totally lacks a conscience."

"If I told you Tom was the prime suspect in the murder of my aunt in San Jose, would that shock you?"

Dorothy did not hesitate. "No," she said. "Where money is concerned, Tom would stop at nothing."

"Would you testify about your experience with Tom?"

"I would be happy to help you in any way. He's a one-man plague, and the entire human race should be protected against him. Please tell the DA I will do whatever I can."

In the course of his investigation, John Kracht had listened to tapes of many of the telephone conversations that Jane made in the months after Tom had left. Many of Jane's calls to friends and relatives of Tom's were of no interest, but there was one notable exception. Shortly after Tom had left, Jane had called Jack O'Donnell in Montana to find out if he had heard any word from his uncle. Jack's wife, Bonnie, spoke to Jane.

"I've only spoken to Tom once in the past year and a half, just after your aunt died," said Bonnie. "I was badgering him about the money he owed us, and he said that your aunt's estate would provide quite a bit of money, more than enough to pay back Jack and me."

"Do you remember what day you spoke with him?" Jane had the complete telephone records in front of her, and saw that there had only been a handful of calls through the fall of 1983.

"Well, I don't know the date. But I know it must have been Saturday, because I wasn't taking care of any kids that day in my babysitting business. And Jack was out, or I would have passed the phone to him."

Jane, who at the time still believed in Tom's innocence, corrected her brusquely. She had the telephone records in front of her, and there had been only one call on a Saturday. "Well, it can't have been that telephone call on Saturday, October 22, because Tom had just come back from Los Angeles. We didn't even know she was murdered until the following day."

Jane, listen to what Bonnie is saying, Kracht thought. Tom was telling her about the murder before he should have known!

Kracht called Bonnie O'Donnell and confirmed her account. Although it would be difficult to prove after a year and a half that Bonnie had indeed spoken to Tom on a specific day, it was still a strong piece of circumstantial evidence.

Kracht asked Jane to call Bonnie back and hear for herself.

"Of course I remember that phone call," Bonnie said. "I remember it because I didn't think that your aunt's death should have anything to do with Tom paying off his debts. I thought that was real strange."

"Are you sure he was calling from my house?" asked Jane.

"Yes, I'm pretty sure he told me he was," said Bonnie.

"And are you sure it was a Saturday?" asked Jane. "Are you sure that Jack had not called Tom first?"

"Positive. I hardly know Tom, and I would not have spoken to him unless Jack wasn't home," said Bonnie.

"Did you talk to him at any other time?"

"It was the only conversation I had with him that year," Bonnie said. "And when I asked him about the money he owed us, he said your aunt's estate would take about ten months to clear, and that he would send us seven thousand five hundred dollars plus interest by August 1984. I relayed all of that to Jack. And I was surprised by how energetic and excited Tom was. I mean, he was really happy he was going to be getting the money."

Hearing this from Bonnie O'Donnell, Jane felt a familiar wave of anger. *Tom, you bastard, to think you were happy the day after you murdered Aunt Gert!* But Jane was also excited. She knew the case against Tom was being built brick by brick and that the weight of all this evidence would eventually crush him.

Just as Jane had kept a detailed diary, she had carefully filed away everything relating to her aunt's murder. She now threw herself into a review of the material. On reading a letter from her daughter-in-law, Rocky (Roxanne) Alexander, she puzzled over one particular passage: "I remember Tom calling Bill and me that Sunday or Monday night to say that Gert had been murdered. He said she had been stabbed and garroted."

"Garroted"? Why had Rocky used that term in her letter? Had Tom used the word garroted when he told them about Gert's death? Jane looked the word up in her dictionary:

GARROTE: A mode of execution by strangulation with an iron collar tightened by a screw.

That was exactly what had happened to Aunt Gert. But how had Tom known it if this information had not yet been made public? Jane herself had not found out about the bicycle chain until weeks after the murder. With a shudder she remembered that terrible day with Irma's lawyer and the antique dealer in Gert's house. Tom, of course, had remained perfectly calm that day.

"Another pebble turned over," Kracht would later tell her. "Thanks, Jane. You have done good work."

The preliminary hearing for the fraud trial took place on March 28, 1985. The courtroom was packed with Jane's friends, all of whom were taken aback by Tom's appearance: his piercing blue eyes were now sunken, his silver-gray hair had tufts of brown dye at the ends, and he seemed thin and pale in a rumpled, ill-fitting suit. Tom glared at everyone in attendance.

"I bet the jury will wonder how I ever dated a man who looked like that," Jane joked to Vaux Toneff.

Although Jane took the stand and testified about her finances and her relationship with O'Donnell, this was not a full trial, merely an effort to establish the parameters of the case. In a victory for Josh Thomas, the judge ruled that the forthcoming trial would take into account the two hundred thousand dollar second mortgage. In the end, Tom was formally charged with four felony counts: one for embezzlement, two for grand theft, and one for obtaining money under false pretenses. But everything related to the McCabe murder investigation, however, would be left out of the fraud trial. It was ruled as too prejudicial.

Bail remained at fifty thousand dollars. In a subsequent hearing, Tom was denied release on his own recognizance. His trial was set for July 22.

In the meantime, Jane had to come to grips with the financial wreckage he had left behind. She had not made a payment on the two hundred thousand dollar second mortgage for more than five months. She could not pay anything on the forty thousand dollar first mortgage. There was the thirty thousand dollar loan he had taken out from the Whelans. In addition, Tom had racked up more than fifty thousand dollars in credit card debt, all under the name of "Alexander." Jane was responsible for it all.

Jane had all of $153 in her own checking account, about seven hundred dollars in a savings account, and twelve thousand dollars in a trustee account with Jim Rohde. She was receiving about four hundred dollars a month from her widow's Social Security benefits, which she had been forced to take at the age of fifty-nine.

Although the house had been appraised for more than four hundred fifty thousand dollars, it was still not selling at its reduced price of $398,000. Realtors had staged a number of open houses without any success; the market seemed to have bottomed out. Every month that went by meant another unpaid check to the Woodson company, and less equity that Jane might recover from an eventual sale.

Somehow Jim Rohde was still juggling Jane's creditors, but things had to change. "Jane, you need to start thinking about getting a job," he told her.

"A job?" she asked. "Doing what?"

Jane could hardly imagine going to work. For nearly four decades she had been engaged to home and family, raising six children. She had also been a volunteer in many causes, and had worked in countless political campaigns. True, she had served as an executive secretary for William Penn Patrick in Holiday Magic, but that had been almost two decades before. Her resume would include a college degree and virtually nothing else. Most people her age were retired or preparing to retire. How would she ever begin to earn a living?

Jane spent the next morning reading the classified ads in the newspapers. It seemed the only job she was qualified for was baby-sitting. She then went to an employment agency, which told her she might be qualified for positions as a cook, housekeeper, or cleaning lady.

"You better swallow your pride," she was told, "because you have no skills."

Jane bit her lip. She had always had someone help her clean her house. Whatever her situation was, she did not think she could stand cleaning for other people.

Jane interviewed at nearby Dominican College, which offered a promising tutoring position. Unfortunately, the job paid only five dollars an hour, and was for just six hours a week. "Well, I'm interested. When does it start?"

"September." It was still months away.

Jane then went to Sausalito, where there was a position available in a warehouse. She would be packing vitamins in cardboard shipping boxes.

"What's the pay?" asked Jane.

"Four seventy-five an hour."

That would just about pay the gas to get here, thought Jane.

In early summer John Kracht called her again to San Jose, this time for a blood sample. "We need it for elimination purposes." Jane took this as a good sign. She knew that Tom had refused to give a blood sample of his own, but that it was only a matter of time before he would be compelled by court order.

What she did not yet know, however, was that the blood results from the lab were about to create an enormous problem in the McCabe case. Because the samples taken from the pillows left in the bathroom had later been taken out of the lab refrigerator and contaminated with bacteria, they had given ambiguous and contradictory results. Nine of the samples allowed for the possibility of Tom as murderer. But two samples—one taken from a ring on the bathtub— seemed to exclude him. (This was before the age of DNA, so the tests were based only on advanced blood type and antigen analysis.)

In domino fashion, more bad news was to follow. A second key piece of physical evidence turned out to be worthless.

"I'm afraid there has been another setback," Kracht told Jane. "None of the lipsticks from your house match the Kleenex."

Jane was surprised. Hadn't Kracht months before told her there was a positive match on the lipstick? Yet it turned out he had been working on visual comparison. When chemical analysis was used, none of the more than three-dozen lipsticks submitted to the lab had been confirmed.

Added to this was the news that Harry Carmichael had threatened a lawsuit against the San Jose PD. He was angry that police had questioned his fifteen-year-old stepson in the case, then executed a search warrant on his apartment. Of course, Harry had no grounds to sue, but it did seem he would be an uncooperative witness if he was ever called to the stand.

"I've run all this past the DA, Jane," Kracht summed up. "They just don't think there's enough to make a case yet against Tom O'Donnell."

"What can I do?"

"Have some more patience," said Kracht.

For Jane, patience was a commodity in increasingly short supply. But she threw herself again into the task of finding the right lipstick. She contacted her beauty parlor, Jay's Salon, which for several years had supplied her a particular brand of lipstick made by the Dermetics corporation. She discovered that the Dermetics factory had been purchased by a larger firm in New York City, and that the old colors were no longer being made. Although she tracked down various suppliers, including the cosmetics depot in Palo Alto that had supplied Jay's Salon, she could not obtain a leftover sample. All she could get was an old color chart. It was a dead end.

Just when it seemed that things couldn't get any worse, Jane got a telephone call from Nancy Martell on June 20, 1985.

"Did you know," she asked, "that Tom is out of jail?"

Tom O'Donnell was a free man again. Harry Carmichael had been able to raise the five thousand dollars, the ten percent required by a bail bondsman, from Tom's first wife, Kay. She also pledged collateral for the remainder of the fifty thousand dollar bond.

The dominoes continued to fall. With the trial just a week away, Tom's public defender wrangled a three-month continuance. The trial was moved to October 26. Then, in another court hearing on October 21, his attorney managed to win another three-month continuance.

Jane was beginning to learn about delays in the criminal justice system.

Chapter Eighteen

The Sixth Amendment to the Constitution guarantees the right to "a speedy and public trial." But things are often different when a suspect is out on bail. The accused and his lawyer begin to call the shots. With help from a crowded court calendar, it was relatively easy to orchestrate delays in Marin County. In the end, nearly a year would pass after Tom's arrest in Las Vegas before he would stand before a jury.

Jane Alexander's entire life had been put in limbo. She continued to speak with John Kracht on a weekly basis. She was having regular conversations with a deputy district attorney in San Jose, Bud Ambrose, who was assuring her he was doing everything he could to file murder charges against O'Donnell. Yet nothing was happening. Jane was learning a sad truth. In the grinding wheels of the judicial system, a victim had no rights.

Chapter Nineteen

"Mom, you are obsessed!"

Bill Alexander, the oldest of Jane's children, had begun to worry about her state of mind, a concern shared by his two brothers and three sisters. Shortly after Tom left in August 1984, they learned how desperate her financial situation had become.

"Why don't you just move out here to Denver?" Bill had asked then. "It would be so much easier for you."

"Thank you, Bill. But no thank you," she said. Jane could not begin to imagine moving in with one of her children. Michael, her son in Seattle, had also extended the same invitation.

All of Jane's children recognized that the horror their mother experienced by the murder of Gertrude McCabe was compounded dramatically by the fact the man she loved, Tom O'Donnell, was now the principal suspect. It had shaken her to the core. They had grown up witnessing their mother's almost missionary zeal for her political beliefs and causes. But nothing prepared them for her new obsession.

Tom O'Donnell murdered Aunt Gert. John Kracht has solved the case.

Tom O'Donnell murdered Aunt Gert. John Kracht has solved the case.

Tom O'Donnell murdered Aunt Gert. John Kracht has solved the case.

The phrase, written in Jane's forceful hand, filled an entire yellow legal pad. Jane called them her "affirmations." She had begun writing them early in the year, shortly before Tom's arrest in Las Vegas. It was the means by which Jane had come to terms with an unpalatable truth, and it helped to trigger her vision of what would happen.

Tom O'Donnell has been convicted of killing Gertrude McCabe.

Tom O'Donnell has been convicted of killing Gertrude McCabe.

Tom O'Donnell has been convicted of killing Gertrude McCabe.

Tom's conviction became a virtual obsession. Whatever happened to her, whatever her financial situation, she would see that justice was done.

Over the course of the year, she filled more than fifty legal pads, each with a different phrase.

"Mom, listen to me," Bill protested every time he called. "You have to move from your house. And you like Colorado, you've said so."

"But if I leave California, Tom will never be convicted."

"Forget Tom, get on with your life," Bill said.

"If someone murdered me," Jane told her son, "I would hope you would have a different attitude."

Jane was unable or unwilling to face the impending loss of her house. Instead she was toying with a concept that would have horrified her a year earlier: bankruptcy. When her lawyer, Jim Rohde, first broached the subject, she got physically ill. But the growing mountain of debt left her little choice. With penalties and interest compounding out of control, she was more than $300,000 in debt.

To add to her misery, in 1986 Marin County was in the midst of the worst real estate recession in the area's history. Interest rates were astronomical. The house was listed at four hundred twenty five thousand, lowered to three hundred ninety thousand, then three hundred sixty thousand dollars. Despite the attractiveness of the five-bedroom house, on a two and a half acre estate with barns and tack rooms, there was not a single offer.

But the loss of her home of nineteen years was too frightening for her to comprehend. She had bought the place with her husband and had raised six children under its roof. The house was filled top to bottom with the accumulated belongings of thirty-five years of marriage. It was her home.

The one hopeful event occurred in her search for work. In August 1985, Jane got a call from Nancy Martell, who was working at The Tamalpais, an elegant high-rise retirement complex about six miles from Jane's home. The "Tam" was in need of a part-time receptionist and telephone operator.

"Come down and fill out an application," Martell told her.

Jane was impressed with the facility. The complex boasted some three hundred residents, ranging in age from sixty-five to one hundred years old. There was a library and a tasteful dining room overlooking San Francisco Bay. There was also a fully-staffed medical and nursing wing.

Jane had to be ready to fill in for any of the three different shifts and often found herself working from 11 PM to 7 in the morning. The pay was $7.50 an hour.

Although the money was not great, the job would be Jane's salvation. On days when she could barely get out of bed otherwise, it was a reason to get dressed and get out the door. In addition, she had contact with other human beings, and the friendliness of the residents went a long way toward helping her function in the real world.

At long last Tom O'Donnell's trial began on January 30, 1986.

Jane was confident in a victory, thanks in no small part to the diligence of Marin County Deputy DA Josh Thomas. She knew that O'Donnell would have to present a defense based on his claim that he had been hunted by vengeful diamond smugglers.

On February 6, after the prosecution presented a case that included two days of testimony by Jane, the moment that many had waited for finally came. Tom O'Donnell took the witness stand. It was not the Gertrude McCabe case, but the packed courtroom prayed it would be the first step in that long journey to justice.

Dressed in a conservative blue suit noticeably below his normal dapper standards, O'Donnell responded to questions from Josh Thomas.

Q. A short time before you left Jane Alexander in San Anselmo, did you have an occasion to be met by two strangers at a location away from your home?

A. I did.

Q. And what did they speak to you about?

A. Well, they were speaking of back in 1974 or 1975. I was involved with an IDB, an "illicit diamond buying" transaction, in Johannesburg, South Africa. People from Egypt came in—a gentleman—and there was one involved from Germany. There were some South Africans, and we put together this—what they call parcels, and you get something, parcels of diamonds, and it could be—can be—these are all rough diamonds, not fine diamonds, rough diamonds they wanted to buy. That is their currency. Three, four times, we tried to transact this thing, and it never went off. Either they didn't show, or something, there is always a reason.

It is a very serious point in your life when you are making a transaction, because you can go to jail in South Africa or whatever country that you are in. And so everyone is a bit scared, and some don't show, or they wait an hour, and they show, but the other is gone.

But there is always something—we went four to six times, and never made it. The night that the transaction was supposed to transpire, I had a previous appointment to look at other jewels, and I told someone to take my place, because I didn't think it was going to go off, as it hadn't before. Unfortunately, that was the night that the government came in on them, when they were transacting—the exchange money for the actual exchange of diamonds, and the government came in and caught them, and they surrounded the place and put them in jail.

And they took the gentleman I had sent, and he was put in jail, too. And I wasn't, because I wasn't there. But I did come by that night to see, when I finished my appointment. I came back that night, and I was right outside where I saw it, as the police came up. They beat me to the time that I came up there, and it was a—so they figured that I was the informer, because I didn't show up. If I had been there, they wouldn't have considered it. But if I had been there, I would have been in jail, and I wouldn't be here.

Because Jane was a witness in the trial, she was not allowed in the courtroom to hear Tom's testimony. But through the glass window in the courtroom door, she could see Tom gesticulating wildly on the stand. Jane could tell the jury did not believe a word. Several of them were trying not to laugh. At one point, she was certain she saw the judge raise a file to his face to hide a grin.

When Josh Thomas laughed out loud in the middle of O'Donnell's long-winded dissertation, O'Donnell lashed out. "This is not funny, Mr. Thomas."

O'Donnell's storytelling skills had been well regarded at football and cocktail parties in Marin. But under the questioning of prosecutor Josh Thomas he sounded garbled, confused, at times almost incoherent. Spectators laughed and shook their heads as they left the courtroom on break.

Tom was mounting a shaky defense. He openly admitted that he had lived a life of dubious deal-making, and yet hoped his jury would believe he never took a dime from a naïve widow. Any possible doubt about O'Donnell's rambling explanation faded when Josh Thomas proved that South African police had no record of any of the events claimed on the witness stand. And Thomas was not above ridiculing O'Donnell as he pressed him about the night he walked out on Jane.

Q. For all that you knew, when this woman you loved, Jane Alexander, came home from that Yurika meeting that night, she might just walk into a couple of foreign agents who might kidnap her. Is that correct?

A. True, sir.

Q. But what they mainly wanted was you?

A. Yes, sir. They wanted me in the worst way but it was agreed and they knew I would show up on September tenth.

Q. The period of time that you were in Las Vegas, or down in the Los Angeles area, why didn't you call Jane Alexander?

A. Because she would have come down while I was still trying to hide from these people.

Q. Well, you didn't have to tell her where you were calling from, did you?

A. I felt that any verbal connection would only reach into the hurt on her side and mine.

Q. Why?

A. Because we loved one another very much. There was no way to get together in my life. I didn't want to endanger her again.

Q. Did you think that by calling her you would be putting her in danger?

A. Yes.

Q. You have said that you have given evidence to your former colleagues to clear Jane of any danger. What evidence did you give them to clear Jane from harm?

A. In the fact that I would meet them, plus she never had been involved and she was—I didn't—there was no way that she is involved in that. One of their comments to me was that Jane was living off of the trust of—you see, when you inform, you get a great deal of money in South Africa, about thirty three percent of whatever the amount of the entrapment is. And they felt that she was living the high life through what I had received by informing, which we all know is very false.

Tom was then asked about his mysterious Swiss trust, which had been named as collateral for the Woodson second mortgage. He could produce no documentation of its existence. It was not an ordinary trust, he explained, but one that was invested in the volatile world of currency exchange operations. In fact, the trust was outside the normal laws regarding such trusts. The sole trustee—a man he named as Hans Bometter—was now dead.

Q. What happened—you mentioned earlier in your testimony yesterday that the trust ran into some problems. What were the problems that it ran into?

A. Well, as I said, I came back in '77. I did not go back to Europe until '79 or '80, and I stopped by Switzerland to find out that in December of 1978, the banker had run into a great deal of financial difficulty, and this is also proven, a fact he shot himself right in the mouth, and he ended his life a young banker. Many people get into trouble in this business.

Q. And did you ever attempt to recoup whatever money you could from that trust?

A. Yes, I did, I tried to see if there was anything now, not just of my two hundred thousand dollars, but the other assumed eight hundred thousand dollars, and being that it was a slush fund and not accountable to the company books, there was no—at that time, they had brought nothing forward of evidence of it.

Q. How long did you hold out any hope to get any proceeds from the remains of that trust?

A. I would still be hoping.

O'Donnell had assumed a deer-in-the-headlights kind of facial expression. Even when his own defense attorney, Dennis Ruel, was questioning him, Tom was nervous to the point of making some extraordinary Freudian slips.

Q. The night you left, when you got to the airport, did you make any telephone calls?

A. I did. I called Mr. Hugh Fine.

Q. And what was your emotional condition when you were talking with Mr. Fine?

A. He said I was sobbing and homicidal. Uh, he said I was sobbing and suicidal.

Q. Was it a fact that you were sobbing?

A. Very much.

Though there was nervous laughter in the gallery, the jury did not get the joke. Because of an earlier ruling, no mention had been made of Tom's possible involvement in the McCabe murder.

After only twelve hours of deliberations, the jury returned a guilty verdict on all four counts. After Judge Smith thanked and excused them, many of the jurors returned to the courtroom to find out what would happen.

"Your honor," said Tom's defense attorney Dennis Ruel, "my client has all his clothes and belongings in a motel in Novato. He has a car here in the county. He is entitled to twenty-four hours to settle his affairs."

The judge would have none of it. Clearly Tom O'Donnell was a flight risk, and the fact that he had a car and clothes at hand was hardly an argument in his favor. Judge Smith raised the bail to one hundred thousand dollars and remanded Tom to custody until his sentencing hearing. The jury watched as Tom was handcuffed and led to jail.

It was a good day for Jane Alexander. She called John Kracht and then went to celebrate the victory at the Elks Club. The next morning a detailed article appeared in the Marin Independent Journal. "Thomas D. O'Donnell awaits sentencing for defrauding a Sleepy Hollow widow and stands as a suspect in a Santa Clara County murder," it began. Jane made fifty copies and mailed them to all her friends.

Judge Dorothy Von Beroldingen's story was introduced at the sentencing proceedings three weeks later. She had written a letter detailing her experiences with Tom O'Donnell. Carnell Rogers, the cleaning woman who had lost ten thousand dollars to Tom in the late 1960s, also came forward to testify. Now seventy-two years old, Rogers produced the canceled check she had written to Tom, as well as a Christmas card Tom had written to her in 1975. Tom promised then that he would be back in three months' time to repay the money, and that he would be taking her and her family out to a famous restaurant in San Francisco. "You are a beautiful woman," Tom had written.

"And that's the last I ever heard from him," said Rogers.

The crowded courtroom was completely silent.

The judge gave O'Donnell the maximum sentence: three years and eight months in state prison, less the 131 days already served. He added a ten thousand dollar fine, to be paid to a victims' fund, and three years' probation after release.

"Ten years ago, I could have sentenced you to fourteen years in prison," the judge said. "You would have been doing a lot more time if it was up to me."

For the first time since Gertrude McCabe's murder, Jane felt a degree of relief. But the whole feeling was tempered by what Judge Dorothy Von Beroldingen had told her. Because of overcrowded prisons, Tom was likely to be out on good behavior after just half his sentence had been served. That meant she had to get the prosecutors in San Jose moving on the murder charge.

Shortly after the Marin fraud trial, though, bad news arrived. Bud Ambrose, the deputy district attorney who had been so close to filing charges against O'Donnell, had taken a six-month sabbatical. Jane heard rumors that Ambrose might not return to the department and there had been disagreements concerning the viability of the McCabe case. John Kracht had brought no physical evidence of Tom O'Donnell's involvement, and the contaminated blood evidence, unless it could be argued away, could hang a jury.

With Ambrose gone, there was now no one in the Santa Clara County DA's office willing to make the Gertrude McCabe case a personal crusade. Jane and Detective Kracht found comfort in a shared sense of irony. "Roses are red, violets are blue," Jane wrote John Kracht on a birthday card. "Tom O'Donnell is laughing at you!"

Chapter Twenty

J ane Alexander's personal life continued its downward spiral as well. On April 24, 1986, she was served with a formal notice that her house was in foreclosure and she was being evicted. The second mortgage had not been paid for more than eighteen months. Besides the heartbreak of losing her home, she was distraught over her inability to repay money Tom had borrowed from her close friends, the Whelans. Their friendship would not survive.

For weeks Jane had been searching for a new place to live. It did not help that she was determined to keep her most loyal and affectionate companion, Duke. Through many painful days he had been her sole source of support. But the dog and her bankruptcy made her rental options very limited.

I bet Tom will never have a problem renting a place when he gets out, she thought.

Jane was also house hunting in Marin County, one of the most expensive places to live in the country. It was difficult to find any habitable apartment for under one thousand dollars a month.

Meanwhile, she was working hard to pack the house. A lifetime of memories and mementos was now a crushing burden. She could never find a place that would hold all the pieces of her former life.

"John, I just don't know how I am going to get on with it," Jane told Kracht. "I thought I would grow old with my husband and enjoy visits from our grandchildren. And then I thought Tom and I would grow old together. I never in a million years thought that I would lose my husband and my home."

"Jane, nothing lasts forever," he told her kindly.

The words stuck in her mind. Maybe that was what she was supposed to learn from all of this. Nothing lasts forever. Nothing is more certain in life than change.

On Friday, May 9, 1986, Jane was issued a court order to vacate her home in three days. She would have to be out by Mother's Day.

Her friends came to the rescue. Vaux Toneff found a storage service that would pick up Jane's belongings. Sandy Sullivan and Erin Rohde pitched in to help her pack and get rid of things she could not take with her.

The phone was the last item to be removed from the house. On Mother's Day, all of her children called.

"Mom, what will you do?"

"Jeanie and Phil Kennedy will let me use their maid's room for the time being."

"And Duke?"

"He will stay with me."

"And Scott?"

Jane's youngest son had been living at home for a few months.

"He will just have to find his own place," Jane said.

"Mom, you can always just move out here with us."

"I wouldn't do that to your marriage," Jane joked.

All of her children knew she wanted to stay in California because of her dogged pursuit of Tom O'Donnell. "I will be just fine," Jane told them. "Nothing lasts forever."

When the new owners arrived, they found Jane trying to clean the place. They took one look at her and said they would do it themselves.

"Lady, you need a rest," they said.

For weeks afterward, Jane struggled through mental and emotional exhaustion. The Kennedys were gracious hosts, more than generous, and mostly left her alone in her quarters. After two months, however, she felt she had to go on her own.

Her son Scott had a friend with a home for rent in nearby Woodacre. Jane was warned that it was located at the end of a dirt road and was somewhat substandard, which was the reason the owners were willing to forgo the usual requirements. She paid a visit with Vaux Toneff. It was an uninsulated cabin, several small rooms heated by a single potbelly stove. A hundred crushed, empty beer cans were piled in the corner of the kitchen. There were no cabinets, no closets, and the place was filthy.

"I'll take it," said Jane.

Vaux was dumbstruck.

"But what choice do I have?" Jane whispered to her friend.

She would share it with her son, Scott, and each would pay five hundred dollars a month. It was a place to live, and she could keep Duke. Jane bought two rugs from Goodwill and spread them on the floor. *At least cleaning the place,* she thought, *would give her something to do all winter.*

The months wore on. Jane soon discovered that she could not afford to store what had been taken from her old house. She took most of it from storage, had a garage sale, and gave away the rest. She adjusted to a new life in the cold, damp darkness of a forest. She got used to a simpler way of living.

Jane spent the winter months of 1987 looking over a photocopy of her diary entries, searching for clues to Tom's activities in the period before and after the murder. She remembered the cane that Aunt Gert had loaned to Tom when he broke his foot. Jane realized she had not seen the cane since Tom's foot healed. He had not returned it to Gertrude, and it was nowhere in the Sleepy Hollow house.

"She was probably struck with a smooth, round instrument like a one-inch pipe," Sergeant Joe Brockman had said when Jane first arrived in San Jose.

A horrible image flashed through her mind, of Aunt Gert opening her door to Tom, holding the cane and smiling. As soon as she turned her back, Tom closed the door behind him, then struck her across the head with the cane. As she fell, he struck her several more times.

Jane saw it all ... the abrasions on Gert's arms and knees as she tried to crawl away from him ... his frustration at not being able to kill or even incapacitate her, producing a knife, holding her down as he stabbed the old woman more than twenty times. The pillow on her face to muffle her cries and hide her eyes.

Stabbed and beaten, Gert still struggled to crawl away from Tom O'Donnell. When that failed, he wrapped the bicycle cable around her neck and used the lock as a tourniquet, pulling out clumps of her hair.

The images haunted Jane. Clarity had not brought her comfort. "Here is this man Aunt Gert knew for years and welcomed into her home," Jane said over and over to herself, "and the last thing she saw in life was Tom on top of her, strangling her."

Despite her vow to get justice for her beloved aunt and see that Tom O'Donnell spent the rest of his life behind bars, she still could not understand how the man she had known for twenty-five years could do such heinous things to such a helpless old lady.

Chapter Twenty

Weeks later, spring finally arrived and Jane's landlady paid a visit. "This looks better than it has in years!" she said. She liked it so much, in fact, she decided to move back in.

Jane was given thirty days' notice. She had been there six months and was still cleaning.

On July 22, she got a call from John Kracht. Tom had been paroled for good behavior. It was just over sixteen months since he had been sentenced.

The time had been spent in a minimum security prison in the High Sierra, and to no one's surprise he'd been a model prisoner, charming personnel and fellow inmates alike. The fact that he was back on the street and murder charges had yet to be filed more than five years after the slaying bore down on Jane's heart like a heavy stone.

Jane called the probation officer, Nancy Boggs, who had evaluated Tom at the time of his sentencing. She was distressed to hear he had been released.

"Are you frightened that Tom is out of jail?"

Jane had not given her own safety any thought. "No, just damn mad at the system."

Her children again petitioned Jane to live with them.

"Not while Tom is a free man."

After visiting dozens of apartments, Jane found a new place, a studio apartment. It had one room and a small kitchen. There were no dogs allowed.

Jane swallowed hard. Did she really have a choice any more about keeping Duke? Scott knew someone in West Marin who would adopt him. A stranger came and took him away. Two days later, Jane heard that Duke had run away from the new owner. He was never seen again.

Her new apartment had a lovely garden attached to it, which Jane replanted for the new owner. But after a few months Jane found a note from her landlady attached to her door.

Please sign both of these agreements and slide mine under the door. I know you're not happy here and I need to have someone here that is happy here. If I had known about your problems – the man you lived with who was obviously a slick embezzling criminal and then the murder – I would never have allowed you to move in. I was having very negative feelings about you long before Christmas.

I went to the Psychic Fair last Sunday and had a Female Energy Reading. My reader said there is something in your home that is causing you great unrest. There is an element of mistrust and fear that is very harmful for you – you must get rid of it.

I hope you find a better place for you soon. I'm feeling bad vibes.

So desperate was Jane to stay in a decent place after her ordeal in the Woodacre Cabin that she tried to reason with the landlady. The woman wouldn't even look at her.

Once again, friends Vaux Toneff and Sandy Sullivan came to the rescue, persuading their friend Jutta Leweicki to rent Jane a converted studio back in her beloved Sleepy Hollow, a mile from her former home on Irving Drive. It was a bittersweet return.

Still, Jane settled into her new patio apartment on Butterfield Road, which was far nicer than her recent living conditions. The apartment had vaulted ceilings, a partitioned bedroom, and sliding glass doors that overlooked a backyard pool. With two skylights, the room was airy and bright. There was a separate entrance for Jane through the garage. Although there was no kitchen, Jane would get by with a refrigerator and a hot plate. She did not cook much any more, as she ate every night while working at the Tam.

As nice as the studio was, though, her kids still had no place they could call home or stay when they came to town. Jane could only see her children and grandchildren by visiting them whenever she could afford it.

All of this was because of Tom O'Donnell. Jane never would have believed how one man's actions could so utterly destroy someone else's life. Twelve grandchildren would never know their family home. Twelve young cousins would never play together at Grandma's.

Chapter Twenty-one

For many months John Kracht had been trying to interest another district attorney of Santa Clara County in pursuing the McCabe murder. He had presented the case in a variety of ways, hoping that something would capture their attention. He pleaded. He presented even more circumstantial evidence. Nothing seemed to work.

Jane, who had done her own lobbying at the DA's office, had been told flatly that the case could never be proven. One attorney tried to get her off his back by telling her he did not think O'Donnell had been involved.

"Then you haven't read the case," she said.

John Kracht finally called Jane again in October 1988. It had been five years since the McCabe murder.

"Maybe someone else can do a better job," he told Jane. "I'm going to ask that the case be transferred to someone else."

"You're quitting?" asked Jane.

"I am burned out."

Jane had sensed for some time that this day was coming.

"There is a chance that another detective might shed new light on the case," said Kracht. "Someone else might have a new approach, or maybe better luck than I have had."

John Kracht liked the attitude of the new detective, a man named Jeff Ouimet (pronounced WEE-may). He worked the night shift and was soon to be promoted to the homicide unit. As was the custom, Ouimet would begin with a cold case.

Jane had lunch with Jeff Ouimet a few weeks after he had been assigned to replace John Kracht on the case. He knew who she was. She had called the police department and the District Attorney's office so often people recognized her voice when she said hello. Many of them quietly wished that Jane Alexander would just go away.

She sent a handmade flyer to all the police officers who had worked on the investigation. She had assembled all their business cards in a collage and over

150

that, in bold red gothic letters, Jane had written, "Who Murdered Aunt Gert?" She mailed the flyers so that they arrived at the San Jose Police Department on the anniversary of McCabe's murder.

"It was a childish act," Jane wrote in her diary. "But what am I supposed to do?"

Jane had lunch with Jeff Ouimet a few weeks after he had been assigned to replace John Kracht on the case.

She was impressed with Ouimet—he was tall, handsome and well-mannered. The two shared similar conservative values in politics. Best of all, he was already immersed in the details of the McCabe murder.

Jane knew immediately that Jeff Ouimet was the kind of detective who had a fire in his belly. The police academy teaches police not to get emotionally involved with victims of crime. But by this point Jane knew that emotional involvement was the only way a difficult case like this could ever get solved.

"I still have a lot of homework to do," said Ouimet. Paramount was his desire to examine the more than 125 recorded telephone conversations Jane had made with Tom's friends, the majority of them with Harry Carmichael. Within them, Ouimet hoped, might be additional clues that would help make the case against O'Donnell.

The case, if it ever found its way to court, was almost certain to be tried on circumstantial evidence. A jury might hear a hundred pieces of evidence and discount ninety percent of it, but they could still convict by what remained. Increasing the sheer weight of circumstantial evidence was crucial.

Piece by piece, Ouimet meticulously dug through the evidence in the boxes of files. He listened to all the tape recordings, reread the witness interviews, studied the autopsy and FBI Behavioral Science Report as well as the crime scene photos. He knew that criminal cases are not usually made by brilliant Holmes-like deductions but by the diligent sifting of minutiae.

He finally found what he was looking for.

In November, Ouimet phoned Jane in Sleepy Hollow. He, like Kracht, was shocked to find that the first investigators had allowed Jane and Tom to spend the night at a murder scene that had not been fully processed. But providence may have intervened: their error created a small but potentially significant break in the case.

He wanted to know about Tom's behavior in Gert's house the night after the murder. He was particularly interested in the check registry, which Jane had discovered in Gert's dresser drawer the day after the police had told Jane and Tom that they could not find it.

"Which drawer did you find it in?"

"The second drawer on the left," said Jane.

"Where was it in the drawer?"

"Leaning on the left side," said Jane, the picture was still clear in her mind. It had been wedged in among Gert's clothes.

"Jane, I have a photograph of that drawer at the time the police discovered the body, and it's empty," said Ouimet.

Empty! Jane had never seen any of the crime-scene photographs, or heard any were taken of the empty dresser drawers.

"I've looked at every photo. The check registry wasn't on the floor, or set aside anywhere else. Someone had it in their possession, and that person put it back, where you found it.

Jane remembered that awful first night. She'd awoken to hear Tom running water in the kitchen. Tom explained that an orange juice can had exploded. He had heard the noise and got up to investigate. Duke did not respond, Tom said, because it was not a human sound. Tom had been in the second bathroom, cleaning the crime scene to cover his tracks.

"We may have a case again," Ouimet said.

Jane's efforts uncovered another clue as well. Since shortly after the murder, she and her cousin Irma had been on bad terms. The estrangement was not helped when Jane phoned Irma sixteen months after the murder to tell her that she suspected Tom O'Donnell was the killer. Irma had blamed Jane for bringing O'Donnell into their lives. And Jane, who blamed herself for much the same reason, did not take the criticism gracefully.

After a few years had passed, however, the two were again on civil terms, at least enough to have lunch together. By then Irma's memory was failing rapidly, although she still had some lucid days. At a Christmas lunch soon after Ouimet's discovery, she was in particularly good form.

"Irma, do you remember when Tom visited you the week after Gert's murder?"

"I do. Tom came over late in the afternoon and brought a lot of papers and a plastic bag full of junk jewelry. He had that old beat-up watch, I remember."

"You mean Gert's diamond watch," said Jane.

"No, you're mistaken, Jane," said Irma. "I certainly would have remembered if Tom brought that to my apartment."

That explained why he took nothing from the crime scene, not even the cash: he assumed Jane would inherit all of it. When he found out that Irma was entitled to half, he showed her the junk jewelry and then told Jane Irma did not want any of it. But there was more.

"And Tom told me Gert's rings were full of blood, so he didn't bring them along that day," said Irma.

Gert's rings were full of blood? thought Jane.

Once again her meticulous diaries proved invaluable. Jane realized that Gert's rings had still been at the coroner's office until the day after Tom visited Irma. How could he have known they were full of blood, unless he had seen them at the murder scene himself?

"Jane, I just don't see why you wouldn't come up to my apartment that day," said Irma. "Tom told me that you were sitting down in the car, that you were just too upset and angry to see me."

"Irma," Jane said, "I was in San Rafael getting a permanent! Tom told me you refused to let me come visit."

After more than five years one small mystery was solved. Tom had not wanted the two women comparing notes and had cleverly sown seeds of mistrust between them. Had they been able to talk, Tom's web of deception might have come unraveled sooner.

Unfortunately, Irma was in her late eighties, too old and infirm to be a reliable witness. Jane passed the news on to Jeff Ouimet.

In November 1989, Jeff Ouimet and his partner, Peter Graves, flew to Los Angeles, where Tom O'Donnell was living while on parole. Tom agreed to speak with them.

"Life has been good to me lately," he said with a self-satisfied air.

Although he was still on parole, the officer he reported to had been impressed by his new business venture. Tom had been selling Electra-Cats, an ultrasonic device that emitted a high-pitched sound that warded off rodents.

Tom O'Donnell had shown him his sales receipts, and explained he needed to travel more to expand his business. There was a good chance he would be released from his parole obligations early.

He also was dating a woman named Lou. She lived in a million-dollar home in Toluca Lake, a suburb of Los Angeles.

Ouimet and Graves made small talk with Tom, feigning an interest in his business and romantic acumen. By now everyone knew how much he loved an appreciative audience. Then the detectives slipped in a serious question.

Ouimet asked Tom to recall his alibi for October 21, 1983. Tom recounted his trip to Las Vegas, and this time he hinted that there was someone who could back up his story. That was all he would say.

Jane later quizzed Ouimet about the encounter.

"Jeff, is Tom using as an alibi some woman friend who was with him in Vegas the night Gert was murdered?"

"You got it," said Ouimet.

"And of course he can't give you her name because he is a perfect gentleman."

"Right again."

"That's wonderful. Imagine the whole courtroom on the edge of their seats, the jury entranced, when the DA asks, 'Will you give us the name of the woman you were sleeping with in Las Vegas?'" Jane paused a moment. "Tom will say, 'No, I will go to the gas chamber to protect this lovely lady.' Won't the press just love it?"

Ouimet laughed. "Well, that's Tom's story now."

"So get him charged, Jeff!"

Jane had learned one of the biggest lessons that a victim's advocate can possibly learn. In many cases it is simply a matter of finding the right investigator and the right prosecutor.

Two full years after Jeff Ouimet took over the case, he finally found a prosecutor who shared his belief that the case could be won on its circumstantial evidence.

Charles Constantinides was regarded as one of the best lawyers in the department. He examined the file and determined that O'Donnell was indeed the killer and that he could win the case. Ouimet told an ecstatic Jane the case was just weeks away from being filed.

Constantinides also had an eye for detail. He wondered why there had been no blood on the gloves in the bathroom and why O'Donnell had bothered to clean up the crime scene. It was unlikely that O'Donnell himself had bled: Jane would have noticed any cuts. Could Tom have vomited at the scene? He was an inexperienced murderer, and perhaps the sight of so much blood made him sick to his stomach.

The deputy DA wanted to be able to answer any question that might come up in the trial. One that made him curious was why Tom had chosen to move against Gert at that particular time. He found out that she had been on the verge of selling her house and moving to a nursing home, where it would have been almost impossible to kill her. Motive based on an urgent need went a long way toward helping a jury understand why a person with no history of violence would suddenly turn to murder.

Jane supplied another piece of information as well. Using reverse telephone directories from the public libraries, she located addresses to match the phone numbers that Tom had called in the weeks prior to the murder. She discovered that he had called eight different airlines to check on flights to Los Angeles. He had done the same before his "dry run" of October 10, 1983.

She could see the details falling into place as Tom plotted the murder. Jane Alexander was learning to be a competent detective, to analyze data and reconstruct a crime. She had good teachers in John Kracht and Jeff Ouimet, and while they were her superiors in crime detection, no one could match her unfailing dedication to the cause.

As before, though, the new case would be shunted off to the side by newer, more pressing cases. In October 1990, seven years after the murder, Constantinides had to shift his attention off the case. There had just been a workplace massacre at the ESL defense plant in Sunnyvale, in which seven people had been killed. Plus, the already overburdened Santa Clara DA's office was racking up prosecutions for violent crime in record numbers. Overextended, Constantinides was less receptive to the McCabe matter.

"Get off my back!" he told Jane one day. "I realize my obligation to Gert as well as you," he said.

"I won't call again," she told him, and hung up. Her enthusiasm turned to despair once again. "How much of this can I take?" she asked herself.

Over a year would pass before they spoke again. Constantinides would prove true to his word, though. On November 22, 1991, Jane returned home to find a message on her answering machine from Jeff Ouimet.

"Jane, Constantinides had decided to file a murder one warrant for Tom O'Donnell's arrest for the murder of Gertrude McCabe."

Eight years after the murder, Jane's prayers had been answered at last. She called everyone she knew. The warrant included "special circumstances," murder for financial gain, and that could mean the death penalty.

When she called Judge Dorothy Von Beroldingen and told her the news, she wasn't sure the death penalty would be the best option. "It would be a better punishment for Tom to just spend the rest of his life in prison, with no chance of parole."

Chapter Twenty-one

Jane agreed. They both knew how that would wear on him.

For a few special friends, Jane saved the news for a Monday night football party. She arrived at the Rohde's at 5:45 PM. Jane managed to contain herself until dinner. When the party retired to the dining room, Jane placed her tape recorder on the table.

"What's going on?" asked Erin Rohde.

"Eight years ago we were all at the Martells' house watching the 49er–Rams football game, when I received the phone call that Aunt Gert had been murdered," said Jane. "Tonight, we are here watching a Rams–49er game. Tom O'Donnell is going to be charged with first-degree murder with special circumstances!"

Although assembling the warrant took time—it had to include a summary of the police records, which by that point amounted to thousands of pages—the charges were finally entered in the national crime computer on December 20, 1991. A judge attached a million-dollar warrant to it, the price of Tom's bail.

At the time Tom was traveling across the country. His Electra-Cat business, although not a roaring success, demanded a lot of time on the road, and he frequently went to Kansas City and other Midwestern destinations. Ouimet finally traced him to his local address by credit card records. He was now living with the wealthy widow in Los Angeles' Toluca Lake.

Detectives cruised past the house for almost a week, reluctant to ring the doorbell for fear that if he was not home, his paramour or neighbors might tip him off. At last they had their chance.

Tom was all dressed up and headed to a St. Patrick's Day party when he exited the house with his partner and was arrested by plainclothes officers. All the way to the Hollywood Police Station, he raved about "this woman in Marin County, Jane Alexander," who he claimed had a vendetta against him.

Jane's diary entry recorded the good news.

> Happy St. Patrick's Day! Went to lunch, and when I triggered my phone later heard the following. "Jane, this is Jeff. I just called to wish you a happy St. Patrick's Day. Tom was picked up this afternoon and is in custody. We will be going down to pick him up in a couple of days."

Chapter Twenty-Two

Tom was taken by bus to the Santa Clara County Jail a few days after his arrest. On April 20, 1992, Jane drove two hours to the courthouse in San Jose for a hearing in which Tom was expected to enter his plea. Although he had been assigned a public defender and had already met with her several times, he refused to address the charges against him. Instead his lawyer asked for a new court date, which was set for June 26.

"So nothing will happen for two more months?" asked Jane, incredulous.

"That's right," said Ouimet, "two more months."

How does anything ever get done? she asked herself. *If the taxpayers knew how the criminal justice system worked,* she thought, *there would be a revolution.*

She drove back to San Anselmo that afternoon in despair. She had come so far and yet still her justice delayed was justice denied. How could victim's families endure this? The suffering caused by crime was compounded a thousand-fold by a judicial system that was so slow to mete out punishment.

Jane Alexander's search for justice would take a fateful turn that day. Just after midnight a murderer named Robert Alton Harris was scheduled to be executed at San Quentin State Prison. He would be the first person in more than twenty-five years to be executed in California. Although state voters had restored the death penalty by popular referendum in 1978, it had taken fourteen years of legal wrangling before he was headed to the gas chamber.

The entire state was in an uproar about the event. Countless protesters had gathered around the prison, where television stations were covering the event live. There were prayer vigils and peace demonstrations. Everyone was waiting for a possible appeal.

Harris was the poster boy for death penalty advocates. He murdered two teenage boys in San Diego, and then ate their fast food lunches.

One woman willing to defend the death penalty was a member of a victim's group in San Francisco. Her name was Jan Miller. Her daughter Veronica had been murdered seven years before in the Northern California town of Chico. The case was still unsolved.

Chapter Twenty-two

As Jane Alexander headed north from San Jose, she heard Jan Miller speaking on a popular San Francisco radio station.

"I personally feel that because we have a law, and the majority of people in California voted for it, it should be used," she said. "The death penalty is there for a specific reason. It's there for a few who commit very heinous murders. When people think of the death penalty, they sometimes confuse it with being for all murderers. It is definitely not. But I would say that I am relieved that justice is finally being done in this particular case."

That's exactly right, thought Jane. The death penalty recognizes the value of the life that was taken away. As she crossed the Golden Gate Bridge and listened on her car radio, the interviewer asked Miller about her work in a victim's group. Jane had never heard of such an organization.

The interviewer mentioned that Jan Miller lived in San Rafael, the town adjacent to the one where Jane lived. When she got home, she found Jan Miller's name in the local phone book. The next day she gave Jan Miller a call.

The following week the two women rode together into San Francisco, where there was a monthly meeting of a victim's advocacy group. Though they had no way of knowing, Jane Alexander and Jan Miller had begun a friendship that would impact the lives of countless victims and have a dramatic effect on the criminal justice system.

On the way Jane told Jan Miller the story of Aunt Gertrude and Tom O'Donnell. It took most of the forty-minute drive.

"And now, thank God, Tom is in prison."

On the way back, Jan Miller told her story. She is the mother of four children and step-mother of three, the latter from her second marriage to Jack Miller. She often jokes that all her daughters had boy's names. Andrea has always been know as Andi, Nicole was Niki and her eldest, Veronica, was Roni.

After high school graduation, Roni enrolled at Chico State University, three hours north of Marin, where she studied nursing. Roni enjoyed her freshman year and continued her relationship with a boyfriend Dominic at home in Marin County. The two saw each other often and intended to spend the summer together at home. But late in her freshman year, Roni decided that she would try to complete the five-year nursing program in just four years. This meant that she would remain in Chico for the summer, working part-time and attending the summer session.

Roni moved into a new apartment for the summer and was happy with her part-time job as a waitress in a local Italian restaurant. On the night of Wednesday, June 27, 1984, Roni phoned her mother to tell her how well she was doing.

"She told me all about her life," said Jan. "Her new apartment was much better than her dorm, and she was enjoying her job and summer school." Jan and Roni talked about the upcoming family week in Lake Tahoe, a much anticipated annual event they had begun five years earlier.

The next evening, Thursday, Roni's boyfriend Dominic phoned to make arrangements to visit that weekend. Roni was relaxed and very upbeat as they talked for forty minutes. Yet just before they hung up, Dominic noticed a distinct change in the tone of her voice, from lively to wary.

Her body was discovered the next day around noon. She was an hour late for work, and her boss called Leslie Miner, who also worked at the Italian Cottage, and asked her to find out why Roni was not answering the phone. Her apartment was a few blocks from Roni's.

Leslie knocked on the front door and heard nothing, then rang the doorbell. She proceeded to go around to the back of the building, where there was a construction site just behind the ground-level apartment. She could see that Roni's window was open, so she pulled herself up and looked in.

The room was covered in blood. Roni was lying on the bed in a T-shirt and shorts, her hair and clothes soaked in her own blood. Her face and part of her head had been savagely bludgeoned.

Construction workers nearby responded to Leslie's screams for help. One of them climbed through the window to see if Roni was still breathing. She was not.

Three hours later, San Rafael police arrived at Jan Miller's house and told her Veronica was dead. A disbelieving Jan asked, "What do you mean, how did she die?"

The patrolman answered, "She was murdered."

"How was she murdered, who did it?" she asked as shock set it.

"She was strangled and she died quickly," they said, the latter a fabrication to spare Jan Miller from the full horror of the slaying.

Four days later, Jan read a newspaper article on the killing that identified the cause of Veronica's death as bludgeoning to the head. She went ballistic, furious at the police officers for saying Roni was strangled. Jan Miller's transition from grieving victim to angry activist was instantaneous. Never again would she rely solely on the efforts of others, no matter who they were. She would somehow find justice for Roni.

Despite a relentless effort to find her daughter's killer, including lobbying police and quizzing Roni's friends, ten years had passed without an arrest.

As Jane Alexander listened, she realized that as much as she loved her Aunt Gert, Jan's story was more heartbreaking than her own. No one should have to outlive their children. *How can someone survive burying their own child?* she asked herself.

"We have to do something about it," Jane told her. "We cannot just lie back and wait for the system to get justice for Roni."

Though eight years had gone by, still Jan and Jane set about reconstructing the crime. Jan had spoken to virtually everyone who lived near Roni at the time of her death. She could draw a map of the complex and pinpoint where everyone lived and what they were doing the night of Roni's murder.

It had been hot in Chico the night of the killing, and since none of the apartments had air conditioning, windows and doors had been left open. Jan believed someone must have heard or seen something.

One day, as she recounted the tales of each of Roni's neighbors for Jane, Jan produced the guest book from Roni's funeral. All but one of Roni's neighbors had attended, a woman named Lois (not her real name).

"Why wasn't she there?" Jane asked. Jan replied that Lois had moved to Los Angeles the next day. She had spent the night of Roni's murder carrying dozens of boxes and armloads of clothes to her car.

When Jane and Jan examined a small sketch of the apartment, they realized Lois had to pass in front of Roni's patio window twice for every trip she made.

"Do you have gas?" Jane asked her. Jan nodded.

They piled in Jan's car and eight hours later arrived in Los Angeles. When they got there, they were lucky to find Lois's name in the phone book. The checked into a motel and scoured a road map until they found the street where she lived.

The next morning, they drove to a seedy neighborhood. They waited all day until Lois arrived home from work. Although they were not familiar with her appearance, they identified her when she opened the mailbox that bore her name. They watched her go up the steps to a second-floor apartment, two children behind her.

"It's showtime," Jane told her. "Let's go."

Jan rang the doorbell, her heart pounding in her throat. When Lois answered the door, Jan smiled and identified herself. "You probably don't remember me," she said, easing her way into Lois's apartment. "But you lived in Chico back in 1984 when my daughter Roni was murdered." With this news the woman's mouth opened in shock.

"I want you to understand why I am here," Jan said. "It's been ten years, and I'm still having a hard time coming to terms with what happened to my daughter. The killer is still roaming around loose somewhere. I'm just trying to find people who knew her and find out what was going on the last two weeks of her life." Jane asked for a few minutes of Lois's time.

"Okay," the woman said, practically choking on the response. When Jan asked her how well she had known Roni, Lois replied, "I didn't know her well at all. I remember that she worked for that Italian Cottage restaurant, because I saw the uniform she wore when she was going to work." To both Jane and Jan, everything Lois said seemed evasive.

With Lois's children playing in an adjacent room, the meeting lasted a torturous half hour. She gradually admitted to knowing all of Roni's circle of friends. But one name troubled her in particular: Aaron Mitchell (also a pseudonym), a neighbor.

"Who is that?" Lois asked when Jan said his name.

"Didn't you know him?"

"Oh, yeah… it's been a long time."

Jan and Jane both felt Lois knew more than she was admitting. Then Jan asked if she had seen or heard anything the night of the murder, reminding Lois that she had frequently passed in front of Roni's window.

There was a long silence. "No. And I told all this to the grand jury years ago."

Jan was stunned. No one in Butte County had ever told her they had convened a grand jury to investigate.

It was time to turn up the heat. Jan looked in the direction of Lois's children. "It is horrible losing a child," Jan said. "Could you imagine one of them being brutally beaten to death?" The comment might seem callous, but

Jan, who now felt Lois held a key to her daughter's murderer, wanted her to feel the pain that she lived with daily.

"Well, I hope you find comfort in life and are able to move on," Lois said, ending the interview.

"I have gotten on with my life," said Jan, "but I won't stop until I find the man who killed my daughter."

Jane handed Lois her phone number. "If you think of anything, you could help a mother find justice."

When Jan returned home, Butte County investigator Perry Reniff confirmed that they had indeed impaneled a grand jury, and that Aaron Mitchell had been considered a suspect. But they could find no evidence to connect him to the crime. All the witnesses who knew him had hired lawyers and refused to talk to investigators.

Jan Miller had run into another dead end. Yet she had also found an ally. Jane Alexander's private quest for justice would expand into an advocacy for victims nationwide.

Jan had been attending different victims group in Northern California for five years and she encouraged Jane to join her. The two traveled to San Francisco every month to join members of other victims' families. But they felt little comfort in the group. Most meetings were long stretches of communal grieving and tears, with no progress toward a resolution in anyone's case.

One night, while returning from an emotionally harrowing meeting, they admitted to each other their full fury and frustration with the judicial system. For all their empathy, Jane Alexander and Jan Miller had had enough tears. They wanted action. They wanted justice and fairness for the families of victims.

They decided to form their own group.

The next day Jane went to see Jim Rohde, who volunteered to create a nonprofit, tax-exempt organization. They decided to call it Citizens Against Homicide. Jan's niece Nancy and her husband, Marv, designed a logo bearing the acronym CAH. Through friends and relatives Jan Miller raised five thousand dollars, while Rohde supplied all legal work pro bono.

They began calling the dozens of victims they had met. Their first newsletter was published in June 1994. It declared Citizens Against Homicide as "A New Voice for Survivors of Homicide in the North Bay Area."

The newsletter featured several unsolved murder cases. Prominent on the publication's first page was the Gertrude McCabe case.

Another was the murder of Michael Assad, husband of Nancy Yingst, who had been murdered behind the counter of his convenience store in Vallejo, just north of San Francisco. Nancy had contacted Jane and Jan and asked for their help in pressuring detectives and prosecutors to keep the investigation alive.

The newsletter also featured the case of Paul Cosner. Paul was the brother of CAH member Sharon Sellito. Cosner allegedly was murdered by one of the most notorious manipulators of the criminal justice system California has ever seen. As of 1994, Charles Ng had sat in jail for nine years on the charges he may have killed as many as thirteen people, many of them young women he and partner Leonard Lake had kidnapped, assaulted, and killed after raping them as sex slaves. (In February 1999, Charles Ng was convicted of eleven murders. The jury did not find sufficient evidence to convict in the slaying of Paul Cosner.)

It profiled the Victim's March on the Capitol and three pending parole hearings of convicted murderers, asking readers to write letters protesting the early release of the killers.

The six-page newsletter was sent to victims' families, prosecutors, detectives, and legislators. It was offered free to anyone who wanted it. Potential supporters were invited to join CAH for a fifty dollar annual fee.

In response, a flood of victims' families started contacting Jane and Jan. Many wanted help with their parole hearings or getting their cases reopened. Others just needed a shoulder to cry on or advice on how to make it through a holiday.

Many wanted to know how to negotiate the labyrinth of the criminal justice system. A few were afraid even to call their local district attorney because they thought they would receive a bill for his or her services.

Jane and Jan decided to attend a parole hearing to support CAH member Anne Poverello. Anne's mother, Mary D'Augusta, had been murdered December 10, 1984, by Michael Leon Grant, who had been in custody since the day after the killing.

Married to a close friend of Anne's daughter and Mary's granddaughter, Grant had been thirty-two at the time and, according to police, had probably become infuriated when the seventy-four-year-old woman had rebuffed a pass he made at her. In his trial, his mother-in-law testified that he had made repeated sexual overtures to her as well.

Though they could not speak, Jan and Jane offered silent support while each member of Anne's family read their plea to keep Grant behind bars. Anne found their presence a great comfort, because the killer continually glowered at the family from ten feet away. When the parole board denied his appeal and sentenced him to five more years without another hearing, he muttered an unintelligible curse directly at Anne.

Anne said something that would become a CAH catchphrase, particularly at parole hearings. "The prisoner made a decision to take the life of another human being in a horrifying fashion. This is not about society's revenge, this is about society's protection." Anne Poverello has since served as CAH's Victim's Representative and is their resident authority on parole hearings.

What started as a group dedicated to helping people in the San Francisco Bay area spread across the country. A woman named Audrey Eller called and said her granddaughter, Kristy Stotler, had been murdered in Cincinnati. Stotler had been pregnant and the mother of a two-year-old boy who was asleep in an adjoining room when it happened.

Though friends and family claimed Stotler was never depressed or despondent, Cincinnati police had ruled she committed suicide by dousing herself with lighter fluid and then setting herself on fire. She lingered in agony for thirty-four days, unable to speak or identify the source of her horror. No one who knew Kristy Stotler believed for a second she would ever commit suicide, particularly with her beloved son so close.

The newsletter containing the Stotler case was sent to every public official in Cincinnati, from the mayor's office to the police department and district attorney. The newsletter reached the state legislature, the attorney general, and the governor's office in Columbus. CAH members lobbied Cincinnati law enforcement and prosecutors for months with letters and phone calls.

After months of diligent work, the case was reopened as an unsolved homicide. It was a triumph for CAH. Friends and relatives of Jane Alexander and Jan Miller began volunteering their efforts, and they soon established monthly meetings. Jan's sister Alice Ostergren, a retired banker, became the treasurer. Alice's three daughters, Carol, Terri, and Nancy, helped organize parole letters, and designed and edited the newsletter.

The group found comfort in their numbers. And they began to see the strength that numbers could bring.

One of their best ideas was to create billboards offering rewards in long-dormant murder cases. The first was for a new CAH member named Jacque MacDonald, whose daughter Debi had been murdered in Modesto, California.

Jacque raised six thousand dollars for a reward for information leading to Debi's killer, while CAH paid for half the expenses and did much of the work in creating the billboard. The billboard company, Outdoor Advertising, gave them the public service rates on a prime location.

Within a few months the face of Debi Whitlock towered above Highway 99 in Modesto, offering the reward and providing the name of the investigating detective. They supplemented the billboard by placing posters on local buses and putting handouts in grocery stores and on posts. Everything bore a prominent photo of Debi and the reward offer. Jacque's daughter went from obscurity to prominence in a short period of time.

Another billboard went up in Chico, bearing the photo of Roni Perotti and offering a ten thousand dollar reward for information leading to the arrest and conviction of her killer. On the day that billboard went up, a Chico newspaper quoted Detective Perry Reniff in their headlines when he said, "There Is a Killer Among Us."

Still no one came forth with information in that case, but Jacque MacDonald's had a heartening outcome. Several months after the billboard and bus posters went up, a man approached a police officer on the street and said, "I know who killed that girl in the billboard." The man said he had known for nine years who the killer was: the man had admitted the crime to him soon after the murder.

Within days the perpetrator was arrested in Arkansas. That surpassed even the reopening of the Stotler case in Cincinnati.

Citizens Against Homicide had their first major success. They had helped solve a long-dormant murder case and taken a killer off the streets. All of them, including Jane and Jan, who were still denied justice of their own, were jubilant.

Another CAH success started before Jane and Jan Miller had left their San Francisco victim's group. They were attending one of their last Thursday night meetings when the chairwoman said, "We got a letter from a man in Seattle named Lee Sansum. He says his sister was murdered by her husband in Palo Alto and that the police won't investigate, the DA won't prosecute, and he's desperate to find someone who will help him with his case." Jane Alexander took the letter, and that night she read it with rapt attention.

On February 22, 1985, Abigail Niebauer, an acclaimed Northern California poet, was killed in the kitchen of her home in Palo Alto, not far from the campus of Stanford University. The cause of death was a shotgun blast to her chest fired at point-blank range.

The man who had fired the shotgun was her husband, James Niebauer. He told police he had been showing the shotgun to his wife and it went off accidentally. He claimed he had not known it was loaded and did not know how the gun could have fired.

◆ ◆ ◆

The police found the stock of the shotgun and the front grip on the kitchen counter. A can of paste wax and a polishing cloth were also found nearby. Yet the lid of the paste wax was closed tightly and the rag did not smell of fresh wax, and no tools for either working or cleaning the shotgun were found in the same room.

As police officers examined the body, they saw that Abigail was lying halfway in and out of the room, so that while her feet were in the kitchen, her head was in an adjacent room. The room was part of an attached apartment where Abigail had been living since deciding to separate and seek a divorce from James.

To even an untrained observer, it appeared she had barely entered the room when she was shot. Even so, Niebauer was released after his interview, as officers were fairly convinced that the shooting had been accidental.

The next day, friends of Abigail began calling the Palo Alto police department to offer their opinions of her death. Most of them suggested or inferred that the killing was not accidental. Several friends reported that the Niebauers had been fighting for months, and that Abigail had moved into the garage apartment to get away from her husband. She had vowed to remain, they said, until their son Jim Jr. graduated from high school that year and went off to college.

They claimed that she had openly been seeing another man, a poet named Greg Hall. He and Abby had been seeing each other several times a week for two years prior to her death.

Her older brother, Lee Sansum, a Seattle computer programmer, was on leave from his job at US West and did not receive word of his sister's death until the day after. When he hung up the phone after receiving the horrible news, Lee had only one thought: Jim Niebauer murdered my sister.

Lee believed he knew why. Barely two weeks before she died, the estate of their late parents, Ernest and Janet Sansum, had cleared after months of legal proceedings. Abilgail had placed her one hundred eighty thousand dollar inheritance in a separate account from her joint holdings with her husband.

The Palo Alto police told Lee they knew about the inheritance, and told him they would get back to him as the investigation continued. Lee went home to Seattle and began calling the Palo Alto police several times a week. The investigating officer, Randy Rafoth, was not available when Lee called. During one of the calls, an officer asked if he had ever spoken to Lieutenant Lynne Johnson, who was supervising the case. He said he had not but would like to. Lee's name and phone number were taken again, but he never heard from Lieutenant Johnson.

Two months after the killing, someone sent him a newspaper clipping.

It stated that Lieutenant Johnson had declared the case an accidental shooting and closed the investigation.

Already stunned by the loss of his parents and sister, Lee Sansum said his whole body went numb. He did not know what to say, or who to turn to. As soon as his senses returned, he did what Jane Alexander had done. He vowed that no matter how long it took, no matter what price he had to pay, he would find justice for Abigail.

The day after reading the file, Jane called Lee Sansum in Seattle and heard the same pain and urgency in his voice that she knew others heard in her own. Yet Lee was civil, soft-spoken, and articulate.

He explained that he had quit his job and spent a considerable portion of his life savings and inheritance in pursuit of justice for his sister Abigail.

Jane advised him to organize everything he had in neat, chronological order, and most important, to begin a diary or log book of everything involved in the case. She told him no matter how insignificant it seemed at the time that he must record everything. By the time he sent the file to Jane, it was thicker than a New York telephone directory.

Jane read every word of the file. Years of fighting the criminal justice system, lobbying DAs, listening to John Kracht and other detectives had changed her from a naïve Marin County widow to a knowledgeable judicial advocate and a wise and compassionate counselor of the bereaved.

But that was not the worst of it. In Jane's lap were two letters that would have intimidated a lesser spirit.

The first, dated June 21, 1988, from the Santa Clara County Grand Jury, stated: "The Santa Clara County Grand Jury has conferred with the District Attorney and reviewed evidence about the Niebauer case. It remains the professional opinion of the District Attorney that there is insufficient evidence to pursue the case any further." Santa Clara County Deputy DA Dave Davies had refused to prosecute and recommended the same to the grand jury.

It further stated "The Grand Jury has found no improprieties in the investigation of the death of your sister Abigail Niebauer and therefore considers the matter closed."

The second was even more distressing. It was a seven-page letter from Michael D. O'Reilly, Supervising Deputy Attorney General of the State of California.

The letter began: "Among the several significant evidentiary problems (in the Abigail Niebauer case) are the following:"

The first dealt with the "chain of evidence," and "the most important piece of physical evidence," the shotgun. One of Niebauer's children had given the weapon to private detective C.C. Crook, and when it was returned to Santa Clara County Authorities, the criminalist who received it said he could not guarantee "there had not been any modifications."

The statement continued that "the re-test done at the Santa Clara County crime lab resulted in significant mechanical problems being discovered. These problems include the gun firing without the trigger being pulled."

The report further claimed that none of Abigail's clothing had been preserved by Palo Alto authorities.

One of the last items bothered Jane: "… an intentional killing committed in a rage generated by an argument is classified as manslaughter. The statue of limitations on manslaughter is only six years and it has run (out) in this matter." If Lee Sansum were ever to get a DA to file charges, it would have to be for first or second degree murder, for which there was no statute.

" …there are ample grounds to suspect this was a deliberate killing," the report continued. "We are simply acknowledging the state of evidence …"

Michael O'Reilly's report concluded, "We are genuinely saddened by the fact this case cannot be brought to a satisfactory resolution."

Although the problems in the Abigail Neibauer case seemed overwhelming, even to the sympathetic Deputy Attorney General, they did not deter Jane

Alexander. "Maybe I'm still just a little naïve," she said, "if I was a lawyer or knew more, I probably wouldn't have jumped in like I did."

She called Lee Sansum and told him the most encouraging words he had heard since Abigail died. "I'll work on your case," she said.

Lee had wanted Jane to send letters to every congressman and senator in the country, but she convinced him that was futile. "We have to go back to Palo Alto and find a way to convince them to reopen the case."

When they left the San Francisco group and started CAH, Jane asked him if she could keep his sister's case. He consented without reservation.

The Sansum case would be Jane's first attempt to put to use what she had learned in her own pursuit of justice for Gertrude McCabe.

She called Palo Alto homicide detective John Lindsay and identified herself as a member of a victim's group, and said she wanted an appointment to discuss the Abigail Niebauer case. Lindsay politely said he didn't know anything about the Niebauer case, but offered to find the files. Jane thanked him and said she would call back. "You never ask them to call you," she had learned. "You always let them know you're going to call again."

By August, Jane was growing anxious about her own case. Tom O'Donnell still had not entered a plea as his public defender made a series of legal maneuvers. One was a request for copies of all one hundred and twenty-five tape recordings she had made of her phone calls with friends of Tom. O'Donnell was demanding his right to a speedy trial, yet he had not even entered a plea. Finally, a trial date was set for September 10.

So Jane went back and forth between monitoring the progress in the O'Donnell prosecution and trying to help Lee Sansum. The new interest—justice for Abigail—helped keep her mind off her own problems and seemed to invigorate her.

Several weeks after speaking to John Lindsey by phone, she drove to Palo Alto and met with him. He told Jane he believed there was a possibility that Abigail had indeed been murdered. Jane left his office upbeat and confident that the case might be reopened. She telephoned Lee, who was exuberant at even the slightest encouraging news.

But before he could do anything about it, Lindsey left the department. Once again, the Niebauer case was back to square one.

But that setback turned out to be Lee Sansum's first break in years. His pursuit of justice had developed a remarkable similarity to Jane's. John Kracht had been the "miracle" in her case. In Lee Sansum's, the miracle was named Mike Yore.

Like John Kracht, Mike Yore had just arrived in homicide. For both men, it was their first murder investigation as lead detective.

When Jane spoke to him in July 1993, Yore had already spent weeks studying the Niebauer file. Almost the first words out of his mouth were, "No question she was murdered." He told her the case, which had been ruled an accidental death, had been reopened twice. Yore stated he would need some new piece of evidence, and he thought that he could get it from forensics.

Yore had spent fifteen years on Palo Alto SWAT and served as their weapons instructor. He is FBI-qualified as an instructor in everything from handguns to automatic weapons and shotguns, and has taken numerous seminars in forensic evidence pertaining to firearms.

In his statement to police, James Niebauer claimed that Abigail was reaching out to hold the barrel of the shotgun, ostensibly to have a look at the serial numbers her husband was offering as proof of the gun's age and potential value. But Mike Yore didn't see any powder burns or residue on the inside of her sleeves. What he saw was a six-inch powder burn in the middle of her left sleeve, on the bottom of her forearms, and a three-inch powder burn on the bottom of the right sleeve, about halfway between her wrists and elbows.

That's when it struck him. Abigail was shot with her arms squeezed in front of her in a defensive position, her hands in front of her face. She was trying to protect herself from the blast.

Still, he knew he would have to prove it. Yore took five of his own white shirts and a half box of shotgun shells that had been taken from the Niebauer place. Then he borrowed several store mannequins and shortened the sleeves on his shirts to the same twenty-seven inches that Abigail's blouse had measured.

He put a bulletproof vest on the mannequin, stuffed the sleeve of the shirt until it approximated human arms, and tied the sleeves to the barrel of the shotgun to simulate the position James Niebauer had claimed her arms were in when she died. With the muzzle a foot from the mannequin's chest, Yore pulled the trigger.

The shot left a hole in the shirt at precisely the point it had entered Abigail's torso, but with no powder burns on the shirt sleeves. The distance from muzzle to torso was too short for the powder to fan out and leave anything but faint traces of smoke. Nothing like the stains found on Abigail's blouse.

Then he changed shirts and repositioned the arms in a defensive position. From fourteen inches he fired again. This time he got distinctive powder burns on both sleeves in the same positions as the one's on Abigail's blouse, but they were larger than hers. Like focusing a camera, Yore moved in and out until he thought he had precisely duplicated the position of Abigail Niebauer at the time of her death. At eleven inches Yore pulled the trigger for the last time, and the powder stains on the shirt were identical to Abigail's.

Jane Alexander had been right about Mike Yore. Not only did he believe in the case, but also he was smart and dedicated enough to find a way to prove it.

Yore took the five shirts to the Santa Clara County District Attorney's office and hung them on corkboards, meticulously re-creating his experiment. There were a lot of nervous faces in the room as he explained his discovery. At the end of his demonstration, they refused to proceed with the case, saying they needed a more expert opinion than his. They walked out without suggesting anyone or offering any advice.

Yore was not discouraged. He called Jane and told her he needed four blouses and four sweaters identical to the ones that Abigail was wearing at the time of her death. He had no budget for them and had already shot up every white shirt he owned.

In a pouring rainstorm, Jane and partner Jan Miller searched every clothing store in Marin County until they found four cable knit sweaters and four white cotton rayon blouses in the size Abigail had worn. Mike would not give them any details, but said he was conducting "experiments" to help prove his case.

Yore went back to the firing range and duplicated his experiment. It took over four hours, but this time he videotaped and photographed all his efforts. He felt the results, which confirmed his first experiments were overwhelmingly convincing that Abigail had not been killed in the position that Jim Niebauer had claimed.

Mike petitioned the Palo Alto Police Department to fly him to Hawthorne, Florida, to show his new findings to Dr. Martin Fackler, one of the world's premier authorities on wound ballistics. They told him there was no money in the department's budget for such a trip.

Yore turned to Citizens Against Homicide. They had begun to raise money for their organization by sponsoring a charity golf tournament and had some money in their treasury. Jane and Jan immediately offered to pay for a round-trip coach class ticket, four hundred dollars.

Yore arrived at Fackler's home in Florida and immediately showed him the evidence he had compiled. Fackler evaluated it and said, "You have it."

A euphoric Mike Yore flew home the next day. Within a few weeks, Fackler's detailed analysis of Yore's experiment arrived in Santa Clara County. In his conclusion, Fackler stated that he felt the evidence was conclusive that Abigail had not been killed as her husband had said she was. She was in a classic defensive position at the time of her death. Fackler offered to fly to California and testify for the prosecution.

However, the D.A.'s office wanted a few months to examine potential defense motions, after which they would consider filing charges. The months would drag and drag. Like the O'Donnell case, the wheels were grinding very slowly.

This did not diminish, though, the efforts of Citizens Against Homicide. The group had played a crucial role in furthering the cause of justice. Now what Jane needed was a little success of her own.

Chapter Twenty-Three

By July 1995, Tom O'Donnell had been in the Santa Clara County Jail for three years and two months and still had not faced his day in court. At first O'Donnell had demanded his right to a speedy trial, but then his pal Harry Carmichael came down with terminal cancer. John Kracht believed that Harry represented a potentially damaging witness who could refute Tom's alibi. Harry knew that police had long suspected him of holding back information and secretly feared being indicted for obstruction of justice or even complicity in Gertrude's murder.

So Tom O'Donnell had gone from his initial demand to "get the trial over with" to working the system to delay it. On numerous occasions he filed a request for a new public defender. He received a mind-numbing twenty-six delays in his hearings and trial dates.

It appeared to Jane as if no one in the Santa Clara County DA's office was available to try the McCabe case. The prosecutor who filed the case, Charles Constantinides, was embroiled in the prosecution of a notorious mob case. Santa Clara County was in the midst of an explosive population and crime growth, and virtually every homicide prosecutor was busy on a difficult case.

Tom had managed to get his original public defender, Randi Danto, replaced by a thirty-year veteran named John Vaughn. He immediately filed a motion to dismiss the charges against O'Donnell on the grounds that the woman he had been with in Las Vegas had died, hence denying his all-important alibi witness. Once again, O'Donnell refused to reveal her name, claiming that she was a friend of Jane's.

Jane, John Kracht, and Jeff Ouimet got their best laugh since the terrible affair had begun. They relished the absurdity of a lifelong con man claiming he would risk life in prison to protect the honor of a dead woman, then asking the judge to dismiss his charges on those grounds.

The judge dismissed the motion.

When that failed, John Vaughn went to work on his primary means of defending Tom O'Donnell. He would mount an assault on Jane Alexander's character. He would cast her as a spurned and vengeful woman with suspicious involvement in Gertrude's murder. Jane was distraught that Vaughn, as a result of the defense's right to discovery, would get a copy of her diaries and access to her most private thoughts.

Following Harry Carmichael's death that year, Tom again demanded his right to a speedy trial. With no prosecutor assigned to the case, he hoped he would catch the San Jose DA's office unprepared.

On July 11, Jane drove to San Jose with Jan Miller for yet another hearing. This time they stayed in the courtroom and waited. Nobody came. The defense attorney was there, and the judge. But the new deputy DA had totally forgotten about the court appearance. After an hour, the judge retreated to his chambers, and later emerged with Assistant District Attorney David Davies. Davies asked for another continuance.

Jane Alexander followed Davies out. She was furious. Years of delays and O'Donnell's manipulation of the system had sent her through the roof. "Don't you have one flunky in this bureaucracy who could call me so that I wouldn't have to drive 175 miles for the DA not to show?"

Davies had never met Jane Alexander. It was an awkward moment. He had to explain that the current deputy DA just had a hung jury on another case and would have to retry it. He had forgotten the O'Donnell hearing. Davies explained that a new deputy DA, Rich Titus, would be assigned to the case.

When Jane returned to court a week later for another hearing, she found out that Titus was in the hospital having an emergency triple bypass. It seemed like even God was out to get her.

"But the good news," Davies said, "is that I got Joyce Allegro to take the case." Jane nearly began to cry. This would be her fourth DA.

"She's great, she's in court downstairs. You can see her in action." With another continuance until September 21, 1995, Jane was not in the best of moods. But as long as she was already there, she decided to watch her new prosecutor in court.

It was not the best moment to observe Joyce Allegro. She was handling a very minor case concerning a car theft. It was a two- or three-day trial, and she was in her final arguments before the jury. Jane could not have been less impressed. It appeared that Allegro was reading her summation off a yellow legal pad. Jane could hardly hear her.

"I don't want a woman trying the case," she told Davies afterward.

"Trust me, she's the best we have," he said.

Jane instinctively did not like Allegro and was worried that a woman would not be tough enough to handle the prosecution.

It would prove to be the best fight that Jane ever lost.

Grant Cunningham had been investigating the McCabe murder for the DA's office for several years. Jane had been impressed with his intelligence and people skills, and so she paid attention when he expressed his concern that she was selling Allegro short. He faxed her the notices for Allegro's Prosecutor of the Year Award, which had been given to her by the California District Attorney's Association in 1994. It included dozens of testimonials from victims' families and colleagues and noted that in 1984 she had been the first female in county history to be assigned to the homicide prosecution team.

Allegro and Cunningham met with Jane at an Italian restaurant in Marin County to discuss the case.

Allegro felt that making a sympathetic witness of Jane was going to be her most important challenge. She feared the jury would wonder how a woman, any woman, could hand over so much to a man like Tom O'Donnell. Jane would have to explain why she let him control all her money and use her credit cards, and then defend him so vociferously after he had left her.

Jane spoke through most of the lunch. She was irritated by a peculiar habit of Allegro, who could write without looking at her notepad, staring into Jane's face as she scribbled away.

When Grant went to the restroom, Jane said to Allegro, "I watched you argue a case a few weeks ago. I have to tell you I wasn't impressed."

Allegro kept her cool. "I may not be flamboyant, I may not pound the table," she said, "but I win. What were you expecting, Clarence Darrow?"

At the end of lunch, Jane Alexander was resigned to the fact that Joyce Allegro was indeed going to prosecute the case.

Jane would learn over the next few months just how wrong she was about Joyce Allegro. She would find out what colleagues had long known about Joyce: she inspires fear in the hearts of defendants.

As Joyce gradually won Jane's trust, Jane's spirits were buoyed enormously by a phone call from the man who had solved the case. "Jane, I'm now working as an investigator for the DA's office," said John Kracht. "I've been assigned to help Grant Cunningham and Joyce Allegro on the O'Donnell case."

"Jane, whenever you two stop circling around and sniffing each other out," Kracht said, "you'll be good friends."

The first step was the voir dire process. Joyce Allegro is famous for picking juries. It is an arcane and mysterious art, and Allegro has a sixth sense about jurors. One of her most enlightening experiences came when she sat on a criminal jury herself on a case that resulted in a hung jury. Allegro realized that juries need more than the facts of a case and the answers to yes and no questions. They need to understand the people on the stand, to judge whether they are credible or not. Juries want answers to the questions they would ask themselves if given the chance.

For the Thomas O'Donnell trial, she needed a jury who not merely had the stamina for a three-month trial, but who could sort hundreds of pieces of evidence presented by the more than sixty witnesses expected to take the stand. Since she knew the defense would mount a no-holds-barred attack on the character of Jane Alexander, she wanted a jury that could look past personal invective and focus on the fact. A smart jury, one that was a bit battered and wise.

Trial selection began on April 15, 1996, twelve and a half years after the discovery of Gertrude McCabe's battered body. Joyce asked Jane to stay at home during the selection process, but would not share her reasons. After a year of working with Joyce, Jane now trusted her implicitly.

A jury of eight women and four men was chosen, ranging in age from mid 20s to late 60s. Largely middle-class, ten were white and two were Filipino. One man was a pony-tailed musician, one a computer programmer, and the jury foreman managed a grocery store. Three of the women on the jury were nurses.

During opening statements on Monday morning, April 22, 1996, Joyce Allegro approached the jury in a power-red suit and tennis shoes. She explained that she had broken her foot and the shoes were all she could wear. It helped break the ice with a jury apprehensive about sitting on a first-degree murder case.

Jane, the prosecution's star witness, was not permitted in the courtroom. But Lee Sansum, his own case still in limbo, had flown from Seattle and was joined by members of Citizens Against Homicide. Several nuns from Notre Dame High School, Jane's alma mater, including her cousin Sister Beth and a close friend, Sister Theresa, were present and would remain throughout the trial.

At home in Sleepy Hollow, Jane finished her diary entry by writing simply, "Thank you Lord."

Joyce Allegro was ready.

"When Tom O'Donnell was introduced to a friend of Jane Alexander's, he said, 'I'm a con man and I'm a good one!' It was one of the few true things he has said," she began.

"The defendant, Tom O'Donnell, is a con man, a very good one. For the next few weeks you're going to hear how he worked his con on a number of people, but especially Jane Alexander. She totally bought into his con, learned to love him deeply, shared everything she had with him, then mortgaged her future on his assurance that he could and would take care of everything. As a result of her trust in the defendant, Jane Alexander not only lost her home and possessions, she lost her freedom, friends, and most terrible of all, her beloved aunt, Gertrude McCabe.

"There are probably fifty different homicide cases in various stages of prosecution by the District Attorney's Office right now," said Allegro. "The issues are different from case to case. Some deal with a known assailant, but question the intent of the assailant. Others are whodunit's; in other words, the identity of the murderer must be proven. This case is a whodunit. The defendant denies killing Gertrude McCabe, but I doubt the defendant will contest that Miss McCabe was clearly murdered in the first degree.

"As you may have gathered from the judge's questions during jury selection, the prosecution's case will be built on circumstantial evidence. There was no confession. There are no fingerprints at the scene or on the murder weapon. There were actually several murder weapons but only one was recovered."

With these words Allegro set the tone for an opening statement that lasted more than two hours. Her style of oratory is measured and simple, attacking a case from many different points of view. Her opening statement described the murder in a least five different ways. It wasn't enough to simply state the point of view of crime-scene investigators at Gertrude McCabe's home. Allegro covered events that led up to it, events that followed it, events from Jane's point of view, Jane's friends' points of view, and finally, events from the perspective of the detectives who cracked the case. This multi-faceted explanation was needed to encompass the enormous amount of evidence. It was also a way of showing the jury that the perspective of the most instrumental witness—that of Jane Alexander, and her diary—was corroborated by many other witnesses.

"I will first discuss the homicide, then the police investigation, then the backgrounds of Jane Alexander and the defendant as they relate to their relationship. Not only will you hear about things that happened in the eighties, there will also be testimony about events from the seventies and even perhaps the sixties. While the importance of some things will not be immediately apparent, at the conclusion of the trial I believe you will see how they all fit into the whole picture to prove the guilt of the defendant beyond reasonable doubt.

"Gertrude McCabe died an awful death on October 21, 1983. Her head was repeatedly beaten. She was stabbed ten times. She was suffocated with a wad of tissue and perhaps a pillow, and finally strangled. It seems unlikely that Miss McCabe struggled with her attacker so that the extensive violence was necessary to subdue her, since Gertrude McCabe was eighty-eight years old, five feet two inches tall, and weighed only one hundred fifteen pounds.

"No, the more reasonable explanation is that the killer wanted to be very sure that Gertrude McCabe was dead, but was probably not criminally sophisticated. He may not have realized just how difficult it can be to actually kill someone."

In broad stokes Allegro laid before the jury Jane's life with Tom O'Donnell. She spoke of their meeting in 1966 and of Tom's friendship with her husband, Al. Allegro told the jury of Al's heart attack at age fifty four and Jane's subsequent depression.

Allegro also related how vulnerable Jane had been to Tom's devious con game. "Now, in spite of, or maybe because of the fact that she was married to a banker, Mrs. Alexander had a pretty cavalier attitude about money. She had always had enough to live comfortably. She did not like to balance her checkbook, so every four or five years she would close out a bank account and open a new one. Her husband apparently indulged her disinterest in financial matters and took care of all major financial details.

"Unlike Jane Alexander, the defendant loved dealing with money. He gradually took control of Mrs. Alexander's finances, to her complete relief, and with her consent. He kept detailed financial records, saved receipts from every purchase, and asked Jane Alexander to do the same. It soon became apparent to the defendant that they did not have enough money to maintain their lifestyle. The defendant was not employed and frequently told people he was 'retired' and waiting for a trust fund to mature in the fall of 1984."

If the jury thought this was a straightforward case, they were quickly made aware of the complexity of Tom's scams. Allegro listed the facts and figures relating to loans, mortgages, and credit cards. They heard tales of intrigue and shadowy international crime figures.

Allegro summed up by explaining that the investigations had been exhaustive and pointed solely at Tom O'Donnell as the murderer of Gertrude McCabe. O'Donnell, she said, had means, motive, and opportunity. After the killing he fled, not because of any pursuit by vengeful diamond smugglers, but because John Kracht was about to zero in on him. Although her style had been methodical and contained, she closed with an emotional flourish:

"After hearing Jane Alexander's testimony, you will not doubt that she loved the defendant deeply. She trusted him so completely that she would have accepted a semi-reasonable explanation for why the "trust" was not going to be able to pay off the Woodson loan. Further, in spite of his terrible record of handling money, the defendant had every reason to believe that she would continue to give him complete control over her finances after she inherited her aunt's estate. However, Miss McCabe was in very good health. Though eighty-eight, she seemed in no hurry to die. If he wanted his lifestyle to continue, the defendant could not wait much longer. Killing her thus became a reasonable means to a desired end.

"Once you have had the opportunity to hear and see all the evidence and apply the law to it, I believe that you, too, will become convinced, beyond a reasonable doubt, that Tom O'Donnell is guilty of the murder of Gertrude McCabe and will return that verdict."

◆ ◆ ◆

After introducing himself as Tom O'Donnell's defense attorney, John Vaughn launched into a high-octane rebuttal of most, but not all, of the allegations against Tom O'Donnell. Vaughn was unsparing in his portrait of Jane Alexander and her key role in forcing the hand of the police. Vaughn suggested that the case was constructed out of Alexander's imagination. He said there was no compelling reason to pursue the case, but that somehow Jane had convinced police to have Tom arrested on St. Patrick's Day, 1992, for the purpose of revenge. Jane Alexander had a vengeful personality, he said, and might have been more involved in the murder than she let on.

"This is a murder case. It is about the killing of Gertrude McCabe on October 21, 1983 ... That was a Friday. It was the last day anybody saw Gertrude McCabe alive. It was the last day anybody talked to Gertrude McCabe. And certainly it was the last day, you will learn, that Jane Alexander talked with Gertrude McCabe. Because you'll see that there is a phone call from Jane Alexander to Gertrude in the early afternoon of the twenty-first.

"When the police first encounter Jane Alexander at Gertrude's home on October 23, 1983, one of the first questions they ask is, 'Do you know the extent of Gertrude's estate?' ... Jane's answer was 'I don't know.' We will question Jane as to whether or not she really didn't know, or was there another reason for saying that she didn't know.

"We know that in 1980 and 1981 Jane borrowed money from Gertrude. We know that during those years that Jane was very close to being destitute. The pension that Jane received as a consequence of her husband's death ... was a whopping sixty-five dollars a month. Sixty-five dollars a month for a lifelong career with a bank, and a small check from Social Security for her last child at home ... That is what Jane was living on when Tom begins his relationship with Jane Alexander.

"This upper-class woman, the lifestyle, the lovely home was perhaps a dream—but it certainly wasn't a reality in 1980 and 1981. What Jane represented at that time was a woman who was not working full-time, could not pay her bills and, quite frankly, was borrowing money from her friends to live, money that she will admit she had no idea how she would ever pay them back. In fact, you will learn that when they received the Woodson Loan in 1982, the first thing that happened was that her friends were paid back the money that they had loaned Jane to live on, an amount in excess of seventeen thousand dollars. That is what Jane was living on those two years. That money, plus the money from her Aunt Gert that had not been repaid."

Friends of Jane present in the courtroom were stunned at how Vaughn was painting Jane as a co-conspirator or suspect rather than a victim of O'Donnell's greed and manipulation.

Next, he portrayed Jane as an extremist. "In 1963 Jane was politically active. You will learn that she was college-educated, in fact, had worked for naval intelligence and even as a volunteer, worked undercover for the FBI on the California Berkeley campus during the sixties as an informant. You will see and meet a smart, savvy, aggressive woman. This same person, sometime later, would obtain a license to sell real estate. That she had that license and that it simply lapsed because she failed to renew it."

Vaughn brought into question the diary entries and Jane's interpretation of them. He attached the crime lab destruction of the blood evidence as a setback that could have cleared his client. Finally, he questioned the odometer readings on the rental car and the police vehicle that checked the route. Was there any effort to calibrate the mileage, or check on highway conditions or detours on October 21, 1983?

In summing up, Vaughn theorized that Tom O'Donnell became the target of investigation only when Jane decided to shift the focus away from herself. He closed with a condemnation of the police department.

"The turning point in this case, the break in this case, we will prove to you did not occur in December of 1991, just before the warrant for Tom O'Donnell was issued. It occurred on December 27, 1984. Sergeant Morin of the San Jose Police Department took a telephone message to John Kracht, the investigator in the case. 'Jane called. She's ready to be a victim on the ten thousand dollar money case and will 'co-op' with you. She realizes that Tom did her wrong. She wants revenge.'

"This case is complicated. There are a lot of players. Tom has pleaded not guilty to this crime. When all is said and done, I will return to you, I will discuss the state of the evidence, such as it is, and I will ask you to return verdicts of not guilty because that will be right, it will be proper, and it will be correct. Thank you very much."

One of the first witnesses was Gertrude's next-door neighbor, Juanita Lennon, who talked of discovering the unclaimed newspapers and the house in disarray. Then the first officers on the scene spelled out the discovery of the body and the examination of the initial evidence.

Judge Robert Ahern was an active presence in the courtroom. He ejected audience members if they giggled during testimony, and on more than one occasion he cautioned jury members to keep their composure.

Ahern also did not dismiss his court early or take excessive breaks. His sessions began promptly at 8:30 and generally continued until 4:30 or 5:00, almost unheard of in modern criminal courts. Breaks were fifteen minutes by the clock, without exception.

When a 4.7 earthquake with an epicenter ten miles from the court struck the afternoon of May 21, 1996, Judge Ahern, in his fifth-floor courtroom, exhibited typical aplomb. After waiting for the considerable swaying of the building to cease, he said to the witness, "Continue." Every other courtroom in the building was evacuated. But the O'Donnell trial pressed on with three more hours of testimony.

By the time Jane Alexander was called to the witness stand on the seventh day of testimony, the jury was anxious to have a look at her. They wanted to see if she was the naïve widow-turned-crusader portrayed by Joyce Allegro, or the vengeful and manipulative woman described by Vaughn.

Some of the jurors expected a flashy socialite, perhaps a few anticipated a fire-breathing, right-wing zealot. What they saw was a trim, articulate, impeccably groomed seventy-four-year-old woman who looked like "Grandmother of the Year" material.

As she approached the witness stand and took the oath, she was nervous, afraid that something she might say could undo thirteen years of painful, exhausting effort.

Jane's testimony began with an account of her relationship to her aunt, and then of her own early life in the navy during World War II. Jane was asked about her courtship and marriage to Al Alexander in 1945, and finally about her family life. Her political activism was addressed, and it was established she had no ties to controversial organizations, as Tom O'Donnell's lawyer had alleged.

Joyce Allegro hoped to undo any negative image of Jane by addressing unpleasant matters directly. She confronted Jane about her conservative politics, her gun ownership, and the way she had surrendered financial control to O'Donnell.

Through Joyce's patient questioning and Jane's soft, deliberate responses, her vulnerability to Tom seemed believable.

Allegro then led Jane through a complete account of the way she was conned.

As the testimony turned to the days leading up to the murder, Tom became more visibly anxious. He had not endeared himself to the courtroom. Although well-dressed, he had a nervous air and seemed arrogant to most observers. Tom was also compulsive in his note taking. He took more notes than any juror, sometimes stabbing angrily at the pages as he wrote.

When Jane was testifying, it was as if he were trying to rewrite what she was saying, to maintain control. At times her testimony seemed to drive him crazy. He fidgeted wildly when Jane was asked about the heavy wooden cane given to him by Gertrude on August 31, which he used for six weeks. When Jane explained the cane had not been found by either her or the police, the inference was there. No one had to suggest that it was the murder weapon. Tom's anxiousness spoke volumes to some.

If the trial had a bombshell, it came in the form of a manila envelope found by John Kracht in Jane's home the week after Tom O'Donnell left. Attached to it, on a sheet of paper with the words "A Little Note From Tom" printed at the top, were penciled several questions.

While Jane was on the stand, Joyce asked her to open and read it to the jury. It was a series of questions Tom had prepared.

"Do you have to sign up for five years? Why not two years?"

"Can you clarify the definition of Accidental Death?"

"Say Ben, what personal questions will be asked, other than medical questions?"

"Do you offer mortgage insurance to pay off home?"

"Are insurance settlements subject to tax?"

"Is this considered a large or small amount?"

"Are there double indemnity clauses, for certain kinds of accidents?"

Also in the envelope was a draft of a life insurance policy on Jane in the amount of $249,999. The beneficiary was Tom O'Donnell.

O'Donnell had requested a life insurance policy on Jane for one dollar less than the two hundred fifty thousand dollar dividing line that would have raised the premiums significantly.

Jane was stunned. She was looking at her own death certificate. As she looked at the date on the draft of the policy, she realized it was shortly before their planned trip to Europe. Kracht had hinted to Jane years before that Tom would have been willing to kill her, too. Here was the proof. A life insurance policy would have solved all of Tom's problems.

Jane would spend nine days on the stand, nearly three of them under John Vaughn's accusatory cross-examination.

One of the centerpieces of the trial was Jane's diaries and her obsessive notation of details. One target of Vaughn's attack concerned gardening. In the days just prior to the murder, Tom had spent hours a day watering Jane's oleander bushes, a plant that does not need water. The bushes had survived a four-year drought, and yet there was Tom, dumping hundreds of gallons of water on it day after day.

To Jane, in retrospect, it showed a man coming unglued, compulsively planning the details of his crime over and over, using a preposterous excuse to avoid her as he plotted.

To the defense, it was Jane who was crazy. Vaughn grilled her as she read from her diaries.

> Q. (Mr. Vaughn) I made a note that on August 11, 1983, Tom watered. Does that conform with the diary?
> A. Tom watered with his crutches on, yes.
> Q. August 12, 1983, Tom watered and still on his crutches?
> A. Tom on crutches, watered two and a half hours.
> Q. August 15, Tom watered; is that correct?
> A. Tom watered.
> Q. August 16, Tom watered?
> A. Tom watered three hours with his crutches.
> Q. August 20, Tom watered. And again, for three hours; is that correct?
> A. That's correct.
> Q. August 26, and I note that he watered for another three hours; is that correct?
> A. Tom, three hours, watering.
> Q. September 2.
> A. Tom watered on the second.
> Q. And September 4, Tom watered?
> A. Yes. Watered.
> Q. On September 6, Tom watered for three and a half hours that day?
> A. That's right.
> Q. September 14, "Tom watered four hours and—
> A. ... his foot hurt."
> Q. It caused his foot to hurt. September 19, Tom watered three hours?
> A. Yes.
> Q. Now, you note that because rain in Marin County in the summer isn't something that happens every day, is it?
> A. That's true.

Q. In fact, to the extent that it rains nonstop in the winter, you don't see any rain in the summer. Would that be a good statement?

A. You could say that.

Q. Now, ma'am, in 1987 you were working with Sergeant Jeff Ouimet because you're still committed to seeing Tom O'Donnell arrested, prosecuted, and convicted for the murder of your Aunt Gertrude, aren't you?

A. Yes, I am. I was.

Q. And you still are?

A. I still am.

Q. And you'll stop at nothing to make sure that happens, correct?

A. I just want justice for my aunt. That's all I want, Mr. Vaughn.

Q. Will you lie to do that?

A. Never.

Q. Ma'am, there was nothing, absolutely nothing unusual about what Tom O'Donnell was doing that summer, perhaps the summer before and the summer before that, watering your yard, was there?

Ms. Allegro: Object to the tone of voice.

The court: Overruled.

A. Mr. Vaughn, I didn't note in the diary that he watered so that he could be convicted of a murder.

Q. No, but you put a nice twist on it in 1987, didn't you?

A. I just stated what was in the diary, and that was four years later.

Q. Four years after the fact you tell Sergeant Ouimet that watering for three or four hours at a time was unusual, and what made it even more unusual is that your recollection is that Tom told you that was his thinking time. Is that correct?

A. I don't quite understand the "unusuals" in there. I told him that he watered and that Tom said it was his thinking time. That's correct.

Q. But you also told us that watering three, four hours at a time was silly, because you even testified in this courtroom last week that when you watered it took you ten minutes to water the pots. So that makes the three hours, four hours, sound pretty unusual, doesn't it?

A. To water oleanders, yes, it's very unusual.

Vaughn noted that after returning home from errands on the day of Gert's murder, Jane's diary noted three hours in the garden before going inside to prepare a meatloaf for Tom's expected return.

Q. Would that have been another day out of the ordinary?

A. I never watered oleanders. I certainly had a lot of other areas that I could water.

Q. Was that your "thinking time"?

A. No, it wasn't my thinking time.

Vaughn also tried to establish that the recollection about Tom's records being thrown out—the two filing cabinets in the basement—were another piece of "evidence" that Jane remembered opportunistically years after the fact. This backfired, however. John Kracht later established that the missing files were mentioned just after Tom's departure, long before Jane suspected or accepted Tom's involvement with the murder.

Despite his obsessive hammering, Jane emerged unscathed from the cross-examination.

♦ ♦ ♦

One of the best witnesses in the case was discovered just as the trial began. Robert Lee "Butch" Johnson was an old friend of Tom O'Donnell's having met him in Arkansas during the 1970s. The two had put together a deal involving coal speculation.

Five months before the trial, Butch Johnson received a call from DA investigator Grant Cunningham. It was a routine investigative call, and it seemed unlikely Johnson would have any direct knowledge of the McCabe matter.

But Johnson had recently spoken to O'Donnell. Tom had called him collect from prison, hoping to get money to make bail. Johnson declined to help but did ask why Tom was in prison.

"Tom said that he went over one day to see some people in San Jose, but they weren't home, or he couldn't find them and because he was over there they charged him with the murder."

Cunningham could not believe what he was hearing. Tom had actually told someone that he had been in San Jose on the day of the murder. "Was he talking about the time of the murder, back in October 1983?" asked Grant.

"Yeah, the day of the murder or the night of the murder, something like that."

"Did he say who he was trying to contact while in San Jose?"

"No, he didn't."

"Did he say anything else?"

"Something to the effect of 'I have no alibi as to where I was,'" Johnson explained. "And that Jane Alexander was blaming him for everything, although it wasn't true."

♦ ♦ ♦

After Jane herself, the most powerful witness against O'Donnell was John Kracht. His quiet, precise demeanor held the jury in rapt attention.

Kracht worked in the building next to the San Jose courthouse, so he was called on several different occasions to fill in for witnesses who couldn't make it to court. The jury saw him on at least five different days. Piece by piece he built the case against Tom O'Donnell.

He also answered the criticism that Jane had harassed the police into action.

"Was Jane motivated by vengeance?" he was asked.

He replied without hesitation. "I would only hope if I were murdered, there would be somebody who would do what she did."

With John Kracht on the stand, Joyce Allegro introduced into evidence a piece of paper that had been discovered on a search of Harry Carmichael's home in Van Nuys. The alibi sheet had been discovered while Tom was in prison in Marin County, awaiting fraud charges. It could only have been written on his visit to Carmichael in the fall of 1984.

It was an account of Tom's trip to Las Vegas, written in Tom's handwriting. It showed mileage along various routes to the city from Van Nuys. It recorded the route that Tom had taken, with the turnoff that took him north to the ghost town of Atolia. It recorded a time figure: "Five to six hours to Vegas." An imaginary friend: "5'7" blonde, 130." Tom also wrote down the names of five casinos.

Tom then wrote a note to himself: "Make up fifty to sixty miles."

Tom had guessed how many miles the rental trip must have taken.

When Roxanne Alexander, Jane's daughter-in-law, took the stand, O'Donnell's fortunes took a decided turn for the worse. Roxanne, nervous and distraught, recalled that O'Donnell had informed her of Gertrude's murder. Within hours of the discovery of McCabe's body, O'Donnell had described the cause of death by saying she had been "bludgeoned, stabbed, and garroted." The word garroted was so alien to Roxanne that she wrote it down on a yellow legal pad. Yet O'Donnell could not have known the cause of death—the bicycle chain around her neck—unless he was present at the murder.

Next, Hans Buhler, an expert in gems, flew in from Spain to testify. He stood out even in a trial with many exotic witnesses. At last the man who had founded the Greenfire Trust, the alleged source of Tom's wealth, could tell his story. The name Greenfire was chosen, he said, because it refers to the brilliance of emeralds.

"But you must understand, however, a trust is something completely different in European business," he testified. "It is something to limit the liability of an individual businessman if that business fails. It is not like your American trusts."

Tom had approached Buhler in his Zurich office more than twenty years before. He would attend his open houses, which were frequented by members of the precious stone trading elite. O'Donnell wanted to get into the business and asked Buhler questions about the trade.

What did Buhler think of O'Donnell?

"He was a showman, he puts on a lot of show with nothing behind it," he said. "How do you say it in English, a bull shits?"

The jury laughed.

Buhler explained that there was a way of holding diamonds or other precious stones in a small packet made of folded paper. Buhler could tell if someone knew the business by the way they opened the packet, holding the paper at the corners, unfolding it with the thumb and forefinger.

"I gave it to him, and right there I could see he knew nothing of diamonds. It's not like opening a piece of mail at home."

Did Tom O'Donnell ever have an investment with the Greenfire Trust?

"No, no, he would pretend, he would pretend."

It is a little-publicized fact that during a trial, the attorneys, particularly the prosecution, will keep an eye out for people attending the trial. If someone interests them, they strike up a conversation.

On May 20, 1996, Grant Cunningham met a well-dressed woman in the audience, Eileen Sherwood. Sherwood identified herself as a friend of Louise Hewitt, with whom she had been close since they both worked in Hody's restaurant in North Hollywood. (Eileen Sherwood and Louise Hewitt are not their real names.)

"How long have you known Tom O'Donnell?" asked Grant.

"Louise and I met him at the same time, at the Money Tree in North Hollywood."

It was Thanksgiving weekend, 1987, and Hewitt and Sherwood were at the bar watching a 49ers game.

"It was about five o'clock, Tom came in and sat nearby. He listened to us talk for a while, then introduced himself, offered to buy us drinks. He said he was visiting from South Africa and was staying with a friend in town. He ended up taking Louise to dinner that night. I remember he didn't have a car. I wasn't interested in him at all, but Louise kind of fought for him as if he were trying to pick the better one of us."

"You know what?" added Sherwood. "First thing I thought was that he was a con."

Louise Hewitt, the mother of three sons, had been married for thirty-six years before being widowed. She had continued to run her husband's motion picture film lab until the time she met Tom.

Within five months he had moved from his apartment into her prestigious residence in Toluca Lake. Hewitt then began to support him in his new business venture, which involved the marketing and sale of electric devices that drove off insects and rodents with ultrasound.

According to Sherwood, scores of these "Electra-Cats" were still stacked in Hewitt's garage, awaiting Tom's release from prison.

Tom's arrest had hit Louise Hewitt hard. She had been embarrassed by his being arrested in front of her neighbors. Until that point she hadn't known he had been convicted of a crime, let alone that he was on parole.

She continued to believe in him more than four years after his arrest. She paid visits to him in prison and accepted his collect phone calls.

Hewitt's loyalty echoed Jane's from the earlier days. "She's in denial, plain and simple," said Sherwood. "She doesn't want to believe that Tom loved her just for her money."

Cunningham told Joyce Allegro about his conversation with Sherwood, and a month later her friend Louise Hewitt was sworn in to testify.

"Did Tom ever tell you he was on parole?"

"No."

"Did Tom ever tell you he had been to prison?"

"No."

"Did Tom tell you he was living with Harry Carmichael?"

"No."

Tom had been living just seven miles from Hewitt at the time he claimed to be commuting from San Jose.

"Did Tom ever tell you his life was in danger?"

"No."

"Did Tom ever tell you that your life could be in danger because you were with him?"

"No."

"Did Tom tell you he smuggled diamonds?"

"Yes."

"Did Tom tell you not to tell people you had seen him?"

"No."

"Did Tom ever tell you why his relationship with Jane Alexander ended?"

"He never told me why."

"Did Tom tell you bad people were after him?"

"No."

Hewitt eventually conceded that at some point Tom said that Jane and the dog had been threatened.

Throughout her testimony Tom O'Donnell showed signs of considerable stress. He stopped taking notes and simply stared into his lap, occasionally rubbing his face.

Hewitt didn't fair any better in cross-examination, when she was supposed to be helping Tom's case. John Vaughn asked her about her feelings for Tom, whether she had ever considered marriage. She didn't want to get married, she said, since she enjoyed her freedom to travel and live her own life.

She also claimed that Tom didn't have much money, but he treated her like a queen.

It was difficult to believe he was capable of the crime, she said. He had never been violent, and she had never heard him threaten anyone.

When Joyce Allegro again questioned Hewitt, it was in relation to her financial support for his business ventures.

"Did you invest seventy-five thousand dollars in the Electra-Cat business?"

"No."

"Did you invest seventy-five thousand dollars in some other business of Mr. O'Donnell's?"

"No."

At that point Joyce Allegro presented John Vaughn with a four page letter by Tom, referencing an Electra-Cat investment by Louise Hewitt in the amount of $75,000. Tom looked sick. His head was in his hands; he could no longer face the court.

Hewitt admitted "buying stock" in the company, but said that she was reimbursed by check when the stock was repurchased. A copy of this check was never admitted into evidence, however.

Little by little Allegro had effectively put the noose around Tom O'Donnell. She rested her case at 11:02 AM on June 18, 1996, two months and six days after the trial had begun.

Defense attorney John Vaughn called ten witnesses to rebut the arguments of the prosecution. Among them were three laboratory criminologists and forensic experts, one of whom had worked directly with the evidence in the case. Each testified about the various scientific methods to match lipstick samples and concluded the smear could not be matched to anything found in Jane's home.

The rubber gloves from the crime scene could not be linked absolutely to those used at the Lockheed Corporation where Mary Carmichael worked. The fiber evidence and hair vacuumed from Aunt Gert's carpets could not be linked to Tom O'Donnell either. The wig that had been found among Tom's belongings when he was arrested in Las Vegas could not be matched to any fiber at the crime scene.

There was never any more than the circumstantial evidence of Tom's guilt, and the defense stressed this point again and again. Tom could not be physically linked to the crime scene.

Chapter Twenty-three

Kay O'Donnell-Hill, Tom's ex-wife, was called in as a character witness. So was Tom's son Brandon. Though neither had seen Tom in more than ten years, both claimed that violence was out of character for him. It was the best the defense could muster.

After three months of testimony, both sides rested and prepared for closing arguments.

On July 9, 1996, Jane rose and had an early breakfast with her niece, RoiAnn Thompson in San Jose, with whom she had been staying throughout the three-and-a-half month trial. It was a day for which she had long awaited, the day when Gertrude's fate would be handed to a jury. Although she had been banned from the trial, as were other witnesses, she was permitted to attend closing arguments.

Jane's friends and supporters packed the courtroom. Jim Rohde's wife, Erin, brought her eighty-year-old parents, Sudee and Les. Jan Miller and CAH members Josie Morgan and Marlena Holoway came to sit with her. The Notre Dame nuns were there, with loyal friend Vaux Toneff. Joyce Allegro's mother and son Kevin came to watch her. John Kracht and Grant Cunningham and a handful of deputy DA's came as well.

Joyce started at the very beginning.

"You remember Roxanne Alexander," she said, summarizing her testimony. "You recall how Tom had spoken to Roxanne the day after Gertrude's body had been discovered and told her that she had been 'garroted.' The information was not revealed to Jane and Tom until six weeks later."

Joyce recalled the testimony of many witnesses and went over the crime scene. Then she displayed the crime scene photos for the jury and observers.

These were painful and disturbing to Jane. It was the first time that she had seen photos of Aunt Gert's body. Some of the pictures came from the morgue and showed Gert naked, with stab marks covering her chest. Jane could not help but cry.

Tom started to stare at Jane during the closing arguments, his eyes burning with hatred. His staring and its effect on Jane and several other observers was so obvious that the bailiff told him to stop and turn around.

Joyce waved Tom's alibi list: "Make up fifty to sixty miles." She hammered on O'Donnell all day and continued the next morning. Her summation was precise and emotional. The jury hung on every word.

She was done by 11:00 AM on the second day.

In his closing argument, Vaughn tried to put Jane Alexander on trial. "Jane Alexander." He kept pointing his finger at her. "And Jane Alexander then called her friend in the police …" he snarled.

He tried to turn Jane's name into a dirty word.

"This Jane Alexander … that Jane Alexander …"

He attacked the police. He called John Kracht a liar.

He mocked the fact that Jane had kept a diary. "We can read it in Jane Alexander's book," he said four times, though Jane had stated under oath that at that time she had no book, no agent, and never talked to a publisher.

He pointed his finger at her. "That liar there … she lied about the size of Gertrude's estate."

Vaughn stated he wasn't accusing Jane of murdering Aunt Gertrude, and then said, "Where was Jane October 21, 1983? We know she was shopping and at the grocery store at 1:50 PM. But it's only one and a half hours from her house to San Jose. Where was she in the evening? What is her alibi? The FBI man said it could have been a woman.

"Tom is the victim of Jane Alexander's, and he has paid enough." That sent many in the courtroom over the edge. One of the nuns cried. Jane Alexander became so upset that afterward she was unable to eat a bite of lunch.

The prosecution always has two rounds at closing, since the burden of proof is on the state. Joyce Allegro stood for one last effort on the third day of summations. She had maintained a calm demeanor through the entire trial, but now she rebutted every one of Vaughn's accusations with a show of emotional indignity.

"John Vaughn wants your sympathy. What about Gert?" He says, 'This trial is about the life of an innocent man, Tom O'Donnell.' This trial is about the murder of Gertrude McCabe, and don't you forget it. Why did Tom lie to Sergeant Ouimet and tell him he was living with Harry when he was living with Louise Hewitt?

"Look at the totality of the evidence. What about the mileage? What about the ten-thirty phone call the night of the murder? Why did Tom burn all of Gert's checks? Maybe he didn't want them to know about the twenty-five thousand dollars they had borrowed. What about Butch Johnson? Tom told him he was in San Jose the day of the murder. Why did he make something sinister out of Jane trying to get this murder solved? Was she just to forget it? What would you do?

"Tom O'Donnell is a cold-blooded killer, the worst kind. He carefully planned this murder. There was no anger, and no remorse. You are the last step on the road to justice for Gertrude McCabe."

On Thursday, July 11, the case was handed over to the jury. John Kracht and Grant Cunningham took Jane and Joyce Allegro to Joyce's favorite restaurant, Palermo's, in San Jose. Jane had bought them all thank-you gifts.

For weeks Grant Cunningham had been trying to warn Jane of the possibility that Tom might be acquitted, that he could walk out of the courtroom a free man. But Jane refused to consider it. Even the thought of a hung jury terrified her. If that happened, the DA's office might not have the stomach to retry the case. The mere thought of such a possibility brought tears to her eyes.

But that evening was different. The three spoke about Vaughn's argument, the jury's reaction, and the finer details of the closing arguments. They agreed that everything that could have been said was said.

"Joyce," Jane said, "I want you to know something. No matter what the verdict is, it will be all right. All I ever wanted was for Aunt Gert to have her day in court. I wanted the justice system to work, and it worked, whether we win or lose. You are better than Clarence Darrow."

The jury deliberated all day Friday, July 12, while Jane spent the day in Grant Cunningham's office, barely able to contain her anxiety. The jury declined to deliberate over the weekend, which did nothing to help her nerves.

The jury deliberated all day Monday while Jane sat in Grant's office again, trying to concentrate on a book. Lee Sansum arrived from Seattle: he had awoken that morning thinking of Jane waiting all alone and jumped on the next plane to San Jose.

At the end of the day, the jury announced they would not return until 1:30 on Tuesday. Jane was about to jump out of her skin.

Tueday, no verdict. "Another day in hell," she wrote in her diary.

Wednesday, July 17, her son Michael's birthday. She awoke thinking it must be the day she would have a verdict.

At 2:30, Jane and Lee were in Grant's office when the phone rang. She heard Grant ask, "We have a verdict in the O'Donnell case?" Her heart stopped. The verdict was going to be read at three o'clock.

Jane called everyone she knew, but all she got were answering machines. As she, Joyce and Grant walked to the court, she saw cops and reporters racing spectators for a seat to hear the verdict. By three, it was standing-room only. One of the most difficult criminal prosecutions in Northern California history was about to end.

The jury came in, and the clerk opened the verdict. Jane's nephew, Bryan, who was holding her hand, said he could feel her pulse beating wildly through her fingers.

"We find the defendant, Tom O'Donnell, guilty of the charge of murder in the first degree."

The place wanted to explode, but they all knew better than to demonstrate in Judge Ahern's courtroom.

When Jane walked into the hallway, the entire jury was waiting for her. One by one they hugged her, they hugged Joyce and all of them, including Jane, wept openly. One juror confided that while she had not formed an opinion on the case before deliberations, she had prayed every night for Jane to survive while she was on the witness stand.

The stoic John Kracht watched the tearful scene in disbelief. "I've never seen anything like it in all my life."

The day stands out in Jane's diary like no other.

"Guilty, guilty, guilty, guilty! Michael's birthday, such a day, can't write."

On October 8, 1996, thirteen days short of thirteen years after the murder, Jane made her last trip to San Jose. She drove with fellow CAH members Vaux Toneff, Jan Miller, and Marlena Holoway. In the courtroom they were joined by John Kracht, Joyce Allegro, Grant Cunninghan, and a dozen court observers. Seven of the twelve jurors returned for the sentencing, a remarkable number considering the trial had ended two months before. It spoke volumes of their feelings about justice for Gertrude McCabe.

O'Donnell's appearance shocked those who had followed the trial. He had not shaved since the verdict and now sported a full white beard. Convicted of first-degree murder, he was no longer permitted to wear the fine suits provided by Hewitt during the trial. He looked pale in his prison clothes.

Judge Ahern brought the court to session. "I have received your sixty-three-page letter," he said to O'Donnell, holding up a wad of yellow legal sheets. "You may speak before sentencing, as long as you don't repeat what you said in the letter, since I stayed late last night reading it all."

"I'm kind of nervous this morning, so please excuse me," Tom began. Having sat in jail for months and months, he had lost his ability to speak loudly and publicly.

For more than forty-five minutes Tom O'Donnell excoriated the court, the judge, his defense attorney, John Kracht, and Jane Alexander. Pointing at her, he railed about her vengeance, and about a cowardly justice system that had been railroaded by political lobbying. He spoke of a gross miscarriage of justice. He said his defense was inadequate, that John Vaughn didn't do what he asked him to do. "I asked him to subpoena Bill Alexander, because he would have proved that his mother's a liar," he said. He demanded a new trial.

In one strange outburst, he explained why he couldn't have been the person who killed Gertrude McCabe.

"I grew up in the outback of Montana," he whispered. "I certainly know how to use a gun. I certainly know how to use a bowie knife," he said, gesturing as if to show a knife ten inches long. "I've killed my share of deer and elk. I know how to kill, and when I kill, I slit the throat from ear to ear. I wouldn't stab someone like that. I would never kill the way Gertrude McCabe was killed. I know better. That would never have been my way."

For one juror, hearing Tom O'Donnell speak was one of the most memorable experiences of the trial. "I expected an overconfident, bossy voice, and it turned out to be mousy. He was so soft-spoken, even though he was emotional and going on and on about how he was misrepresented. He spoke almost in a stage whisper."

Judge Ahern finally explained the law to O'Donnell, pointing out that he was not his own attorney and therefore could not introduce a motion for a new trial. He then sentenced O'Donnell to the full statutory term of twenty-five years to life, with time off for years served.

John Vaughan asked if his client could delay for a week his departure from county jail to San Quentin, so that he could "clean up some business" before leaving.

Judge Ahern responded tersely. "Mr. O'Donnell, you are sixty-eight years old, and before you meet your maker, I would hope you have some remorse for your actions."

Then he looked at John Vaughan and said, "Mr. Vaughn, your client will be on the next bus to San Quentin."

Jane turned to John Kracht, who was sitting behind her.

"John, when's the next bus?"

John Kracht looked at his watch, deadpan as ever. "One PM," he said.

That was the last time Jane Alexander ever saw Tom O'Donnell.

She had fought the good fight and she won.

Epilogue

By the winter of 1998, Citizens Against Homicide had become a nationally-known organization, active in all fifty states and with a mailing list well into the thousands. They survive on donations from friends and the kindness of strangers. No one draws a dime in salary. Jane Alexander and Jan Miller have appeared as victim's advocates on numerous radio and television programs, including the Gordon Elliot and Maury Povich shows. They are supported solely by donations.

Jane and Jan, along with a Northern California core group of fourteen people, including Anne Poverello, Jacque McDonald, and their officers Jack Miller, Ed Sullivan, Bill Miller, Alice Ostergren, Terri de la Cuesta, Chuck Mitchell, and Carol Silveira, are actively involved in more than fifty homicide investigations.

Their membership writes hundreds of letters every month to block the paroles of convicted murderers. Since their creation in 1994, they have not lost a single hearing.

In 1998, Joyce Allegro was elected to the Superior Court of Santa Clara County. She credits Jane Alexander with bringing Tom O'Donnell to justice.

John Kracht and Grant Cunningham are still investigators for the Santa Clara District Attorney's office. John Kracht is still the quietest man in San Jose.

Jeff Ouimet is still with the San Jose Police Department.

Jacque MacDonald hosts a twice-monthly cable television show, Victim's Voice, interviewing victims and investigators involved in homicide cases. Sponsored by CAH, it now reaches more than a dozen communities throughout California.

In 1997, Jane Alexander was awarded the Patricia Lewis Witness of the Year award from the California State District Attorney's Association for her efforts in finding justice for Gertrude McCabe.

That same year, Citizens Against Homicide was given a special citation by the California state legislature and Governor Pete Wilson during the annual Victim's Rights march on the state capitol.

But that's not all. The principal aim of CAH is not winning awards and citations, but getting justice and putting the bad guys where they belong.

In the summer of 1998, thirteen years after the shotgun death of Abigail Niebauer at her home in Palo Alto, a Santa Clara County grand jury returned a first-degree murder indictment against James Niebauer. Palo Alto Detective Mike Yore, who had so fastidiously reconstructed the case by blowing apart his last five white shirts, flew to Seattle and arrested James Niebauer. Mike Yore and Jane Alexander had spent five torturous years in pursuit of justice for Abigail and her bereaved brother, Lee Sansum.

Joyce Allegro had examined the case against Niebauer and encouraged her own department to go ahead with the prosecution.

"You don't know what's going to happen," Jane told Lee Sansum after James Niebauer was behind bars in the Santa Clara County jail. "A jury is composed of twelve people who were minding their own business when suddenly they were called upon to sit in harsh judgment of someone they never met. It's not easy. You must be happy that the system worked and that Abigail will have her day in court."

For Mike York, who faced resistance at almost every turn, just getting to court was also a triumph. "Criminals don't just kill the victim, they kill whole families," he said. "An entire network of friends, relatives, and coworkers. Justice belongs to the living as much as the dead."

The case was given to a young homicide prosecutor named Linda Condron, whose preparation and determination reminded many of Joyce Allegro herself.

Three days after Christmas 1998, Lee Sansum got the only present he had wanted: justice. James Niebauer was found guilty of murder in the first degree by a jury of his peers and received a sentence of twenty-seven years to life.

Jane Alexander summarizes her efforts quite simply. "Once you're a victim, you will always be a victim. It changes you forever. But 'victim' does not mean 'helpless.' I'm not a warrior or a crusader. I simply believe that if you have a debt, if you borrow fifty dollars, you must repay fifty dollars. If you take someone's life, you must pay with your own freedom. I'm in the debt collection business. It's as simple as that."

CAH Family photo
(Left to right CAH Member Shellie Cervantes and
founders Jane Alexander and Jan Miller)

About The Author

James Dalessandro was born in Cleveland and educated at Ohio University and UCLA Film School. In 1973, he founded the legendary Santa Cruz Poetry Festival, along with Lawrence Ferlinghetti, Ken Kesey, Allen Ginsberg and Michael McClure. He was the writer of the "House of Blues Radio Hour," and is currently the instructor of advanced film and television writing at the Academy of Arts University in San Francisco. A member of the Writer's Guild of America since 1983, he has sold more than a dozen film projects and published four books. He is writer/director/producer of the award-winning documentary film, THE DAMNEDEST, FINEST RUINS. His books include CANARY IN A COAL MINE, poems and short prose; BOHEMIAN HEART, a San Francisco noir mystery novel; 1906, a best selling novel that re-creates San Francisco during the great earthquake and fire, and CITIZEN JANE, the true story of a woman who spent 13 years tracking down and putting away the murderer of her 88-year old aunt. He lives in the San Francisco Bay Area with his wife, Katie.

BUY A SHARE OF THE FUTURE IN YOUR COMMUNITY

These certificates make great holiday, graduation and birthday gifts that can be personalized with the recipient's name. The cost of one S.H.A.R.E. or one square foot is $54.17. The personalized certificate is suitable for framing and will state the number of shares purchased and the amount of each share, as well as the recipient's name. The home that you participate in "building" will last for many years and will continue to grow in value.

Here is a sample SHARE certificate:

YES, I WOULD LIKE TO HELP!

I support the work that Habitat for Humanity does and I want to be part of the excitement! As a donor, I will receive periodic updates on your construction activities but, more importantly, I know my gift will help a family in our community realize the dream of homeownership. **I would like to SHARE in your efforts against substandard housing in my community!** *(Please print below)*

PLEASE SEND ME _____ SHARES at $54.17 EACH = $ $_____

In Honor Of: _____

Occasion: (Circle One)   HOLIDAY   BIRTHDAY   ANNIVERSARY

       OTHER: _____

Address of Recipient: _____

Gift From: _____ *Donor Address:* _____

Donor Email: _____

I AM ENCLOSING A CHECK FOR $ $_____ **PAYABLE TO HABITAT FOR HUMANITY** <u>OR</u> PLEASE CHARGE MY VISA OR MASTERCARD *(CIRCLE ONE)*

Card Number _____ Expiration Date: _____

Name as it appears on Credit Card _____ Charge Amount $ _____

Signature _____

Billing Address _____

Telephone # Day _____ Eve _____

PLEASE NOTE: Your contribution is tax-deductible to the fullest extent allowed by law.
Habitat for Humanity • P.O. Box 1443 • Newport News, VA 23601 • 757-596-5553
www.HelpHabitatforHumanity.org

LaVergne, TN USA
28 August 2009
156333LV00002B/1/P